Afghanistan and the Vietnam Syndrome

Deepak Tripathi

Afghanistan and the Vietnam Syndrome

Comparing US and Soviet Wars

 Springer

Deepak Tripathi
London, UK

ISBN 978-3-031-23554-2   ISBN 978-3-031-23555-9 (eBook)
https://doi.org/10.1007/978-3-031-23555-9

© The Editor(s) (if applicable) and The Author(s), under exclusive licence to Springer Nature Switzerland AG 2023
This work is subject to copyright. All rights are solely and exclusively licensed by the Publisher, whether the whole or part of the material is concerned, specifically the rights of translation, reprinting, reuse of illustrations, recitation, broadcasting, reproduction on microfilms or in any other physical way, and transmission or information storage and retrieval, electronic adaptation, computer software, or by similar or dissimilar methodology now known or hereafter developed.
The use of general descriptive names, registered names, trademarks, service marks, etc. in this publication does not imply, even in the absence of a specific statement, that such names are exempt from the relevant protective laws and regulations and therefore free for general use.
The publisher, the authors, and the editors are safe to assume that the advice and information in this book are believed to be true and accurate at the date of publication. Neither the publisher nor the authors or the editors give a warranty, expressed or implied, with respect to the material contained herein or for any errors or omissions that may have been made. The publisher remains neutral with regard to jurisdictional claims in published maps and institutional affiliations.

This Springer imprint is published by the registered company Springer Nature Switzerland AG.
The registered company address is: Gewerbestrasse 11, 6330 Cham, Switzerland

Foreword

In this book, Dr. Deepak Tripathi draws the broad contours of the long wars fought by the United States, first in Vietnam, last in Afghanistan. To cover this vast canvas and also discuss the US role in the Arab Spring prior to the sudden American withdrawal from Kabul in 2021, he draws on the skills acquired as a seasoned journalist, as well as his academic credentials. The latter were earned by a PhD and a trilogy of books, *Breeding Ground, Overcoming The Bush Legacy in Iraq and Afghanistan,* and *Imperial Designs*.

In the present study, inspired by the logic laid out in Paul Kennedy's *Rise and Fall of the Great Powers*, and the subsequent amendments to that theory, Tripathi concludes that "the idea of war without end eventually confronts reality, beyond which war cannot continue." This predicament has plagued the United States on several occasions, and it may well be that in the longer-term perspective, the forward push against the former Soviet Union and Russia which began in 1945, and continues today in the struggle waged over Ukraine, the same logic will in the end call a halt to that protracted campaign too.

The original Vietnam Syndrome, the presumed lack of will to impose US preferences on the world by military means, in the author's view was rooted in the alienation of the American public from its military, and was to shape the particular form of subsequent US foreign interventions. On the other hand, and in line with his theoretical point of departure, Tripathi argues convincingly that this "syndrome" is too US-centric. It is a general feature of great powers exhausting themselves in protracted wars.

Well might the elder Bush claim, at the close of the First Gulf War, that the Vietnam Syndrome had been buried definitively. But it already contained the seeds of another disaster—Afghanistan. "In a state of hubris," writes Tripathi, "the United States risked living in a world of its own imagination. But a country in such a state renders itself oblivious of failure lurking around, ignores early warning signs, and long-term costs in the years to come. America was entering that phase [in 1991], as future events would demonstrate."

Exploiting his intimate knowledge of South and Central Asian as well as Middle Eastern affairs, the author roams far beyond the direct topics of Vietnam and Afghanistan, Iraq, and Libya, exploring related topics, such as the Cold War, Chinese-Soviet rivalry, and others.

Detailing the abuses that America's military adventures entailed, which "drained America's moral capital," the book provides insight also in the role of Pakistan, especially its pivotal intelligence service ISI that sought to turn Afghanistan into a strategic asset providing depth in the confrontation with India over Kashmir. An overview of events in the Arab Spring, appendices with chronologies, and relevant documents concerning the closure of the Afghan War make this a highly valuable, timely book recommended for close study and further debate.

University of Sussex Kees van der Pijl
Brighton, England

Preface

This is a sequel to my book, *Breeding Ground: Afghanistan and the Origins of Islamist Terrorism* (Potomac, 2011), and adds to a Middle East trilogy that includes two other volumes, *Overcoming the Bush Legacy in Iraq and Afghanistan* (2010) and *Imperial Designs: War, Humiliation and the Making of History* (2013). These works reflect my interest in the vast region that is South and West Asia, and great power rivalries there. This interest stems from my life, travels, and work since I was in my early twenties. Born in India, I was fortunate to secure a job in the South Asia Branch of the Voice of America in Washington in 1974, and spent three formative years in journalism. It was a turbulent period in America's domestic politics and foreign affairs—the Watergate scandal leading to the resignation of President Richard Nixon, the worldwide economic crisis triggered by the 1973 Arab-Israeli War and OPEC's oil ban, and the US military withdrawal from Indochina and the fall of South Vietnam, Cambodia, and Laos to communist nationalist forces. In 1977, I moved to London to work for the BBC, where I was to spend more than two decades until 2000.

My interest in Afghanistan goes back to the late 1970s. The country endured communist coups in 1978 and 1979, an invasion by the Soviet Union in December 1979, and a proxy war between the Soviet occupation forces and US-backed Afghan Mujahideen. The Afghan conflict was the last major East-West confrontation of the Cold War, ending in the Soviet Union's defeat and withdrawal from Afghanistan in February 1989. The Soviets left behind their client regime of President Najibullah in Kabul, and the civil war continued between the communist rulers and fundamentalist Islamic groups that made up the Mujahideen movement.

In January 1990, the BBC sent me as its correspondent to Kabul, where I set up a bureau, making it possible for the corporation to establish a permanent presence in Afghanistan. I traveled via Moscow and Tashkent, and landed in Kabul, where the climate was hostile and destruction of war was to be seen everywhere. During the fifteen months based in the Afghan capital and traveling in the country, I learned a great deal about the Afghan people, their culture, their hospitality, and indomitable spirit when fighting the enemy. That character has shaped the history of Afghanistan, which has lured great powers and, at the same time, thwarted their attempts to subjugate the country over centuries. Foreign interventions and wars have rendered landlocked Afghanistan into a devastated country in a state of extreme poverty. But Afghans have maintained their own way of life despite repeated attempts by others to change it.

My book *Breeding Ground* was about the Afghan conflict during the Cold War and its aftermath leading to the first Taliban regime (1996–2001), and their overthrow by US-led international forces. Based on a study of Cold War Soviet and American National Security archives, it attempted to show how Afghanistan became a terrorist sanctuary in a series of conflicts lasting over three decades. The attacks on September 11, 2001 created such shock and revulsion that the United States and allies invaded Afghanistan, with the backing of the United Nations Security Council, and an overwhelming majority of UN members. Many people thought a total reformation of the Afghan state was possible. It could be made a modern peaceful country, leading to a new era.

How unrealistic those hopes were became clear as the Americans and their allies soon found themselves entrenched in war with a resurgent Taliban. Afghanistan and external players near and far showed little signs of change in their motives and behavior. The Afghan conflict entered a new phase and merged with the overarching geopolitical ambitions of the United States. The expansion of war by the George W. Bush administration and his successor, President Barack Obama, once again demonstrated a failure to learn from America's past experiences. Those experiences tell us that the tendency of great powers to get involved in foreign wars and to remain there comes with inherent risks, especially when the occupier is perceived as dictating the occupied for too long, having overstayed its welcome.

Western Europe, chiefly Germany, and Japan after WWII were apparent exceptions. But the circumstances and the manner of America's role in both cases had marked differences. First, the level of Europe's societal development, pool of expertise, and history were in a different league. The Nazi rule did not change that, even though the war brought enormous destruction. Second, there was the Soviet threat. The victory against Nazi Germany was achieved by the Allies, among them the Soviet Union. But soon after WWII, the USSR brought eastern Europe under its own control, becoming the main adversary of the US-led Western bloc. Somewhat similar circumstances existed in the Far East, where Japan's defeat came with the emergence of not only the Soviet Union, but also communist China as major powers. These factors convinced the new ruling classes in both Europe and the Far East that America's presence and massive assistance were essential for their defense and reconstruction. Even so, the repercussions of the Soviet empire's breakup were not entirely peaceful in Europe, as the conflict in the 1990s in former Yugoslavia, and more recently the Russian aggression in Ukraine in the face of NATO expansion, showed.

Outside Europe, in South and West Asia and North Africa, the magnitude of crises in the post-Soviet era turned out to be much more complex and serious. Populations in these regions have very different values, beliefs, and sentiments that determine their behavior. They have very different political and social environments. Countries are ruled by authoritarian strongmen, not liberal democracies. Local customs rather than constantly evolving laws are the primary source of governance. Internal conflicts instigated or fueled by great power interventions influence these regions. Vulnerable and unstable, they are more likely to succumb to great power politics. From South Asia through the Middle East to Africa, the Soviet Union's disintegration created conditions in which rulers, once reliant on Soviet patronage, found themselves without Moscow's guarantees, luring the United States in to fill the vacuum.

The main substance of my Middle East trilogy went back to the 1970s, a decade of major upheaval that left a lasting effect in the region. In particular, 1973 was a watershed year when the Arab-Israeli War in October ended in an Israeli victory, but at great cost to the United States and the world economy after the Organization of Petroleum Exporting Countries (OPEC) led by Saudi Arabia imposed an oil embargo on the United States and allies. That war brought a US-Soviet nuclear confrontation closer than at any point since the 1962 Cuban missile crisis. The economic consequences of the 1973 Middle East crisis led President Nixon to instruct his Secretary of State, Henry Kissinger, to embark on his shuttle diplomacy aimed at peacemaking between the two sides.

The other event of historic importance that received less attention was the overthrow of Afghanistan's King Zahir Shah by his cousin, General Daud Khan, who also abolished the monarchy and declared the country a republic. That palace coup took place in July 1973, but did not attract the attention that the Middle East crisis received for several reasons. Daud Khan, a prince in the Afghan royal family, carried out a bloodless coup while the King was away in Italy for medical treatment. However, life under President Daud continued as before for most Afghans. Daud had more liberal, pro-western leanings, which were also a factor in the relative lack of reaction in the West. And, of course, tensions in the oil-rich Middle East drew greater international attention than the events in one of the poorest and least developed countries in the world. In the long run, it turned out that events in 1973 in Afghanistan were no less significant than those taking place further west in the region.

Fifty years on, I came to believe that the Afghan coup of 1973 upset the delicate balance King Zahir Shah had maintained between the different social and religious forces during his reign of four decades, and triggered a long-drawn-out conflict drawing local, regional, and international players. President Daud's imposition of western-oriented policies caused alienation among conservative and religious groups in Afghan society, on the one hand, and young military officers mostly trained in the Soviet Union on the other. A deep and dangerous split occurred between rural and urban Afghanistan, provoking a civil war that tempted the Soviet Union to invade in 1979, and the Americans in 2001. After a decade of occupation in the 1980s, the Soviets were forced to retreat, and the USSR disintegrated thereafter. Then, after the September 11 attacks in 2001, the Americans invaded Afghanistan, but left after 20 years of war, having failed to transform the country. The history of Afghanistan is part of a pattern showing that when great powers get bogged down in long wars, they eventually become tired and lose support at home before finally admitting defeat and retreating.

The twenty-first century started badly for me. In the year 2000, my career came to an abrupt end due to ill health and inability to work 10- or 12-h shifts in a BBC newsroom. Such a life-changing event makes one think about the future. Fortunately for me, it turned out to be an opportunity to discover new interests in academia, concentrating on history of war and humiliation, and its consequences. And so to my book *Breeding Ground*, though it was the second volume in my trilogy because it took several years to research, write, and publish. *Breeding Ground* was published a decade after the US-led invasion of Afghanistan. The war was on, but hopes were alive that the people of Afghanistan might have a happy ending after all. That the Taliban would ultimately force the United States out was not envisaged, even though the US-led international forces were beginning to face stiff resistance. As the conflict went on year after year, it was time to reflect and reexamine the unfolding chain of events.

Time to reflect helped to see Afghanistan's long conflict in a wider perspective. As well as the Arab-Israeli War, and the overthrow and abolition of the Afghan monarchy back in 1973, America's protracted military involvement in Indochina was coming to an end. I remember the final phase of the Vietnam War ending in the collapse of the US-backed regimes in South Vietnam, Cambodia, and Laos in 1975. I was in Washington during the period. Two years before that historic upheaval in 1973, American combat troops had been withdrawn from Indochina, after which the inevitable was only a matter of time. The United States was in a state of shock, anger, and humiliation at what happened, conscious of its status as the greatest power, but largely unaware of the rise of nationalist forces and the flow of history. The Vietnam debacle was viewed as America's own reluctance to deal with the enemy with full military force, caused by dwindling public support for the war. The term "Vietnam Syndrome" entered the political rhetoric and analysis to describe the paralysis in America's foreign policy, and capacity to exert power abroad.

Despite the rhetoric about the Vietnam Syndrome, the reality was that the United States under President Jimmy Carter began to send covert aid to the Afghan Mujahideen, who were fighting the communist regime that had seized power in Kabul in a coup by young military officers in April 1978. Carter's modest aid package, channeled through the CIA, started in mid-1979. His National Security Advisor, Zbigniew Brzezinski, an ardent anti-Soviet American of Polish descent, claimed years later that it was he who had advised Carter to help the Mujahideen to lure the Soviets into Afghanistan, and give them "their Vietnam." That is exactly what happened in December 1979, when the Soviet Union invaded Afghanistan. After Carter's defeat by Ronald Reagan in November 1980, Afghanistan became a major US-Soviet battleground, with the Reagan administration pouring money and weapons into Afghanistan.

It is true that the North Vietnamese and their South Vietnamese allies Viet Cong looked to China and, to an extent, the Soviet Union for support. But they were essentially nationalist revolutionaries who had fought French colonial rule before France relinquished the territory under the 1954 Geneva Agreements, which mandated unification on the basis of elections under international supervision to be held in July 1956. In the interim, Vietnam was divided into North Vietnam and South Vietnam as a temporary measure until elections would be held 2 years later. The United States and South Vietnam rejected the accords and never signed them. The South Vietnamese leadership asserted that free elections were impossible in the communist North. Nonetheless, France did withdraw, and there followed a growing American involvement in Vietnam and subsequent war in Vietnam, Cambodia, and

Laos—a war that ultimately forced the United States to withdraw its combat troops in 1973. In 1975, pro-US South Vietnam was captured by the North Vietnamese forces, Cambodia led by General Lon Nol fell to Khmer Rouge, and the royalist government of Laos to Pathet Lao.

At this point, perhaps the meaning of defeat in war should be discussed. The term "defeat" can mean different things to different people. Some may argue that the United States was not defeated in Vietnam since American combat troops were withdrawn from the region in 1973, well before the fall of South Vietnamese, Cambodian, and Laotian regimes. Others may contend that Vietnam was not a defeat, because American troops did not surrender to the enemy. Or the United States had the power to obliterate the enemy with nuclear weapons had Washington chosen to do so. In their view, what happened was a political failure rather than military defeat. Still others may assert that the American withdrawal from Vietnam was voluntary under the 1973 Paris Peace Accords between the United States, North Vietnam, South Vietnam, and the Provisional Revolutionary Government of the Republic of South Vietnam (PRG).

What really matters, however, is that after a 20-year conflict, the Nixon administration was compelled to sign the Paris Accords to end the war and withdraw its combat forces without achieving victory. Thereafter, the governments it backed surrendered to enemy forces. Therefore, it was a defeat. This analytic approach helps us take an overview of which side prevails and ultimately achieves its aims. In other words, what decides victory or defeat.

A decade after the publication of *Breeding Ground* in 2011, I began to think of America at war in Afghanistan, and the manner of the Taliban's 2021 victory, and how America's war in Indochina had ended with opposition forces in South Vietnam, Cambodia, and Laos emerging victorious in 1975. The United States could not live with the humiliation in Indochina. And only 4 years later, President Carter went along with his National Security Advisor Zbigniew Brzezinski's advice to entice the Soviets to invade Afghanistan and give them Vietnam treatment, even though China, not the USSR, was the main backer of North Vietnam, as discussed in Chap. 2.

In 1998, Brzezinski expressed his undisguised triumph over the Soviet Union's comprehensive defeat including the retreat from Afghanistan, the collapse of President Najibullah's government the Soviets had left behind in Kabul, and the dissolution of the Soviet state.[1] But by then, Afghanistan had

---

[1] Zbigniew Brzezinski's interview in French in Le Nouvel Observateur (Paris), January 15-21, 1998, translated by William Blum and David N. Gibbs in "Afghanistan: The Soviet Invasion in Retrospect," International Politics 37, no 2, 2000, 241–242.

fallen to the anti-US Islamic fundamentalist Taliban, who defeated Mujahideen groups Washington had supported in the war against the Soviets, and Afghanistan had become a sanctuary for al Qaeda led by Osama bin Laden. Barely 3 years later on September 11, 2001, America was attacked, prompting President George W. Bush's decision to invade Afghanistan and remove the Taliban from power. And there began a new phase of war—this time between US-led multinational forces and the Taliban.

The length of America's 20-year war, and the manner in which its troops were withdrawn, made me think about the end of the Vietnam War, and similarities between them. Each war lasted about 20 years. America employed some of the most advanced weaponry against an enemy that was poorly equipped and poorly supplied. In Indochina, America's secret bombing caused very heavy military and civilian casualties in North Vietnam, Cambodia, and Laos. In the final 20-year phase of the Afghan War, American drones were used against suspected enemies across the Afghan-Pakistan frontier. But, in the end, the underdog prevailed in Afghanistan, as had happened in Indochina.

This long gaze at history opened the route for me to write *Afghanistan and the Vietnam Syndrome.* How a seemingly undefeatable power submitted to circumstances in which it was forced to accept that it could not continue the war, because the cost was simply too high? That is the question this book attempts to answer. In my effort, Paul Kennedy's book *The Rise and Fall of the Great Powers* (1987) was particularly helpful in advancing my argument that the idea of war without end eventually confronts reality, beyond which war cannot continue.

What created such conditions for the United States in Vietnam and Afghanistan? The nature of local and foreign forces that collided in both cases is a fascinating subject to explore. Their interests and motives that drove them to act as they did caused enormous destruction and human suffering, ending in unforeseen outcomes. In both cases, what prevailed was courage, endurance, capacity to take losses, and overcome what seemed impossible. Continuing the march of history, nationalism that has a close relationship with cultural and ethnic identity, and the people's will, was vital to the outcome. The nature of forces that ultimately prevailed in both wars was fundamentally anti-imperialist. *Afghanistan and the Vietnam Syndrome* is a study that explores these forces.

Before continuing to Chap. 1, a few words need to be said about the Russian invasion of Ukraine, which became a new theater of East-West confrontation within months of America's withdrawal from Afghanistan. The origins of Russia-Ukraine conflict went back to 2014, when pro-Kremlin President of Ukraine, Victor Yanukovych, was ousted in a popular revolution and fled to Russia.² Yanukovych was resisting growing demands for Ukraine to sign an agreement with the European Union. Parliament of the autonomous region of Crimea supported Yanukovych, but the rest of Ukraine opposed him. The split pushed the country toward a civil war. On February 27, 2014, Russian troops without insignias launched a coup, capturing government buildings in Crimea, and Russia eventually annexed the region. After that, a state of war existed between Ukraine and Russia.

On February 24, 2022, Russia launched a full-scale invasion of Ukraine, from Moscow's ally Belarus in the north, from Russia in the east, and from occupied Crimea in the south.³ Against all expectations in Moscow that President Volodymyr Zelensky's government would soon collapse, the Ukrainian nation united against the invading forces. Able-bodied Ukrainian men and women took up arms, and Russian forces began to encounter strong resistance. The United States, Britain, and allies began to send vast amounts of military, economic, and humanitarian assistance. Thus, Ukraine became a major battleground between Russia and the Western Alliance. At the time of writing, advances by Russian forces were slow, but they had captured large areas in eastern Ukraine. On September 30, 2022, President Putin signed "accession treaties" formalizing Russia's annexation of four Ukrainian regions occupied by his forces after holding referendums, which were widely condemned as illegal.⁴ It was the beginning of what looked like a long, brutal conflict, with economic warfare between Russia and the West, and Russia weaponizing supplies from its vast gas and petroleum resources to the West.

A proper assessment of the Russia-Ukraine War will have to wait until such time in the future when its conclusion is known. But this study is about the Greater Middle East, and it is in that direction that this book will proceed.

Afghanistan and the Vietnam Syndrome: Comparing US and Soviet wars aims to study the long war between George W. Bush's decision to invade Afghanistan in 2001 following the 9/11 attacks on America, and its complete withdrawal in 2021, leaving the Taliban to return to rule the country. The Soviets had in the past met the same fate, being forced to retreat from Afghanistan after a decade-long occupation in the 1980s. This book examines attempts by US-led occupation forces to defeat the Taliban and al Qaeda, and undertake a state-building program including an American-style democratic system in place of

---

[2] "Putin's Gamble: Russia's 2014 Invasion of Crimea—A Short History," History.co.uk.
[3] "Hundred days of war in Ukraine—A timeline," CBS News, June 3, 2022.
[4] The four regions of Ukraine occupied by Russia, and annexed, were Kherson, Zaporizhzhia, Luhansk, and Donetsk. See Pjotr Sauer, "Putin annexes four regions of Ukraine in major escalation of Russia's war," Guardian, September 30, 2022.

the centuries-old tribal system in Afghanistan. This study further looks at how the Bush administration extended its mission to conduct a global war on terror, invade Iraq to overthrow the Saddam Hussein regime, and rebuild the Iraqi state.

The US venture did not stop there. It stretched further west in the Middle East to Libya and Syria to overthrow regimes that had long challenged American hegemony. The book examines how the mission also assumed a drive for democracy promotion in the region, but was forced to halt when friendly authoritarian regimes were challenged by mass revolts demanding democracy. And so arrived the point when the United States had overreached itself beyond which an endless war could not continue.

At the time of the 2021 US withdrawal from Afghanistan and Iraq, and scaling down of American ambitions in the wider Middle East, it looked like the Vietnam War, and retreat after failing to defeat anti-US forces in Indochina. That withdrawal was forced on the United States after it had overreached in its war in Vietnam, Cambodia, and Laos. Taking an overview of America's military venture in the wider Middle East, and the limits of the world's only superpower on display, the book explores parallels between Vietnam, on the one hand, and US and Soviet wars in Afghanistan on the other. The study is based substantially on qualitative research into original archives listed in the bibliography.

London, UK   Deepak Tripathi

Acknowledgments

I am grateful to many individuals and institutions for their help when I was writing this book. Richard Falk, my mentor and friend, had contributed the foreword to my 2011 volume *Breeding Ground: Afghanistan and the Origins of Islamist Terrorism*. He encouraged me to write this sequel. Richard went through an earlier version of the manuscript and gave valuable suggestions, which improved the book. A lot had changed in Afghanistan, the region, and global affairs in over a decade, and the time had come for this volume. I am also grateful to Martin Shaw, who guided me to my PhD and made recommendations for improvement. He and Richard Falk gave generous testimonials after reading the manuscript. I thank Kees van der Pijl for his foreword, and Amin Saikal and Lisa Hajjar for their endorsements. Barnett Rubin and William Maley gave of their time to suggest useful reading lists and also gave endorsements. They are all renowned academics, whose support is much appreciated. Among the many institutions whose archives provided me with source material, the National Security Archive and the Woodrow Wilson Center were especially useful. I am thankful to them. My wife was unstintingly supportive during a difficult period. She knows how much that means to me. Finally, I must express my gratitude to Niko Chtouris, my editor at Springer, who was always willing and ready to help. Without his commitment, this project would not have been possible. While I am indebted to all whose contributions made this book possible, the responsibility for its contents is entirely mine.

About This Book

Great powers have often found that military adventurism to force their will in distant lands comes with the risk of spending excessive military, economic, and moral capital to the extent that war is no longer sustainable. In modern times, the Americans met that fate in Vietnam, and so did the Soviets and Americans in Afghanistan. America's 1975 retreat from Vietnam was a consequential event, prompting US commentators to explain it as reluctance to get involved in foreign wars, a mindset described as the Vietnam Syndrome.

Deepak Tripathi points out that the Vietnam experience made the Americans determined to give the Soviets their Vietnam. The 1979 Soviet invasion of Afghanistan, and retreat after a decade of occupation represented the revenge America sought. However, President George W. Bush's decision to invade Afghanistan after the 9/11 attacks was the beginning of a long military venture that ended in retreat in 2021. In this book, Tripathi explores parallels between Afghanistan and Vietnam.

Testimonials & endorsements

"Anyone with an interest in world affairs should read Deepak Tripathi's superb book *Afghanistan and the Vietnam Syndrome*. Although drawing on his deep knowledge of Afghanistan exhibited in his masterful 2011 study *Breeding Ground: The Origins of Islamist Terrorism,* Tripathi's focus in this book is far broader, analyzing US foreign interventions since Vietnam, convincingly dissecting policy failures, above all in Iraq and Afghanistan. Tripathi's essential argument is that the US has continued to suffer from 'imperial overreach' ever since its disastrous experience in the Vietnam War."
—Richard Falk, *Milbank Professor of International Law Emeritus, Princeton University; Chair of Global Law, Queen Mary University of London*

"Deepak Tripathi has written widely on United States foreign and military policy, and his new book offers a concise, reliable, and readable narrative of the long wave of US intervention in the Middle East. Extending the case that overreach is the cause of US failures, Tripathi traces recent events to the seminal disaster in Vietnam, reworking the idea of the 'Vietnam Syndrome' as a general definition of this type of imperial hubris. Although the book focuses on the developments which led to the US withdrawal from Afghanistan in 2021, its argument is widely applicable."
—Martin Shaw, *Emeritus Professor of International Relations, University of Sussex*

"Deepak Tripathi's *Afghanistan and the Vietnam Syndrome* offers a compelling and comparative argument about the wars in Vietnam and Afghanistan: The United States lost both along with much blood and treasure, and hawkish officials' hubristic delusions about US invincibility and the imminence of victory against militarily inferior enemies prolonged both. Losing long wars and an incapacity to understand why has become 'the American syndrome.'"
—Lisa Hajjar, *Professor of Sociology, University of California – Santa Barbara, and Author of The War in Court: Inside the Long Fight against Torture*

"Combining the sharp judgments of an experienced foreign correspondent with the insights of the trained historian, Deepak Tripathi has produced an informed, insightful and wide-ranging study that helps us make sense of the challenges that both the Soviet Union and the United States encountered in Afghanistan's mountains and on Afghanistan's plains. No one will fail to benefit from reading it."
—William Maley AM FASSA, *Emeritus Professor of Diplomacy, Australian National University*

"Deepak Tripathi has written an excellent and highly readable overview of imperial overstretch by both the USSR and the United States in the late twentieth and early twenty-first century. He draws persuasive parallels between the war in Vietnam, the wars (Soviet and American) in Afghanistan, and the interventions that followed the Arab Spring. The book reads as a warning to anyone planning once again to use armed force to spread either a system of government or stability to a society that they are equipped neither to understand nor to engage with."
—Barnett R. Rubin, *Distinguished Fellow, Stimson Center; Non-Resident Senior Fellow, Center on International Cooperation, New York University; and Quincy Institute for Responsible Statecraft*

"*Afghanistan and the Vietnam Syndrome* uniquely informs us of the parallels that have existed between America's Afghanistan and Vietnam fiascos. It stands out for its analytical depth and discussion of the issues that have so far received inadequate coverage. As another admirable sequential work, Deepak Tripathi shows how major powers do not learn from their past misguided policy behaviour. It is a book of our time that deserves to be read very widely."
—Amin Saikal AM FASSA, *formerly Distinguished Professor and Director, Center for Arab and Islamic Studies, Australian National University; Adjunct Professor of Social Sciences, University of Western Australia*

Contents

1 9/11 Reprisal 1
  1.1 Pakistan Dimension 5
  1.2 Return to Afghan-Pakistan Theater 12

2 Overreach 15
  2.1 Vietnam Syndrome 19
  2.2 North Vietnam 22
  2.3 South Vietnam 24
  2.4 Laos 26
  2.5 Cambodia 27

3 War on Terror 35
  3.1 Guantanamo Bay 40
  3.2 Drones 44
  3.3 Abu Ghraib 46

4 Afghan War 51
  4.1 War on Soviet Communism 51
  4.2 War on Al Qaeda and the Taliban 57

5 Iraq War 65
  5.1 Desert Storm 66
  5.2 Containment 70
  5.3 Operation Iraqi Freedom 73
  5.4 Uprisings 77

5.5	New Iraqi State	79
5.6	Obama's Withdrawal and Reentry	81
5.7	Retreat	82

6 Arab Spring 83
6.1	Egypt	86
6.2	Libya	89
6.3	Yemen	94
6.4	Syria	95
6.5	United States in Syria	97

7 Return to Kabul 101
7.1	Taliban Regroup	103
7.2	Haqqani Network	106
7.3	Miran Shah Shura	107
7.4	Peshawar Shura	107
7.5	Karachi Shura	108
7.6	Political Crisis	109
7.7	Toward the End Game	111
7.8	Trump and Afghanistan	115

8 Conclusion 121

Appendix A 129

Appendix B 135

Appendix C 141

Bibliography (Summary) 149

About the Author

Deepak Tripathi, PhD, is a Fellow of the Royal Historical Society and a Fellow of the Royal Asiatic Society of Great Britain and Ireland. A former BBC Afghanistan correspondent, he set up the corporation's bureau in Kabul in the early 1990s. Tripathi is the author of a Middle East trilogy published by Potomac: *Overcoming the Bush Legacy in Iraq and Afghanistan* (2010); *Breeding Ground: Afghanistan and the Origins of Islamist Terrorism* (2011); and *Imperial Designs: War, Humiliation and the Making of History* (2013). He has lectured at universities and other institutions in Britain and India.

September 29, 2022

1

9/11 Reprisal

A week after the September 11, 2001 attacks, on the United States, President George W. Bush signed a joint resolution passed by the Senate and the House of Representatives, authorizing the use of military force against those who perpetrated and provided support for the attacks.[1] In his signing statement, Bush said: "Those who plan, commit, or aid terrorist attacks against the United States and its interests—including those who harbor terrorists—threaten the national security of the United States. It is, therefore, necessary and appropriate that the United States exercise its rights to defend itself and protect United States citizens both at home and abroad." Three days later, the President followed it up with an ultimatum. Identifying al Qaeda as the perpetrator and the Taliban for hosting its leaders, including Osama bin Laden, Bush told the Taliban, who controlled much of Afghanistan: "Deliver to US authorities all the leaders of al Qaeda that hide in your land."[2] The message was to hand over terrorists "or share in their fate."

The Taliban's response was immediate. Kabul's diplomat in Pakistan, Mullah Abdul Salaam Zaeef, said that they were "not ready to hand over Osama bin Laden without evidence."[3] For the next several weeks, while the United States was engaged in military mobilization and gathering international support against al Qaeda and its Afghan hosts, the Taliban were playing for time. They continued to ask for evidence while the Bush administration insisted that there was no scope for negotiation. The British Prime Minister,

---

[1] See "President Signs Authorization for Use of Military Force Bill," September 18, 2001, George W. Bush White House Archives.
[2] "Bush delivers ultimatum", CNN, September 21, 2001.
[3] "Taliban defy Bush ultimatum," Guardian, September 21, 2001.

© The Author(s), under exclusive license to Springer Nature Switzerland AG 2023
D. Tripathi, *Afghanistan and the Vietnam Syndrome*,
https://doi.org/10.1007/978-3-031-23555-9_1

Tony Blair, was among the first world leaders to express support for President Bush, saying: "The hour is coming when America will act."

Any US administration would have felt compelled to respond, such was the shock and rage of the American people following the 9/11 attacks. But what would be the nature of America's response? And how far would it go? These were the most audacious attacks on the US mainland, comparable to the Japanese attack on Pearl Harbor in America's Pacific island of Hawaii during World War II.[4] The end of the Cold War more than a decade before had given America a new sense of security, which turned out to be short-lived, with new nonstate entities like al Qaeda emerging in the space vacated by the Soviet Union to take on the world's only superpower. While countries of the erstwhile Soviet bloc in Europe looked for new accommodations with Western Europe, mostly forming the European Union, states like Iraq, Syria, and Libya in Asia and Africa, previously allied to the Soviet Union, were left behind in the wreckage of the Cold War. China and the European Union could challenge America's position as the only economic and military superpower. The United States had to maintain its supremacy after the end of the Soviet Union.

This was the rationale of America's leading neoconservatives, who launched a think tank, the Project for the New American Century (PNAC), in 1997 with a mission "to promote American global leadership."[5] The 9/11 attacks strengthened the neoconservatives' resolve to impose US domination as America's retaliation, going beyond Afghanistan to Iraq and elsewhere, demonstrated. For the United States, continued access to the Middle East's oil wealth for the industrialized world was vital. Al Qaeda and its Taliban hosts were the new enemy.[6] The extremist ideology that al Qaeda and the Taliban embodied was seen as the biggest threat to Western civilization. Osama bin Laden had been living in Afghanistan, had fought along with anti-Soviet Mujahideen, who were supported by the United States, and had invested in the country from his wealth. The Taliban were unwilling to hand him and other al Qaeda leaders over to the United States. The positions of the Taliban and the United States were thus entrenched as shown by events leading up to December 2001, when America's military operations to remove the Taliban regime in Kabul began. The conditions in which the Taliban militia emerged in 1994, 2 years after the communist regime of President Najibullah collapsed, provided an insight into the nature of Afghanistan's long war, and

---

[4] On December 7, 1941.

[5] Formed in 1997. Dissolved in 2006. "Project for the New American Century," Militarist-Monitor.

[6] For example, "Osama bin Laden's statement broadcast on Al-Jazeera Television," translated text provided by Associated Press, reproduced in Deepak Tripathi, *Breeding Ground: Afghanistan and the Origins of Islamist Terrorism* (Washington, DC: Potomac, 2011), 161.

the Taliban themselves.[7] The Afghan state was rapidly disintegrating amid an internecine conflict between rival Mujahideen factions. The government of President Burhanuddin Rabbani was dominated by ethnic Tajiks, whose military commander was Ahmed Shah Massoud. His forces were based in the north of Kabul. Rival Pashtun commanders controlled eastern and southern parts of Afghanistan close to Pakistan. Neither Pashtuns nor Tajiks were united. There were smaller ethnic forces in the north such as one of the Uzbek warlord, Abdul Rashid Dostum, and another of the Tajik commander, Ismail Khan.

From that chaos arose the Taliban, a group of young Afghans who had spent almost their entire lives in refugee camps in Pakistan, and had been educated in Deobandi fundamentalist madrassahs.[8] Male family members went to fight the communist regime in Afghanistan. Many never returned, or came back severely injured. Refugee children were left to fend for themselves, and protect female family members. These childhood experiences shaped the Taliban's ideology, and their readiness to use violence as the primary means to run society. Their character was formed in ways that they would endure extreme hardship, be willing to make great sacrifices, and go to extents many would find unthinkable to ensure survival—all according to their own interpretation of the Quran. Their character proved more durable than that of their opponents.

So the stage was set for war between very contrasting forces. On one hand, the world's most powerful country, on the other, al Qaeda, a dark nonstate group harboring in Afghanistan, and the ruling Taliban. America's demand was unequivocal—hand over Osama bin Laden and other leaders of al Qaeda. The Taliban were unwilling to submit, and seemed to be playing for time. So President George W. Bush embarked on a diplomatic campaign to build a worldwide coalition for what he called "war on terror."[9] He warned: "Our war on terror begins with al Qaeda, but it does not end there. It will not end until every terrorist group of global reach has been found, stopped and defeated." As part of that diplomatic offensive, the State Department reported that President Bush had "met with leaders from at least 51 different countries to

---

[7] For a detailed examination of the Taliban's rise in 1994, see Ahmed Rashid, *Taliban: Islam, Oil and the New Great Game in Central Asia, Revised Edition* (London: IB Tauris, 2008). Also, for a US government perspective, see Peter Thomsen, *Wars of Afghanistan: Messianic Terrorism, Tribal Conflicts, and the Failures of Great Powers* (New York: PublicAffairs, 2011).

[8] Deobandi is an Islamic revivalist movement within Sunni Islam. Formed in the late nineteenth century around Darul Uloom Islamic seminary in Deoband, India, the Deobandi movement in Pakistan was influenced by Wahhabism, a Saudi-inspired movement in Pakistan and Afghanistan since the late 1970s communist takeover in Kabul, becoming more orthodox.

[9] "Text of George Bush's State of the Union speech," Guardian, September 21, 2001.

help build support for the war against terrorism."[10] A total of 136 countries had offered a "diverse range of military support." And the UN Security Council and General Assembly had condemned the 9/11 attacks.[11] Among those who condemned the attacks was the NATO Secretary-General, Lord Robertson, who described the attacks as barbaric and intolerable and called on members of the alliance and the international community to unite to fight against the "scourge of terrorism."[12] For the first time, NATO invoked Article 5, saying that an attack against one member would be regarded as an attack against all members of the alliance.[13]

Another leader who played a central and controversial role in America's war on terror was Pakistan's military ruler, General Pervez Musharraf. He had become isolated since his coup in 1999. The events on September 11, 2001, presented him with an unexpected opportunity to take center stage. Hardly a day had passed when General Musharraf made a statement in support of the United States. He called the 9/11 attacks a "heinous crime against humanity." And he said: "We regard terrorism as an evil that threatens the world community. Concerted international effort is needed to fight terrorism in all its forms and manifestations." Ironically for the military ruler of a country where religious extremism had been a festering phenomenon, General Musharraf offered to continue to extend cooperation to combat terrorism as it had done in the past.[14] And he assured President Bush and the US government of Pakistan's "unstinted cooperation in the fight against terrorism." These responses emboldened the Bush administration's determination.

---

[10] See the US State Department Archive for "The Global War on Terrorism: The First 100 Days."

[11] See "Security Council Condemns, in 'Strongest Terms', Terrorist Attacks on United States," Resolution 1368, September 12, 2001. Also, "First Resolution of the 56th UN General Assembly (2001)," September 12, 2001, Avalon Project, Yale Law School.

[12] "Statement by the Secretary-General of NATO Lord Robertson; September 11, 2001: Attack on America," Avalon Project, Yale Law School.

[13] "Collective defense—Article 5," North Atlantic Treaty Organization.

[14] "Statement by the President of Pakistan," September 12, 2001, Avalon Project, Yale Law School. On extremism and political violence in Pakistan, read, for example, Bruce Riedel, *Deadly Embrace: Pakistan, America, and the Future of the Global Jihad* (Washington, DC: Brookings Institution Press, 2011). For an in-depth study of Pakistan's insecurities, the army's leading role in determining defense and foreign policies, and Pakistan's use of nonstate actors in pursuit of its goals, read C. Christine Fair's scholarly work, *Fighting to the End: The Pakistan Army's Way of War* (New York: Oxford University Press, 2014). Also, Eamon Murphy, *The Making of Terrorism in Pakistan: Historical and Social Roots of Terrorism* (New York: Routledge, 2013).

1.1 Pakistan Dimension

At this point, it would be useful to critically examine how consequential Pakistan's role was in the US-led war in Afghanistan, the wider war on terror after the 9/11 attacks, and how that role related to the past. Through much of its history as a separate state for Muslims founded on religious ideology, after the British withdrawal from, and partition of, India in 1947, Pakistan had been a rentier state. Taking advantage of its strategic location, it allowed powerful and wealthy foreign patrons, in particular the United States, Saudi Arabia, and China, to use its territory and facilities in return for financial and military assistance. Surrounded by a much bigger India to the east, and previously a hostile Afghanistan to the west, Pakistan's borders are porous. The country was cut down in size after the 1971 war of liberation by the Bengali population of East Pakistan more than 1300 miles from its western heartland, with India in between. Landlocked on both east and west, Pakistan's leaders looked to the United States while India turned to the Soviet Union at the beginning of the Cold War. Maintaining order was a challenge in a country of diverse population of Punjabis, dominant in national politics and military, as well as Pashtuns, Baloch, Sindhis, and Mohajir immigrants from northern India. The divided territory of Kashmir has been a long-festering dispute with India. Such anxieties rooted in external and internal threats made Pakistan a highly insecure state right from its birth.

Democracy struggled in Pakistan from the beginning. Its founding father and first Governor-General, Muhammad Ali Jinnah, died only a year after the country's formation as a dominion. His death followed a period of upheaval. The tenure of Jinnah's successor, a Bengali politician Khwaja Nazimuddin, was short-lived. He became Prime Minister when Liyaquat Ali was assassinated in 1951. Iskander Mirza, another Bengali, took over as President when Pakistan became an Islamic republic with its first constitution in 1956.[15] Two years on, the army seized power in a coup in 1958, and General Ayub Khan became President. In 1969, amid nationwide protests and riots, Ayub Khan resigned.[16] He was succeeded by another military strongman, General Yahya Khan. In the 1970 elections, the Bengali nationalist party, the Awami League, won a majority in the National Assembly. The Pakistan People's Party of Zulfiqar Ali Bhutto and military declined to accept the Awami League leader,

---

[15] Between 1947 and 1956, Pakistan had a provisional constitution, a modified version of the Government of India Act (1935).

[16] See, for example, Pamela Constable, *Playing with Fire: Pakistan at War with Itself* (New York: Random House, 2011), 39–40.

Sheikh Mujibur Rahman, as Prime Minister of Pakistan. Civil war ensued in what was then East Pakistan. Amid widespread suppression by the army, and mass migration of Bengali refugees across the border, India intervened with military force. The war led to the cessation of East Pakistan becoming an independent country, Bangladesh.[17]

There were more military takeovers in Pakistan—by General Ziaul Haq in 1977 and General Pervez Musharraf in 1999. Former Prime Minister Zulfiqar Ali Bhutto was executed under General Zia's martial law regime in 1979. His daughter, Benazir Bhutto, also a former Prime Minister, was killed by an assassin in 2007 during General Musharraf's rule.

Pakistan's fragility has several manifestations. One of the most important is the military's tightening grip on power. The Inter-Services Intelligence (ISI), a highly secretive spy agency, was set up to be operationally responsible for gathering and analyzing information relevant to national security. In fact, the ISI acquired the central role in determining and executing defense and foreign policies. Pakistan's military has a history of seeking constant supplies of modern weapons for external and internal security. Its concept of strategic depth has focused on maintaining a safe distance between frontline positions facing the Indian armed forces and Pakistan's core military-industrial and civilian centers. Greater the distance between frontline positions with India to the east and areas to which military can withdraw to the west, the more space the military would have to prepare for defense.[18] Comments made in 2010 by Pakistan's Chief of Staff, General Ashfaq Parvez Kayani, explain the country's thinking. Kayani said: "We want a strategic depth in Afghanistan, but do not want to control it." A friendly Afghanistan that Pakistan can manage is key to this goal. Kayani described it as essential to address Pakistan's long-term concerns in the region.[19]

Since its founding, Pakistan's main preoccupation has been with how to counter India's mammoth population, economy, military, and position on the international stage. Pakistan's alliance with the United States was a reaction to India's developing ties with the Soviet Union. To this end, Pakistan and the United States signed a Mutual Defense Assistance Agreement in 1954. Pakistan's accession to the Southeast Asia Treaty Organization (SEATO) followed in the same year, and membership of the Baghdad Pact a year later. Washington saw Pakistan as an important part of its strategy against

---

[17] Willen van Schendel, *A History of Bangladesh* (Cambridge, UK: Cambridge University Press, 2009), 159–172.

[18] C. Christine Fair, *Fighting to the End*, see chapter "Pakistan's Quest for Strategic Depth," 103–135.

[19] Aziz Hakimi, "Af-Pak: What Strategic Depth?," openDemocracy, February 4, 2010.

communism—the Soviet Union and China. But Pakistan's true value to the United States was in gathering intelligence.[20]

In the 1950s, technology was not advanced enough for America to send spy planes over the USSR, let alone satellites. Pakistan and Iran, both members of the Baghdad Pact, were close enough to monitor Soviet nuclear testing sites. Pakistan had a common border with China's Xinjiang Province, so was more useful. For these reasons, the United States signed the 1954 Mutual Defense Assistance Agreement with Pakistan, followed by deals negotiated with the ISI to establish facilities for intelligence gathering. This exchange was supposed to be of equal value to both sides, but each side was distrustful of the other. Who was to be the arbiter to decide what equal value meant? America's need to collect intelligence about the Soviet nuclear program seemed to give Pakistan's intelligence services the upper hand. For its part, the ISI was suspicious that the Americans were not sharing all the information collected on Pakistan's territory, and wanted to obtain maximum financial and military gains from the United States.

Despite suspicions, the patron–client relationship between the United States and Pakistan survived. There were crises and breaks from time to time, but the ISI managed to turn them to Pakistan's advantage. An early crisis came in May 1960, when the Soviet Union shot down an American U-2 reconnaissance plane, capable of flying at an altitude of 70,000 feet, over what was then Sverdlovsk, later to be known as Yekaterinburg, in Russia. The U-2 had taken off from Peshawar in northwest Pakistan. The pilot, Francis Gary Powers, was captured, tried, and sentenced to 10 years in prison in the Soviet Union. During his trial, Powers admitted that he was on a reconnaissance mission. The plane had crashed, but parts of it were recovered, and put on display in Moscow as evidence of American deceit.[21]

Powers was exchanged for a Soviet spy, Rudolf Abel, in 1962, but the incident had serious consequences. Declassified documents show that Powers had been flying missions for the Central Intelligence Agency (CIA).[22] Initially, President Eisenhower's administration denied that the plane was spying, and said that it was on a weather mission that originated from Adana in Turkey. When it did not return, it was assumed that the plane was lost.[23] But the confession by Powers, and public display of parts of the crashed aircraft, left no

---

[20] Owen L. Sirrs, *Pakistan's Inter-Services Intelligence Directorate: Covert Action and Internal Operations* (New York: Routledge, 2018), 34–35.
[21] See "U-2 Overflights and the Capture of Francis Gary Powers, 1960," Office of the Historian, US State Department.
[22] See declassified documents under the title "U-2 Spy Plane Incident," Eisenhower Presidential Library.
[23] Ibid, see "Cover plan to be used for downed U-2 flight," May 2, 1960.

doubt about what it was doing. President Eisenhower finally acknowledged that he had been fully aware of America's reconnaissance program. The Soviet leader, Nikita Khrushchev, was furious. He demanded that Eisenhower apologize, and discontinue the U-2 program, but Eisenhower refused. Consequently, the Soviet Union ended its cooperation with the Eisenhower administration in the "open skies" plan in which each country was permitted overflights over the other to conduct aerial inspections of nuclear facilities and launchpads. Khrushchev waited until John F. Kennedy's inauguration as President.[24] The U-2 crisis led to the collapse of the summit between the United States, the USSR, France, and the United Kingdom. The Soviet leader also accused Pakistan, Turkey, and Norway, the final destination of the U-2 mission, of being accomplices in the episode. And he warned Pakistan that "if another incident occurred, the Soviet Union would retaliate immediately."[25] The affair caused a temporary breach between Pakistan and the United States, with Pakistan's military ruler, Ayub Khan, saying he could not be sure of American "friends."

Pakistan was also not pleased when America's relations with India seemed to be improving. India's border conflict with China in 1962 was one such instance. President Kennedy offered India military and economic assistance. When he learned about it, President Ayub Khan expressed disapproval for not being consulted in advance.[26] The 1965 India-Pakistan War prompted Washington to suspend military assistance to both countries. Again, Pakistan complained that the US suspension affected it much more adversely.[27] When the India-Pakistan War broke out in 1971, Washington stopped military assistance once again. Pakistan, meanwhile, had begun to develop political, economic, and military ties with China in the 1960s.[28] Three main factors were at play: their shared antagonism toward India, geographical closeness with common border in Pakistan's north-east with China, and Beijing seen as a more reliable ally that the United States was not. Although China's ability to provide economic assistance was limited, this changed as China became a

---

[24] "U-2 Overflights and the Capture of Francis Gary Powers," Office of the Historian, US State Department.

[25] See the summary of Chap. 5, "An Eye for An Eye: Mohammad Ayub Khan and the Collapse of Regional Relations," in Elisabeth Leake, *The Defiant Border: The Afghan-Pakistan Borderlands in the Era of Decolonization, 1936–1965* (Cambridge, UK: Cambridge University Press, 2016).

[26] For various exchanges between the State Department and US embassies in Pakistan and India, and other correspondence on the situation created by the Sino-India border war, see "Foreign Relations, 1961–1963, South Asia," US Department of State Archive.

[27] "A chronology of US aid suspension to Pakistan," News of Pakistan, July 22, 2019.

[28] Bruce Riedel and Pavneet Singh, *US-China Relations: Seeking Strategic Convergence with Pakistan*, Brooking Institute Policy Paper Number 18, January 2010.

major economic and military power with a veto in the United Nations Security Council.

Pakistan's relations with the United States faced a serious crisis at the end of 1971, when the Nixon administration's support was seen as insufficient and ineffective in preventing Pakistan's breakup. Only a few months before, President Nixon's National Security Advisor, Henry Kissinger, had secretly flown to Beijing from Pakistan, paving the way for Nixon's first visit to China a year later.[29] Those visits began a process of normalization of US relations with communist China, leading to America's full diplomatic recognition, and Beijing securing a permanent seat in the UN Security Council. America's inability to prevent the breakup of Pakistan, and the creation of Bangladesh after India's military intervention, underlined Pakistan's view that the United States was unreliable. The breakup left Pakistan as a single territorial entity in what was West Pakistan before the 1971 Bangladesh War.

When General Ziaul Haq overthrew Prime Minister Zulfiqar Ali Bhutto's government in a military coup in July 1977, and subsequently Bhutto was executed, the United States cut off military and economic aid to Pakistan.[30] President Jimmy Carter was averse to military coups removing elected leaders, and Pakistan was suspected of developing nuclear weapons.[31] Pakistan had received military and economic assistance to the tune of six billion dollars between 1953 and 1979. The USSR had already tightened its grip on Afghanistan following a coup led by young pro-Soviet military officers. But two major events changed the situation in the region. First, the Islamic revolution in Iran that overthrew the pro-US regime of Shah Mohammed Reza Pahlavi in early 1979; then, the Soviet invasion of Afghanistan in December 1979 that turned Pakistan into a frontline state facing Soviet forces. Addressing the American Congress after these events, President Carter warned the Soviet Union: "An attempt by any outside force to gain control of the Persian Gulf region will be regarded as an assault on the vital interests of the United States,

---

[29] Henry Kissinger's secret trip to China, facilitated by Pakistan on July 9–11, 1971. President Nixon's visit to China, February 17–28, 1972.

[30] In a separate move on July 3, 1979, President Carter signed a secret order, officially called "finding" granting aid to Mujahideen. Disclosed by the National Security Advisor, Zbigniew Brzezinski, in an interview with French newspaper La Nouvel Observateur, cited in Kyle Tadman, "An American Provocation: US Foreign Policy during the Soviet-Afghan War," Western Illinois Historical Review Volume V, Spring 2013, 42–43.

[31] See Leo E. Rose and Noor A Husain (Ed), *United States–Pakistan Relations* (Institute of East Asian Studies, University of California, Berkeley, 1985), 5.

and such an assault will be repelled by any means necessary, including military force."[32]

General Zia's fortunes changed, and Pakistan was back in the American fold. However, it took Carter's defeat by Ronald Reagan in the November 1980 presidential election when a new age of close security ties between Washington and Islamabad began. It was to last through the 1980s. Afghan refugees had started arriving in Pakistan following the first communist coup in Kabul in April 1978. After the December 1979 Soviet invasion, that trickle became a flood of millions of refugees crossing into Pakistan and Iran.[33] But it was Pakistan where the numbers were greater, and where the United States and allies were interested in. Men, women, and children were being housed in numerous refugee camps.[34] Many fighting-age Afghans from those camps would go on to fight as Mujahideen in Afghanistan. Children would receive an Islamic education in madrassahs and would become the next generation of Taliban. American interest in Pakistan was renewed in what became the final phase of the Cold War that would ultimately lead to the Soviets retreating from Afghanistan, and the disintegration of the USSR. During that period, General Zia's Pakistan became a recipient of massive American aid, all of which had to be channeled through Pakistan's military, with the ISI becoming the main player receiving and allocating the aid to Afghan groups, as well as training them to fight the Soviet and Afghan government forces. Pakistan was allowed to decide how much aid each Mujahideen faction got.[35] Three of the most hardline Pashtun warlords received the most generous share. The ISI's policy was to use fundamentalist Islamic groups in Afghanistan and Pakistan not only to fight in Afghanistan, but also to use them in the Indian part of the disputed territory of Kashmir, and manage the population at home.

The arrival of millions of Afghan refugees meant social and economic pressures on Pakistan, but they also brought international attention and humanitarian, financial, and military assistance to the country. The Soviet invasion was universally condemned, including by the Islamic world. Within months of his inauguration, President Reagan's administration announced details of a

---

[32] "The State of the Union Address Delivered Before a Joint Session of the Congress" by President Jimmy Carter, January 23, 1980, American Presidency Project.
[33] The number of Afghans leaving their country was estimated at over six million, with more than half going to Pakistan. See "Refugees from Afghanistan: The world's largest single refugee group," Amnesty International, November 1999.
[34] See Deepak Tripathi, *Breeding Ground* (Washington, DC: Potomac, 2011), 59.
[35] Main beneficiaries were Gulbuddin Hikmatyar, Yunis Khalis, and Abdul Rasul Sayyaf. See Deepak Tripathi, *Breeding Ground* (Washington, DC: Potomac, 2011), 80.

package worth three billion dollars in economic and military aid.[36] The decision raised questions in the US Congress about whether it was wise to supply highly sophisticated military hardware such as F-16 fighters and Stinger missiles to Pakistan. There was disquiet in India. However, Reagan insisted that Pakistan needed the weapons "to deter or repel" air attacks or incursions out of Afghanistan. America's need to use Pakistan in confrontation with the Soviet Union was greater than all those concerns over Pakistan's instability, military coups, and human rights. Pakistan's military rulers prevailed over the skeptics.

Other countries—Britain, France, Italy, Saudi Arabia, the United Arab Emirates, and Egypt—all funneled military and financial aid to Mujahideen via Pakistan. As the Reagan administration began sending aid to Pakistan, Saudi Arabia agreed to match the American levels of assistance.[37] The commitment of such a large coalition emboldened General Zia's military regime, and world leaders began to visit Pakistan. Zia became a leading actor on the international stage. But on August 17, 1988, he was killed in a mysterious plane crash while returning from a military demonstration at Bhawalpur to the capital, Islamabad. Among the dead were a number of senior military officers, the US ambassador to Pakistan, Arnold Raphael, and the head of the US Military Aid Mission, General Herbert Wassom.

Finally, the Soviets gave up Afghanistan, agreeing to withdraw their forces under the Geneva Accords signed on August 14, 1988.[38] When their withdrawal was officially completed on February 15, 1989, there was joy of victory and relief that the war was over. The attention switched to efforts to form a Mujahideen coalition government in Kabul. No sooner had those attempts begun did they run into trouble. Conflict between rival factions made it impossible to form a stable government. And the United States, having achieved its main objective to force the Soviet Union to retreat from Afghanistan, began to wind down its involvement. By then, Ronald Reagan's successor, George H.W. Bush, was in the White House, and managing the aftershocks of the Soviet empire's collapse was his priority. As the 1980s decade came to an end, the interest in Pakistan declined.

---

[36] US-Pakistani joint statement on June 15, 1981, at the end of a visit by Undersecretary of State for Security Assistance, James Buckley. See Deepak Tripathi, *Breeding Ground* (Washington, DC: Potomac, 2011), 67–68. For 1979–1990, the US aid figure was reported to be $5 billion, "A Timeline of US Aid to Pakistan," Newsweek, October 20, 2009.

[37] Ali Ahmad Jalali and Lester W. Grau, *The Other Side of the Mountain: Mujahideen Tactics in Soviet-Afghan War* (Quantico, VA: Military Press, 2000), vii. Also, Robert Gates, *From the Shadows: The Ultimate Insider's Story of Five Presidents and How They Won the Cold War* (New York: Simon & Schuster, 1997), 251.

[38] "Agreement on Afghanistan signed in Geneva," Washington Post, April 15, 1988.

1.2 Return to Afghan-Pakistan Theater

Events on September 11, 2001, brought America back to Pakistan and Afghanistan. The enemy this time was not the Soviet Union, but al Qaeda and its Taliban hosts. When America's demands that al Qaeda leaders be handed over, and terrorist camps closed, were refused, President Bush ordered first attacks on Afghanistan to remove the Taliban from power.[39] The assault began with aerial bombardment of Taliban military installations and al Qaeda camps. British bombers joined in, with intelligence and logistical support from France, Germany, Australia, and Canada. The initial bombing focused on targets in areas around Kabul, Kandahar, and the Taliban-controlled cities of Mazar-i-Sharif, Kunduz, and Jalalabad.[40] The bombing continued through November and December. On the ground, the Northern Alliance, a coalition of Tajik and Uzbek forces, was used with air support from the American-led coalition. The Bush administration was reluctant to deploy its own ground forces to fight, and go in too quickly to overthrow the Taliban in case a Northern Alliance leader became head of the new government in Kabul, and factional fighting broke out.[41] In the end, as the Taliban resistance wore down in the face of weeks of heavy bombardment, the Northern Alliance's patience ran out. On November 13, 2001, Northern Alliance forces entered Kabul and took over the capital.[42] The Taliban retreated from Kabul to their heartland in southern Afghanistan, or escaped into Pakistan.

Once again, the United States faced the same predicament as it had done throughout its dealings with Pakistan since the early 1950s. America needed Pakistan, but to what extent could Pakistan be trusted? Close links between Pakistan, especially its military intelligence, Afghan Mujahideen, and now the Taliban posed difficulties for Washington. In the face of the US-led military intervention, leading members of the Taliban and al Qaeda had melted away, many escaping to Pakistan, where they would find sanctuary. Pakistan's military intelligence would surely know their whereabouts. Successive governments of Pakistan and its armed forces had developed close ties with Afghan and Pakistani religious fundamentalist groups. How could the same

---

[39] "Bush announces opening of attacks," CNN, October 7, 2001.
[40] "US and UK Bomb Targets in Afghanistan: Bush: 'Battle Joined'," New York Times, October 8, 2001.
[41] The first contingents of one-thousand-three-hundred US troops arrived in Afghanistan in November 2001; their presence was reinforced to two-and-a-half thousand in December 2001 to search for Osama bin Laden in the Tora Bora Mountains. US troop numbers were around one-hundred thousand in 2010 and 2011 at their peak. See "A timeline of US troop levels in Afghanistan since 2001," Military Times quoting the Associated Press.
[42] "Key dates in US war in Afghanistan since September 11, 2001," CBC.

military-political establishment be trusted in America's new war? The Bush administration faced such dilemmas but nonetheless decided to use Pakistan.

The United States gave Pakistan nineteen billion dollars between 2002 and 2010, excluding commitments such as under the Enhanced Partnership with Pakistan Act 2009.[43] On average, this amounted to more than two billion dollars every year. In 2010, the amount allocated was just over three-and-a-half billion dollars. In years from 2002 to the final year of the Bush administration in 2008, about three-fourths of the money went "explicitly for military purposes," only 10% "explicitly for Pakistani development." Clearly, the Bush administration was interested in using Pakistan's territory and military primarily for operations to fight the war on terror.

Despite so much money spent, the trust between Washington and Islamabad was low, with Washington accusing the Pakistani government and military of duplicity, and protecting leading militants in Pakistan.[44] On the other hand, some Pakistanis insisted that it was not a global or Pakistani war, but America's war that was costing Pakistan much more than the aid, and tens of thousands of lives. The reality, though, was that sympathizers of militant groups inside Pakistan's army were found to protect militants in Pakistan, and were involved in violence themselves. Eventually, the Central Intelligence Agency traced Osama bin Laden near the Pakistani Military Academy in Abbottabad, where he had been living under the army's gaze. Bin Laden was killed in a combined US military-CIA operation ordered by President Barack Obama on May 2, 2011.[45] The Taliban's supreme leader, Mullah Omar, was reported to have died at a hospital in Pakistan in 2013. The White House said it believed the reports of his death were credible.[46]

Still, the Bush administration remained cautious for fear of alienating the Pakistanis. In November 2001, the Northern Alliance had forced the Taliban out of Kabul, but the United States would not accept a non-Pashtun from the Tajik-Uzbek ranks as Afghanistan's new leader, deciding that only a Pashtun could head a new government. Otherwise, resistance from dominant Pashtun tribes in southern Afghanistan, and in Pakistan across the border, would be fueled, causing greater instability. Pakistan's government and military would be upset, and America's whole scheme could fail. An obvious contender for leadership was the ex-King Zahir Shah, who had been living in exile in Rome

---

[43] S. Akbar Zaidi, "Who Benefits from US Aid to Pakistan?," Policy Outlook, Carnegie Endowment for Peace, September 21, 2011, 5.
[44] Ibid, 1.
[45] Tim Lister, "Abbottabad—The military town where bin Laden hid in plain sight," CNN, May 2, 2011.
[46] "Mullah Omar: Taliban Leader 'died in Pakistan in 2013'," BBC, July 29, 2015. Also see, "Mullah Omar is Dead: Father of Afghanistan's Taliban Died in Pakistan," NBC, July 29, 2015.

since he was overthrown by his cousin, Daud Khan, in 1973. Zahir Shah was revered by many Afghans, but was 87 years old. Was he the right man to oversee Afghanistan's transition to a new government? Leading neoconservatives in the Bush administration did not think so. Among them was Zalmay Khalilzad, an Afghan-born American diplomat, a Pashtun himself, and close to the White House.

President Bush entrusted Khalilzad with finding a compromise candidate to head a transitional administration in Kabul. Former King Zahir Shah and ex-President Burhanuddin Rabbani were both sidelined, and 44-year-old Hamid Karzai, a Pashtun from Kandahar Province, was chosen to head the interim administration, and subsequently as chairman of the transitional government and president.[47] Karzai's family had been close to the royal family, and he was well-regarded by the CIA. Although the head of the new administration was Pashtun, three of the most powerful positions went to the Northern Alliance—defense ministry to Mohammed Fahim, foreign ministry to Abdullah Abdullah, and interior ministry to Younus Qanooni.[48] The initial military and political success appeared to have surpassed expectations. Within 6 weeks, the United States and allies had deposed the Taliban from power and killed or captured hundreds of al Qaeda members. However, that success concealed the fact that thousands of Taliban fighters had simply gone home with their weapons. Their leaders had escaped and were hiding.

When President Bush ordered the first air attacks against the Taliban and al Qaeda on October 7, 2001, he told American forces: "Your mission is defined. The objectives are clear."[49] Their mission was to disrupt al Qaeda's use of Afghanistan as a terrorist base of operations and attack the military capability of the Taliban regime. But when Bush addressed cadets at the Virginia Military Institute in April 2002, his objectives had become much more ambitious. He declared that the United States was obliged to help Afghans build a country free of terrorism, have a stable government, a new national army, and an education system for boys and girls alike. Bush asserted: "True peace will only be achieved when we give the Afghan people the means to achieve their own aspirations." There was a paradigm shift in war, not only in Afghanistan, but would go beyond, and require a much longer and more expensive commitment from America. The Bush administration had a messianic mission to impose America's global leadership, and the consequences would be far and wide.

---

[47] Carter Malkasian, *The American War in Afghanistan: a history* (New York: Oxford University Press, 2021), 76–78. Also, see Rahimullah Yusufzai, "Analysis: Khalilzad emerges as the king-maker in Afghanistan," Gulf News, June 13, 2002.

[48] Thomas H. Johnson, "The Prospects for Post-Conflict Afghanistan: A Call of the Sirens to the Country's Troubled Past," Strategic Insights, Volume V, Issue 2, February 2006.

[49] Craig Whitlock, *The Afghanistan Papers: A Secret History of the War* (New York: Simon & Schuster, 2021), 6 & 14.

2

Overreach

Throughout the history of warfare, great powers have often shown a temptation to start with limited objectives, only to expand when overwhelming force achieves success, and their seduction for more is too strong to resist. However, this pattern has an end, because with growing military and political commitments come mounting costs, which drain economic capability, and ultimately make it difficult or impossible to continue. Prior to the communication revolution in the second half of the twentieth century, there were limited means at home to receive information about war on distant fronts, constraining how news shaped public opinion. In the age when imperial rivalries were common, defeat came when military-political commitments over a long period became far greater than the economy could sustain. Military power and economic capability were two essential factors determining victory or defeat. In his 1987 book, *The Rise and Fall of the Great Powers: Economic Change and Military Conflict from 1500 to 2000,* Paul Kennedy advanced his theory of "Imperial Overstretch"—also known as "Imperial Overreach"—in the context of the last five centuries. Kennedy's thesis was that if too large a proportion of the state's resources was diverted from wealth creation to military purposes, it would likely lead to a weakening of national power over a longer term.[1]

More recently, Dennis Florig suggested that Kennedy's "Imperial Overstretch" did not take account of policy choices playing a role in the mismatch between commitments and resources.[2] He asserted that if Kennedy's

---
[1] Paul Kennedy, *The Rise and Fall of the Great Powers: Economic Change and Military Conflict from 1500 to 2000,* First edition (New York: Random House, 1987), xvi.
[2] Cited in Peter Bennett-Koufie, "Hegemonic Overreach in the British Empire: Economic Distress, Hegemonic Overreach, and the Fall of Singapore," Inquiries Journal, 2017, volume 9, number 04, 1/1.

dictum were to be believed, then it would appear that all empires eventually would grow beyond the ability to defend themselves. But Kennedy is not explicit that great powers fall necessarily because of extending themselves too much. Their demise may occur for other reasons—conflict among rulers, revolution, natural disaster causing unbearable economic and social burden on the state for instance. In any case, Florig proposed an alternative theory to Kennedy's, taking into account policies implemented by key decision-makers that cause an imbalance between military obligations and available resources. He termed it "Hegemonic Overreach."

The communication revolution which began in the second half of the twentieth century, and still continues at a rapid pace, has given rise to an instant flow of news with its ability to influence mass opinion, becoming a third important factor that serves to determine outcomes. Kennedy focused on the age of empires over five centuries for his theory of "Imperial Overstretch" that established an inverse relationship between military commitments abroad and economic strength at home. But if we introduce public opinion at home and abroad as an additional factor, things become more complex. Then, on one hand, it is an actor's military pursuit, and, on the other hand, its economic capability, and how its conduct is viewed by the masses. There are numerous examples—the Iranian revolution, the fall of the Berlin Wall leading to Germany's reunification, political change sweeping the rest of the former Soviet bloc, to name a few.

The aim here is not to overindulge in a detailed comparison between Kennedy and Florig and attempt to reach a conclusion in favor of one or the other. Rather, it is to recognize that both offer something useful for this study, and move further. While Kennedy's analysis of overstretch and its consequences is based on vast historical evidence, Florig's enquiry, his introduction of the idea of hegemony in particular, complements what we had already learned. The conduct of great powers tends to be hegemonic is a reality, because their objective is to control and shape the behavior of others. To this end, great powers may use military intervention, or they may use threats. They may lure smaller actors with rewards for compliance, and threaten punishment for defiance. Often, there is a combination of both, in case obedience comes without fighting.

We see numerous examples of great powers building hegemony in history. In the twentieth century, the superpower race between the United States and the Soviet Union, and wider arms race, after World War II gripped almost the whole world, from Asia to Africa, Europe, and the Americas. Building hegemony was central to the Cold War. Coming from the Greek word hegemonia, which means leadership and rule, hegemony in international relations refers to an actor's overwhelming capability to shape the international system by coercive and noncoercive means.[3] Hegemonic behavior usually refers to an actor, for instance, a single state such as Great Britain in the nineteenth century or the United States in the twentieth and twenty-first centuries. The Soviet Union was a hegemonic actor until its dissolution, and that of the Eastern Bloc it dominated. But hegemony can also refer to the dominance of a cohesive political community of states, the European Union for example, with external decision-making ability by influencing other states rather than by controlling them, or their territory.

For this study, however, hegemonic behavior of a single state in the exercise of domination and leadership is more useful. Political realists often describe the most powerful state in the international system as the hegemon, identified as the state possessing vastly superior material capabilities—military, economic, and, sometimes, diplomatic or soft power.[4] In the realist view, military power is the principal foundation of hegemony, because violent conflict is forever a possibility in the anarchical international system. America's unmatched military superiority in sea, air, and space, therefore, provides the military foundation of hegemony.

This is why the notion of a state possessing multiple capabilities leads us toward the United States in the current international system. To those mentioned above, we should add at least three more capabilities that enhance its power. First, the United States has a vast territory. Its mainland located in North America dominates both North and South America. It is surrounded by seas in the east, west, and south. Distances between the Americas and Asia, Africa, and Europe are great. Second, the United States ranks number three in the world in terms of population, after China and India, providing the country with a large pool of labor and military potential. Third, the United States attracts scientists, engineers, IT experts, and economists from all over the world, pulling the best. Winning the science and technology race continues to give it an unparalleled edge over the rest of the world. China may be catching up, but the US economy was ahead by approximately one-third, according to the World Bank report in 2020.[5]

John Mearsheimer has defined hegemony as "domination of the system, which is usually interpreted to mean the entire world."[6] The end of the USSR and the Eastern Bloc under Soviet domination led to the conclusion by some

---
[3] Carla Norrlof, Hegemony, Oxford Bibliographies, September 2015.
[4] Barry Posen, cited in Brian C. Schmidt, "Hegemony: A conceptual and theoretical analysis" (Berlin: Dialogue of Civilizations Research Institute, 2018), 5.
[5] See "World Bank GDP 2020," when United States GDP was $20.9 trillion, China's GDP $14.7 trillion.
[6] John Mearsheimer, *The Tragedy of Great Power Politics* (New York: WW Norton, 2001), p 41.

that the sole superpower left was the United States, which could act anywhere at will, and its command of the international system was complete. Francis Fukuyama, in a 1989 article in the *National Interest*, and subsequently his book, *The End of History and the Last Man*, asserted that "a remarkable consensus concerning the legitimacy of liberal democracy as a system of government had emerged throughout the world over the past few years, as it conquered rival ideologies like hereditary monarchy, fascism, and, most recently, communism."[7] He argued that liberal democracy constituted the "endpoint of mankind's ideological evolution" and the "final form of human government." How different the world looked more than three decades later? The United States could choose most, by no means all, targets to intervene, but there were limits and unwanted consequences.

Fukuyama's assertion was rooted in his belief in a unipolar world. In the bipolar world, which existed from the end of World War II to the collapse of the USSR, the Cold War period between 1945 and 1991, significant features of international politics were conflict between capitalist and communist ideologies, nuclear weapons race, and competition for strategic resources, mainly oil in the Middle East. Waterways had to be kept open for trade, enforced by US-led military presence.[8] For Fukuyama and neoconservatives in the Project for the New American Century, the end of the Cold War and the Soviet Union's collapse meant the end of ideological confrontation and much else which came with that. It was for America to impose its leadership, control, and restructure the international system unchallenged.

However, the world evolved differently once the Cold War had ended. Richard Haass argued that globalization transformed the system into a nonpolar world of many power centers with significant power.[9] We have interwoven economies and intergovernmental institutions like the United Nations, NATO, and the European Union. The United States has to rely on consent to exercise its power beyond its borders.[10] In the case of the 2003 invasion of Iraq, and subsequently the civil war in Syria, America's leadership was challenged. And China, an emerging rival, needed to be accommodated despite turbulence in relations with the West as we entered the 2020s decade.

---

[7] Francis Fukuyama, *The End of History and the Last Man* (London: Hamish Hamilton, 1992), p xi.

[8] For an overview of the Cold War Middle East, see, for example, Deepak Tripathi, *Breeding Ground: Afghanistan and the Origins of Islamist Terrorism* (Washington, DC: Potomac, 2011), 21–29.

[9] Richard N. Haass, "The Age of Nonpolarity: What Will Follow US Dominance," Foreign Affairs, May/June 2008.

[10] Yasemin Oezel, "The Impact of the "Unipolar Moment" on US Foreign Policies in the Mid-East," E-International Relations, September 13, 2015.

It is an undeniable fact that all great empires of the past have declined after reaching their peak. Various scholars have tried to explain the reasons for their decline. Whether it was because of disparity between their military commitments and economic resources required to support the military, as Paul Kennedy explained in "Imperial Overstretch" or due to "Hegemonic Overreach" which takes into account broader policies instigated by decision-makers leading to excessive cost, as Dennis Florig suggested, is more a matter of nuance than the fact of overreach. We know that cost cannot be measured only in economic terms. When foreign wars and decisions taken to militarize a society upset other sectors of the economy, restricting consumer choice and lifestyle for instance, the impact on the people's collective view is felt. Population may unite behind a government, especially when a threat is close or seemingly imminent. But the longer a distant conflict goes on, the more fragile public support may become.

Let us take the example of compulsory military service or draft. The first deployment of American troops in South Vietnam by President Lyndon Johnson in March 1965, in response to reports of two clashes between American and North Vietnamese forces in the Gulf of Tonkin in August 1964, led to growing opposition to the draft in the United States.[11] The Anti-Vietnam War Movement (1964–1973) was a key factor in Johnson's decision to withdraw from the 1968 presidential race. And the hostage crisis at the American Embassy in Tehran (November 4, 1979—January 20, 1981) was chiefly responsible for President Jimmy Carter's defeat by Ronald Reagan in the 1980 election. The corrosive effects of foreign crises, and their capacity to bring political change, should not be underestimated.

2.1 Vietnam Syndrome

America's defeat in the Vietnam War left a traumatic legacy which still reverberates. How the US war began, and how its involvement deepened in subsequent years until its complete retreat in 1975, needs a critical look at some of the events. After Japan's defeat in the Far East in World War II, the French had attempted to reestablish their colonial rule in Indochina—Vietnam, Cambodia, and Laos—but were defeated by the Viet Minh (League for the Independence of Vietnam) in 1954. In the same year, Vietnam was

---

[11] Jennifer Rosenberg, "When Did the US Send First Troops to Vietnam?," updated March 23, 2020, ThoughtCo. The United States federal government has employed draft in six conflicts: the American Revolutionary War, the American Civil War, the First and Second World Wars, the Korean War, and the Vietnam War.

partitioned into communist North Vietnam and non-communist South Vietnam under the Geneva Accords.[12] Amid intensifying superpower race, the United States supported the South and the decision of its leader, Ngo Dinh Diem, to prevent elections, fearing they might result in a communist victory and Vietnam's reunification.[13] North Vietnam began to support communist revolutionaries in the South. President Dwight Eisenhower, concerned that the fall of one country could lead to other countries in the region falling under communist control like a domino, sent about 700 military personnel, and military and economic aid, to prop up South Vietnam's government. So began the involvement of the United States in Indochina.

President John F. Kennedy followed it up within months of his inauguration by deploying 500 troops of the US Special Forces and military advisors to support the pro-US South Vietnamese government. Their number rose to 11,000 by 1962. American lives began to be lost, so more advisors were dispatched to support the South Vietnamese military. Their number reached 16,000 by 1963. The Gulf of Tonkin incident was a dramatic escalation in the Vietnam War. Subsequent investigations showed, and prominent individuals close to the events at the time acknowledged, that the Johnson administration misrepresented what had actually happened. Johnson's aim was to escalate and expand America's war in Indochina, including playing a direct combat role in Vietnam, the secret bombing of Cambodia, and numerous violations of international law.[14]

In *Revisiting the Vietnam War and International Law*, Richard Falk provided an extensive examination and interpretation of the Gulf of Tonkin affair, the Johnson administration's version of what happened, and how the United States justified its escalation of the Vietnam War.[15] The consequences of those actions were so grave and far-reaching that we should inform ourselves about the whole sequence of events as they were reported by both sides. On August 4, 1964, President Johnson announced that US air attacks were underway in response to "open aggression on the high seas against the United States of America" in the Gulf of Tonkin. He was referring to North Vietnamese PT-boat attacks on American destroyers—the USS *Maddox* and USS *Turner*

---

[12] See "Agreement on the Cessation of Hostilities in Viet-Nam," July 20, 1954, PeacemakerUN.org

[13] "Military Advisors in Vietnam: 1963," John F. Kennedy Presidential Library.

[14] Richard Falk, Editor: Stefan Andersson, *Revisiting the Vietnam War and International Law—Views and Interpretations of Richard Falk* (Cambridge: Cambridge University Press, 2017). Also, Jesse Greenspan, "The Gulf of Tonkin Incident, 50 Years Ago, August 1, 2014, History.com; Lieutenant Commander Pat Paterson, "The Truth About Tonkin," Naval History Magazine, Volume 22, Number 1, February 2008 (Annapolis, Md, US Naval Institute).

[15] See Richard Falk, Editor: Stefan Andersson, *Revisiting the Vietnam War and International Law—Views and Interpretations of Richard Falk* (Cambridge: Cambridge University Press, 2017), 352–377.

Joy. Johnson said that he had ordered bombing of North Vietnam in retaliation. Soon after, the Secretary of Defense, Robert McNamara, called the American reprisal an "appropriate action in view of the unprovoked attack in international waters on United States naval vessels." Falk pointed out that the *New York Times*, throughout its coverage on August 5, 1964, and the following days, reported the attacks on the two US vessels on August 4 as established facts.[16] Separately, on its editorial page on August 5, the newspaper referred to the first attack on the *Maddox* on August 2 and offered its support to the American retaliation. It echoed Johnson's assertion that he wanted "no wider war," though, as Falk remarked, bombing inside North Vietnam amounted to a major US military escalation. There was no journalistic scrutiny of these reports.

Falk commented that the Johnson administration's version, reflected in the *New York Times* and other newspapers, was not accurate. While seeking "no wider war" in its retaliatory bombing, "the Johnson administration had already authorized secret military and paramilitary actions inside North Vietnam with the aim of provoking an incident that the administration could exploit as a pretext for escalating US military involvement in Vietnam." Seven years after the Gulf of Tonkin affair, the *New York Times* published the first of a series of articles on the *Pentagon Papers*, exploring how the United States became so deeply involved in the war. Quoting documents previously classified, the *New York Times* reported that "an elaborate program of covert military operations began on February 1, 1964, under the code name Operation Plan 34A … Through 1964, the 34A operations ranged from flights over North Vietnam by U-2 spy planes and kidnapping of North Vietnamese citizens for intelligence operations, to parachuting sabotage and psychological warfare teams into the North, commando raids from the sea to blow up rail and highway bridges, and the bombardment of North Vietnamese coastal installations by PT boats."[17] America's secret military operations against North Vietnam had begun before Johnson's claims of unprovoked attacks on the *Maddox* and the *Turner Joy*. Preparations for those operations had been underway for some time.

At the time of the Tonkin Gulf affair, North Vietnam denied having attacked American ships.[18] No independent observers were on board the two ships to confirm or deny the attacks, and no casualties among the crew or damage to the *Maddox* on August 2 had been reported. In the United States,

---

[16] Ibid, 353–354.
[17] Ibid, 354.
[18] Ibid, 355–357.

the attention was focused on the administration's announcements that American ships had been attacked. But critics later focused on the possibility that the vessels had not been attacked by North Vietnamese boats. Richard Falk referred to *Secrets*, the memoir of Daniel Ellsberg, the American military analyst who leaked the *Pentagon Papers*, which tell the story of the US government decision-making during the Vietnam War. In his memoir, Ellsberg says that "within a few days it came to seem less likely that any attack had occurred on August 4; by 1967 it seemed almost certain that there had been no second attack, and by 1971 I was convinced of that beyond reasonable doubt."[19]

Falk then went on to former US Defense Secretary Robert McNamara's 1995 memoirs in which he admitted how North Vietnam's defense minister during America's war in Vietnam, General Vo Nguyen Giap, told him that the August 4 incident did not occur. McNamara wrote in his memoirs: "I have no reason to believe he is in error."[20] About the earlier incident 2 days before, McNamara said that General Nguyen Dinh Uoc, director of the North Vietnamese Institute of Military History, confirmed that the August 2 attack on the *Maddox* had occurred in response to Operation Plan 34A attacks on North Vietnam. However, the attack on the *Maddox* was not ordered by "the central authority in Hanoi but rather by the commander of the torpedo boat squadron in the Tonkin Gulf." Therefore, "Hanoi could not read the signal" that McNamara intended to send with the US reprisal bombing, because the North Vietnamese central authority "did not order the attack."

2.2 North Vietnam

On August 6, 1964, the Chinese Premier, Zhou Enlai, and North Korean Ambassador, Pak Se-chang, met at a reception and discussed the situation in North Vietnam. China had already been informed about the Tonkin Gulf affair and America's retaliatory actions inside North Vietnam. According to the North Vietnamese account, "there flew over 60 sorties," and "for four hours, coastal bases were bombed."[21] The statement claimed that "five aircraft were shot down, and another three were damaged." The United States had admitted the loss of two aircraft, but, Hanoi said, three more "possibly fell

---

[19] Daniel Ellsberg, *Secrets: A Memoir of Vietnam and the Pentagon Papers* (New York: Viking Penguin, 2003), 7.
[20] Falk, *Revisiting the Vietnam War and International Law*, 359.
[21] See "Record of Conversation from Premier Zhou's Reception of the North Korean Ambassador, Pak Se-chang, August 6, 1964, 4 pm" in *Vietnam War* document collection (Washington, DC: Wilson Center History and Policy Program Digital Archive, CWIHP).

into the sea, or they could have been recovered from the water." One airman was captured. North Vietnam accused Defense Secretary McNamara of "outright fabrication," because on August 2, "the Vietnamese took action in self-defense. The American side suffered no injury; the Vietnamese had damage to one ship." Referring to the second confrontation which was claimed to have taken place on August 4, the Vietnamese statement said that "it was entirely planned beforehand by the US side. At that time, there were no Vietnamese ships there."

Things were moving at a hectic pace in Washington. On August 7, the American Congress drafted the Gulf of Tonkin Resolution in response to the two purported attacks on US ships. It was proposed and approved as a joint resolution, and enacted 3 days later on August 10.[22] It was a significant move, because it gave President Johnson the authority to use conventional military force in Southeast Asia without declaring war, and to use whatever force was necessary to assist any member of the 1954 Southeast Asia Collective Defense Treaty, also known as the Manila Pact.[23] South Vietnam was not a member of the Manila Pact, but France was, even though its colonial rule in Indochina had ended before joining the pact.

American military operations had increased by April 1965. At a meeting of ambassadors from communist countries at the Soviet Embassy in Hanoi on April 2, it was reported that the United States had "increased its war material and troops in the south," and had intensified its attacks.[24] A note said that apart from "amplification of bombing attacks," the United States was also using "its own troops in battle action." The note went further: "One can say that the US participates in equal parts in the operations of the South Vietnamese government troops." Referring to the South Vietnamese communists, the note cited Soviet Ambassador Ilya Shcherbakov being informed by North Vietnam's General Vo Nguyen Giap that "the raids in the South have to be increased, regardless if the US is going to increase its attacks on the DRV," meaning North Vietnam. It was also asserted at the meeting that "Vietnam is a homogenous country and the Vietnamese nation is a homogenous nation, that's why the Vietnamese have the right to carry out this war jointly and to help each other."

---

[22] Public Law 88–40, Statute 78, 364 cited in Jennifer Rosenberg, "When Did the US Send the First Troops to Vietnam," updated March 23, 2020, ThoughtCo.

[23] Members of the Manila Pact were the United States, the United Kingdom, France, Pakistan, the Philippines, Thailand, Australia, and New Zealand.

[24] "Note by the East German Embassy in Hanoi on a Conversation with Ambassadors of the other Socialist States in the Soviet Embassy on 2 April 1965," April 25, 1965, in *Vietnam War* document collection (Washington, DC: Wilson Center History and Policy Program Digital Archive, CWIHP).

At a meeting with the Chinese Communist Party Chairman, Mao Zedong, held in Changsha (Hunan), the North Vietnamese leader, Ho Chi Minh, asked for assistance: "If China is able to help us build some roads in the North, near the border with China, we will send forces reserved for the job."[25] In response, Mao Zedong said that because "we will fight large-scale battles in the future, it will be good if we also build roads to Thailand."

> President Ho: "If Chairman Mao agrees that will help us, we will send our people to the South."
>
> Mao Zedong: "We will do it. There is no problem."

It was clear that while the United States was reinforcing its own troops in South Vietnam, North Vietnam, the National Front for the Liberation of the South (NFL), and allied groups of armed people in South Vietnam were preparing for a long war.

2.3 South Vietnam

Once it became clear that President Ngo Dinh Diem would not hold elections in South Vietnam, fearing they could lead to the reunification of Vietnam, his opponents began to consider other ways of achieving their objective, and some came to the conclusion that violence was the only way to force Diem.[26] Following the cancelation of elections, there was a large increase in the number of people leaving their homes to form armed groups in Vietnam's forests. Initially, they were not capable of taking on the South Vietnamese army, so they began hitting soft targets, resulting in the killings of about 1200 South Vietnamese government officials in 1959. In December 1960, Diem's opponents announced the formation of the National Front for the Liberation of South Vietnam, also known as the National Liberation Front (NFL). Their aim was to "overthrow the camouflaged colonial regime of the American imperialists and the dictatorial power of Ngo Dinh Diem."[27] The NFL had its origins going back to the mid-1950s and the Viet Cong, a collection of groups opposed to the South Vietnamese government. The Viet Cong were supported with weapons, guidance, and reinforcements from

---
[25] "Discussion Between Mao Zedong and Ho Chi Minh, Changsha (Hunan), May 16, 1965" (Washington, DC: Wilson Center History and Policy Program Digital Archive, CWIHP).
[26] "National Liberation Front," Spartacus Educational.
[27] "The Viet Cong," alpha history.

North Vietnamese soldiers, who infiltrated into South Vietnam.[28] In later years, the overwhelming majority of Viet Cong were recruited in South Vietnam, and in 1960 became the military arm of the NFL. By 1969, the NFL joined other groups in parts of South Vietnam that had come under the control of the Viet Cong, and formed the Provisional Revolutionary Government. Vietnam's reunification was their objective.

South Vietnam was in a prolonged crisis, including protests, attempted and successful military coups in the 1960s. In a major incident in May 1963, South Vietnamese troops opened fire on Buddhist demonstrators in the central city of Hue, killing several people including children.[29] It came to be known as the Buddhist Crisis. In June, a monk publicly immolated himself at a busy intersection in Saigon in protest against Diem's regime, leading other Buddhists to follow. In November 1963, a group of military officers, led by General Duong Van Minh, assassinated President Ngo Dinh Diem and his powerful brother Ngo Dinh Nuh.[30] US President John F. Kennedy was assassinated in Dallas, Texas, just 3 weeks later on November 22, 1963. Evidence emerging later suggested that Kennedy was more disposed to support the overthrow of Diem than previously thought.[31] In a tape recording of a meeting with the newly appointed US Ambassador to South Vietnam, Henry Cabot Lodge, in August 1963, before he went to Saigon, the President was clear.[32] Kennedy did not directly speak about a coup, but said: "The time may come, though, we've gotta just have to do something about Diem, and I think that's going to be an awfully critical period." We also know about meetings between Vietnamese Generals and CIA officers, among them Lucien Conein, who was a point of contact for one of the coup leaders, General Tran Van Don. Lyndon Johnson, who became President after Kennedy's assassination, was to continue the policy of containment of communism, and deal with Kennedy's Vietnam legacy.

So America's war against North Vietnam truly became Johnson's war after his election victory in 1964. On November 1, just before Americans went to vote, communist guerrillas launched a daring attack on Bien Hoa air base, killing four American and two South Vietnamese personnel, and destroying

---

[28] "Viet Cong," Britannica.

[29] "Vietnam War Timeline," History.Com

[30] See, for example, "The Diem Coup," (Charlottesville, VA: Miller Center, University of Virginia). Also, Peter Kross, "The Assassination of Ngo Dinh Diem," HistoryNet.

[31] "New Light in a Dark Corner: Evidence on the Diem Coup in South Vietnam, November 1963," (Washington, DC: National Security Archive, George Washington University).

[32] Ibid. See specifically "Transcript of Kennedy-Lodge meeting tape, August 15, 1963," in "New Light in a Dark Corner," Document 03.

more than 25 aircraft.[33] In Washington, the Joint Chiefs of Staff recommended that the United States retaliate, but Johnson waited until November 3, when he set up an interagency task force headed by William Bundy to review Vietnam policy.[34] One of Bundy's recommendations was "pursuing a strategy of graduated response." A detailed plan was devised, and the first phase was launched on December 14 with Operation Barrel Roll. It involved bombing Laos along what the Americans called the Ho Chi Minh trail—a combination of jungle and mountain supply routes running from North Vietnam to South Vietnam via Laos. The trail was used for North Vietnamese troops and military supplies into the South and Cambodia.[35] We will now look at how Johnson's "graduated response" escalated, and enlarged the conflict.

2.4 Laos

Laos had been an independent constitutional monarchy since the French withdrawal from Indochina in 1954. Communist-orientated Pathet Lao, officially the Lao People's Liberation Army, had joined the Viet Minh, the Vietnamese independence movement, against the French to force them out.[36] In 1956, Pathet Lao's political wing, the Lao Patriotic Front, was formed. It participated in government with the monarchists for a period. However, the Lao Patriotic Front fell out with the royalists, triggering a civil war between them and the US-supported government in Vientiane in 1959. Supported by North Vietnam and Viet Cong, Pathet Lao captured enough Laotian territory from north to south to form the Ho Chi Minh trail. Hence, Laos became a target for US bombing on President Johnson's orders in December 1964.

The Ho Chi Minh trail made it possible for the North Vietnamese army and Viet Cong in South Vietnam to continue the war in Vietnam, and for the communist forces in northern Laos fighting US-trained guerrillas.[37] For the United States, sending ground forces into Laos to fight would have been much more damaging, because Laos was officially a neutral state. The land-

---

[33] David Coleman and Marc Silverstone, "Lyndon B. Johnson and the Vietnam War," in Presidential Recordings (Charlottesville, VA: Miller Center, University of Virginia). Also, "1 November 1964: Bien Hoa Air Force Base Attacked," in VIETNAM The Art of War.

[34] "Lyndon B. Johnson and the Vietnam War," (Charlottesville, VA: Miller Center, University of Virginia).

[35] Erik Mustermann, "Deadly Legacy of US Bombing Campaign in Vietnam War," December 10, 2018, War History Online.

[36] See "Pathet Lao," Britannica.

[37] "Laos and the CIA's "Secret War" in the Most Bombed Country Per Capita," August 17, 2021.

scape and climate would have made it difficult and costly. Between 1964 and 1973, American aircraft flew some 580,000 missions, and dropped more than two million tons of bombs on Laos, not only around the Ho Chi Minh trail, but also in other parts of the country.[38] It was equal to one planeload of ordnance every 8 min for 9 years, "making Laos the most heavily bombed country per capita." In addition, 270 million cluster bombs were dropped. Although the US secret war in Laos was in support of the royalist government against the Pathet Lao, it also took a heavy civilian toll. Many Lao villages were destroyed, and hundreds of thousands of people were displaced during the 9-year period. It is estimated that as many as one-third of the bombs did not explode, leaving the Laotian population exposed to extreme danger, killing or wounding more than 20,000 people.[39] After the CIA ended its operations in Laos in 1973, hundreds of thousands of refugees fled Laos, many settling in the United States.

2.5 Cambodia

Much was written about the secret bombing of Cambodia between 1969 and 1973 on President Nixon's orders—a decision with which his National Security Advisor, Henry Kissinger, was closely involved. In later years, it emerged that the United States began bombing Cambodia in 1965 under the Johnson administration, not long after his 1964 decision to bomb Laos. Those military operations between 1965 and 1969 were kept so secretive that the information was not made public until 2000. The American bombing of Cambodia was shrouded in illegality—"wiretaps, perjury, falsification of records, and general determination to deceive."[40] Information from the US Air Force database, released much later, showed that during three-and-a-half years between 1965 and 1968, more than two-and-a-half thousand missions flew over Cambodia, and over 200 tons of bombs were dropped.[41] These early bombings appeared to be "designed to support nearly 2000 ground incursions conducted by the CIA and US Special Forces."

---

[38] "Secret War in Laos," in Legacies of War. Legacies of War is a leading educational and advocacy organization based in the United States. Its focus is on collecting information on the impact of conflict in Laos during the Vietnam War.
[39] "The Bombing of Laos: By the Numbers," ABC News, September 6, 2016.
[40] Henry Grabar, "What the US Bombing of Cambodia Tells Us About Obama's Drone Campaign," Atlantic magazine, February 14, 2013.
[41] Taylor Owen and Ben Kiernan, "Bombs Over Cambodia: New Light on US Air War," in Asia-Pacific Journal: Japan Focus, Volume 5, Issue 5, May 2, 2007.

On December 9, 1970, President Nixon called his National Security Advisor, Henry Kissinger, to discuss the continuing bombing in Cambodia. By then, more than 475,000 tons of bombs had already been dropped on Cambodia since 1965. Cambodia had been a neutral country under its head of state Norodom Sihanouk until March 1970, when pro-US General Lon Nol seized power, deposing Sihanouk while he was abroad. It meant that Cambodia, Laos, and South Vietnam—all had American-backed governments, but North Vietnam was communist, and the United States was at war with communist-oriented nationalists throughout Indochina.

America's military power was being seriously challenged abroad. At home, Nixon's policy was coming under growing criticism in Congress after the failure of a joint US-South Vietnamese ground invasion of Cambodia to root out communists. The President, in the second year of his term, was angry, determined to escalate. So Nixon told Kissinger that the US Air Force was being unimaginative, and wanted more secret bombing deeper inside Cambodia, with the aim of destroying the Viet Cong's mobile headquarters in the Cambodian jungle. He told Kissinger: "They have got to go in there and I mean really go in … I want everything that can fly to go in there and crack the hell out of them. There is no limitation on mileage and there is no limitation on budget. Is that clear?"[42] In his response, Kissinger admitted America's problem. The Air Force was "designed to fight an air battle against the Soviet Union. They are not designed for this war … in fact, they are not designed for any war we are likely to have to fight."

Within minutes, Kissinger called General Alexander Haig to convey the new orders from the President, saying: "He wants a massive bombing campaign in Cambodia. He doesn't want to hear anything. Anything that flies, or anything that moves. You got that?" And so, the secret bombing of Cambodia became more intensive, as did the insurgency against the pro-US government of General Lon Nol in Phnom Penh. The data released under the Clinton administration in 2000 showed that the total payload dropped in those years was about "five times greater than the generally accepted figure." The revised total payload of 2.7 million tons dropped on Cambodia was more than the Allies total of just over two million tons during all of WWII. Previous estimates had suggested that between 50,000 and 150,000 Cambodian civilians were killed. But in view of the five times greater payload now known, the casualties would have to be much higher.[43]

---

[42] Ibid.
[43] Ibid.

Nixon ordered his own ground invasion of Cambodia on April 28, 1970, a month after General Lon Nol seized power in Phnom Penh, ending Cambodia's neutrality. His administration kept it concealed until 2 days later.[44] Details now known show that American and South Vietnamese army units crossed the border from South Vietnam into Cambodia. South Vietnamese army launched a total of thirteen major operations between April 29 and July 22, with US troops joining them in May and June. The aim of the invasion was to prevent North Vietnamese attacks into South Vietnam from Cambodian sanctuaries. But the secrecy of Nixon's decision meant that not even the Secretary of State, William Rogers, and the Defense Secretary, Melvin Laird, were told. When it became public, two members of the National Security Council headed by Henry Kissinger resigned in protest. President Nixon tried to justify the invasion in a television address, but it triggered new antiwar demonstrations. Four students at Kent State University in Ohio were killed when the National Guard opened fire on demonstrators. Many members of Congress were angered by Nixon's decision, accusing him of having widened the war illegally.

It is important to remind ourselves that the United States entered the Vietnam War as part of the Cold War to contain communism, which meant confronting the Soviet Union and China. It is also known that, just after the Tonkin Gulf affair in 1964, North Vietnam had informed China about the situation. And China, an old ally, had pledged its backing for Hanoi. In November 1964, the Soviet Politburo increased its military support to North Vietnam with supplies of aircraft, artillery, small arms and ammunition, air defense system, food, and medicines as China sent military engineers to help build infrastructure.[45] But there were growing signs of a Sino-Soviet split in the 1960s. In one conversation with a Romanian delegation, the Soviet leader, Nikita Khrushchev, described Mao Zedong as "sick, crazy, that he should be taken to an asylum."[46] In October 1964, Khrushchev was deposed from power. And, by the late 1960s and early 1970s, there were signs that the United States wanted rapprochement with China, because there was a feeling in Washington that, with the Vietnam War escalating, such a policy might isolate North Vietnam, and increase the US leverage against the Soviet

---

[44] Andrew Glass, "Nixon authorized invasion of Cambodia, April 28, 1970," POLITICO, April 28, 2015.
[45] "Vietnam War Timeline," History.com.
[46] "Note on the Conversation between the Romanian Party and Government Delegation led by Leon Gheorghe Maurer and Soviet Leader Nikita Khrushchev," September 27, 1964, in the *Sino-Soviet Split, 1960–1984* collection, History and Public Policy Program (Washington, DC: Wilson Center History and Policy Program Digital Archive).

Union.[47] Diplomatic efforts to achieve rapprochement between Washington and Beijing continued, but America's calculations about isolating North Vietnam were to be proved wrong.

Two battalions of three-and-a-half thousand US Marines arrived on the beaches of Danang on March 8, 1964.[48] They were the first combat troops to be sent to South Vietnam to support the government there to defeat the communist insurgency. As they were being dispatched, President Johnson said—

> I guess we've got no choice, but it scares the death out of me. I think everybody is going to think, we're landing the Marines, we're off to battle.
> —President Lyndon B. Johnson, March 6, 1964[49]

Initially, the mission was to protect an air base used by the Americans to launch bombing raids on North Vietnamese targets supplying the insurgents in South Vietnam with military aid. Those US raids were the beginning of a sustained bombing campaign, and an escalation of America's war in Vietnam over the next 3 years. The scale of US reinforcements being sent to South Vietnam was dramatic. After President Johnson's first dispatch in March, the number rose to about 23,000 by the end of 1964, compared to just over sixteen in the previous year.[50] At their highest level in 1968, there were 536,000 American troops. From that point, their strength began to decline in 1969, until just fifty were left in 1973. As the US troop strength began to drop in 1969, so did the size of the South Vietnamese armed forces increase, reaching more than a million in 1973. Allied troops from Australia and South Korea, as well as limited numbers of troops from New Zealand, the Philippines, and Thailand, were also deployed during these years. However, they all returned to their home countries by 1973. America's 3-year bombing campaign and more than half-a-million soldiers had failed to subdue the communist forces in Indochina.

The United States paid a terrible price in the Vietnam War, as did other combatants. More than 58,000 Americans were killed, and over 150,000 were

---

[47] "Rapprochement with China, 1972," Office of the Historian (Washington, DC: US Department of State).
[48] David Coleman and Marc Silverstone, "Lyndon B. Johnson and the Vietnam War," Presidential Recordings Digital Edition (Charlottesville, VA: Miller Center, University of Virginia).
[49] Conversation WH6503-02-7026, 7027 cited in Coleman and Silverstone, "Lyndon B. Johnson and the Vietnam War."
[50] US and Allied troops levels in Vietnam, as well as South Vietnamese troops present in their own country, are compiled by the American War Library (CA: Long Beach, American War Library).

wounded, with about 1600 missing.[51] South Vietnam lost between 200,000 and 250,000 fighters. Viet Cong lost more than a million. Around two million civilians were killed in the territories of North and South Vietnam, Cambodia, and Laos. How many North Vietnamese died is not known.

Johnson's escalation meant that America's final retreat from Vietnam, and subsequent collapse of pro-US governments in Cambodia, Laos, and South Vietnam, did not happen under his presidency. The war continued through his successor Richard Nixon's administration. It was when President Gerald Ford was in the White House that the South Vietnamese capital, Saigon, fell at the end of April 1975.[52] Images of tens of thousands of people on the roof of the US Embassy, and at other points, desperately clambering to be airlifted by helicopters are still alive, followed by the reunification of North and South Vietnam. The impact of that experience on American foreign policy remains a subject of debate. As well as foreign and domestic opposition to the Vietnam War, the United States was facing two more crises in the early 1970s. The OPEC oil embargo resulting in dramatic price rises hit the economy hard. And the American people's confidence in their government was sinking because of the Watergate scandal involving multiple abuses of power by the Nixon administration. Fighting a costly war abroad was the last thing Americans were willing to support.

What amounted to a defeat in Vietnam was a shock to America's international standing, prompting an examination of its causes, and lessons to be learned. Conservatives reacted to the outcome with anger and disbelief. Norman Podhoretz, editor of *Commentary* magazine, wrote a piece titled "Making the World Safe for Communism," in which he accused those who had opposed the war of being "isolationists."[53] In one of the most telling comments, Podhoretz wrote—

> Do we lack the power? Certainly not if power is measured in brute terms of economic, technological and military capacity. By all those standards we are still the most powerful country in the world … The issue boils down in the end, then, to the question of will … Have we lost the will to defend the free world—against the spread of Communism? Contemplating the strength of isolationist sentiment in the United States today, one might easily conclude that we have.

---

[51] "Vietnam War US Military Fatal Casualty Figures," US National Archives. Also, "Vietnam War Casualties (1955–1975)," MilitaryFactory.com; and "Casualties and Statistics of the Vietnam War," (CA: Mountain View, Study.com).

[52] See Effie Pedaliu, "Forty five years after the fall of Saigon, the Vietnam War still holds lessons for US foreign policy," (London: Phelan US Centre, London School of Economics).

[53] Norman Podhoretz, "Making the World Safe for Communism," Commentary Magazine, April 1976.

These remarks led others in the press and policy circles to explain why America failed to repel North Vietnam's invasion of South Vietnam. A new term—the Vietnam Syndrome—came into use. One academic, Benjamin Buley, described it in these words—

> The American people had grown increasingly alienated from the military, and increasingly distrustful of the publicly stated objectives of national security policy.[54]

In January 1981, President Reagan's nominee to be his defense secretary, Caspar Weinberger, appeared in his Senate confirmation hearings. Weinberger picked up the theme of the Vietnam Syndrome, and spoke at length about lessons of the Vietnam War, asserting that the United States should not go to war unless vital national interests were at stake.[55] More than 3 years later in November 1984, in a speech at the National Press Club in Washington as Secretary of Defense, he formally announced what came to be known as the Weinberger Doctrine. He explained that six major tests should be applied while the United States contemplates the use of its combat forces abroad. They were—

- Vital national interest at state
- The nation is prepared to commit enough forces to win
- Clear political and military objectives are established
- Forces are sized to achieve those objectives
- Reasonable assurance of support of the American people and Congress
- Other options have been exhausted before US forces are committed

So these principles of the Weinberger Doctrine became the origins of America's policy position, designed to overcome the Vietnam Syndrome. Drawing from these principles, journalist and academic, Marvin Kalb, put it like this—

> It is the belief, born of the brutal experience during the Vietnam War, that never again will the United States gradually tiptoe into questionable wars without a clearcut objective, overwhelming military force, an endgame strategy and, most important, the support of Congress and the American people.[56]

---

[54] See Benjamin Buley, *The New American Way of War: Military Culture and the Political Utility of Force* (New York: Routledge), 63.
[55] John T. Correll, "The Weinberger Doctrine," Air & Space Forces Magazine, March 1, 2014.
[56] Marvin Kalb, "It's Called the Vietnam Syndrome, and It's Back," January 22, 2013, Brookings Institute, Washington, DC.

It is noteworthy that American conservatives like Podhoretz asserted that the country's lack of will was responsible for the failure in Vietnam. Buley emphasized the American people's alienation from the military, and distrust in public officials. And Kalb was critical of lack of advance planning and support of elected representatives in Congress and the wider public, reflecting what Reagan's Secretary of Defense, Casper Weinberger, admitted were causes of the failure in Vietnam. All had a common theme that national reluctance to fight major wars abroad was responsible for America's failure in Indochina. But these definitions are too US-centric, for they do not acknowledge factors which should also be taken into account, such as—

- The intervenor's hegemonic or imperial ambition
- The economic, psychological, and physical drain
- Lack of familiarity with the political, cultural, territorial landscape of the target
- Failure to understand how the intervenor brings unity in the target country
- Above all, the will to fight the intervenor, and the march of history against imperialism

Taking such factors into account helps us toward a more inclusive definition of the Vietnam Syndrome. It is—

> A condition in which a state intervenes with military force in another state or region, or escalates conflict, using false assertions as justification, and in doing so spends excessive military, economic, and moral capital to the extent that is viewed nationally and internationally as having violated the rule of law, making war unsustainable.

In this context, we will now look at America's wars in Afghanistan and Iraq, and involvement in the wider Middle East, from 2001 to 2021. We will examine how the world's only superpower overreached itself. And how the forever war that began following the events of 9/11 came to an end.

3

War on Terror

President George W. Bush's ultimatum to the ruling Taliban in Afghanistan to hand over al Qaeda leaders, and his declaration of the war on terror, came together.[1] His message was that America's war began with al Qaeda but would not end until every terrorist group with global reach had been found, and defeated. Twenty years later, that war was still continuing when President Joe Biden came to office in January 2021. It remained focused on targeting non-state groups and their leaders but without success in preventing the advance of ideology that motivates people to commit violent acts. The war had cost more than five trillion dollars by the end of 2020 and claimed the lives of 7000 American military personnel, as well as countless civilian lives.[2] Osama bin Laden, al Qaeda leader, and Abu Bakr al-Baghdadi, the ISIS leader, were dead.[3] But many thousands of fundamentalists belonging to the movements they founded, and their offshoots, remained active.

There had been failures nonetheless. Arguments about what caused them would go on. As Henry Kissinger had said in a prescient comment about the Vietnam War: "We fought a military war; our opponents fought a political one. We sought physical attrition; our opponents aimed at our psychological exhaustion. In the process, we lost sight of one of the cardinal maxims of

---

[1] "Bush delivers ultimatum," CNN, September 21, 2001.
[2] See commentary by Bruce Hoffman, "The War on Terror 20 Years on: Crossroads or Cul-De-Sac?," March 18, 2021 (London: Blair Institute for Global Change).
[3] Osama bin Laden was killed by American Special Forces in a raid in Abbottabad, Pakistan, on May 2, 2011, on President Obama's orders. The death of al-Baghdadi was announced by President Trump on October 27, 2019. Al-Baghdadi self-detonated a suicide vest after being captured in a US special operation inside Idlib province in Syria.

guerrilla war: the guerrilla wins if he does not lose. The conventional army loses if it does not win."[4]

The scope of the war on terror was global and limitless. Its military, intelligence, economic, and financial dimensions could be compared to the Cold War. Practices used in the war on terror—such as US-led military operations and extrajudicial killings anywhere in the world, surveillance, abduction of suspects, indefinite detention without trial, techniques to extract information and confession, economic sanctions, and restrictions on financial transactions—all required the United States and allies to reinvent or reinterpret established definitions. One striking example was the CIA's harsh interrogation techniques as part of the enhanced interrogation program, which human rights organizations and many legal experts called torture under a different name.[5] Devising and implementing a vast regime to prosecute the war on terror involved huge financial costs. It overstretched America's professed legal and moral commitments.

The events of 9/11, and the declaration of the war on terror, posed a challenge to the rule of law, which was central to Western civilization. The rule of law is defined by United States courts as a principle under which "all persons, institutions, and entities are accountable to laws that are publicly promulgated, equally enforced, independently adjudicated, and consistent with international human rights principles."[6] The courts play a vital role in ensuring the rule of law, especially where they hear cases involving minority groups, or those who hold minority opinions. Equality before the law is an essential part of the rule of law. More generally, we value this principle for protecting individuals from the arbitrary exercise of state power. As part of the war on terror, powers granted to US agencies to act beyond their national boundaries, and the exclusion of courts from hearing cases, created a very different paradigm.[7]

The legal framework for the war on terror was the Authorization for Use of Military Force (AUMF), passed in the American Congress days after the 9/11 attacks, and becoming law.[8] It allowed President George W. Bush to use

---

[4] Niall Ferguson, "After Vietnam: Richard Nixon, Henry Kissinger, and the Search for a Strategy to End the Vietnam War," October 26, 2017 (Yorba Linda, CA: Richard Nixon Foundation).

[5] "CIA tactics: What is 'enhanced interrogation'?," BBC News, December 10, 2014.

[6] "Overview—Rule of Law," United States Courts (Washington, DC: Administrative Office of the United States Courts).

[7] Except, for example, the military commissions at the Guantanamo Bay detention center created by President George W. Bush in 2001 to try foreign terrorism suspects in proceedings that lacked protections under the due process of law of US federal courts. See "The Guantanamo Trials," Human Rights Watch.

[8] "S.J. Resolution 23—Authorization for Use of Military Force," September 18, 2001.

military force against those who planned the attacks, and those who aided and harbored them.[9] Over time, the AUMF became the basis for war on al Qaeda and the Taliban. As the United States expanded military operations from the Philippines in Southeast Asia to Niger in West Africa, successive presidents decided not to seek authorization from Congress for further actions, but to rely on increasingly farfetched interpretations of the AUMF. Rendition and torture of suspects were approved under these interpretations, and the Executive determined the war's scope outside the full set of checks and balances that Congress was supposed to apply. The AUMF contained no termination date or geographic boundaries and granted the president authority to decide which countries, groups, or individuals would be subject to the use of force. It also allowed certain individuals, who had been captured, to be detained at the Guantanamo Bay detention camp in Cuba.

Records show that the CIA's secret detention program and rendition program were ordered and approved at the very top of the administration. On September 17, 2001, President George W. Bush signed a Memorandum of Notification (MON), granting the CIA unprecedented counterterrorism powers to capture and detain individuals "posing continuous threat of violence or death to US persons and interests, or planning terrorist activities.[10] The memorandum provided the foundation of the CIA's secret prison system. In a speech 5 years later, Bush himself acknowledged the existence of the CIA detention centers, and that suspects had been held secretly outside the United States.[11] Vice President, Dick Cheney, spoke publicly about the entire approval process for CIA interrogation. He was among the main administration figures briefed on abduction and rendition programs and discussed these operations with President Bush.[12] Cheney, along with the National Security Advisor, Condoleezza Rice, also chaired National Security Council meetings where CIA rendition operations were discussed. He advised President Bush to approve rendition operations and requested formal authorization from him. At a meeting in July 2003, Cheney, with other senior NSC members,

---

[9] "Overkill: Reforming the Legal Basis for the US War on Terror," Report No 5, International Crisis Group, September 17, 2021.

[10] Report of the Senate Select Committee on Intelligence, "Committee Study of the Central Intelligence Agency's Detention and Interrogation Program," December 9, 2014.

[11] "Transcript of President Bush's Remarks" from the East Room of the White House, NPR, September 6, 2006.

[12] "Getting Away With Torture: Bush Administration and Mistreatment of Detainees," Human Right Watch, July 12, 2011.

"reaffirmed that the CIA program was lawful and reflected administration policy."[13] The program included simulated drowning called waterboarding.

The Defense Secretary, Donald Rumsfeld, "created conditions for members of the armed forces to commit torture and other war crimes by approving interrogation techniques that violated the Geneva Conventions and the Convention against Torture."[14] He made statements indicating that the US was not bound to treat detainees in accordance with international law. Rumsfeld described the first detainees to arrive at the Guantanamo Bay detention camp as "unlawful combatants." And he declared: "Unlawful combatants do not have any rights under the Geneva Conventions," disregarding that the conventions provided explicit protections to all persons detained in an international armed conflict, including those not entitled to POW status.

While President Bush was laying down a sweeping legal framework for arbitrary arrests, detention, and harsh interrogation involving torture techniques as part of his global war on terror, there were senior officials who objected to the extent they went. Among them was the Secretary of State, Colin Powell, who objected on January 26, 2002, to White House Counsel Alberto Gonzales's contention that al Qaeda and the Taliban detainees were not POWs, and therefore not entitled to protections under the Geneva Conventions.[15] The State Department's Legal Advisor, William Taft, agreed. Later that year, the General Counsel at the Defense Department, William Haynes, urged caution in authorizing some of the harsher techniques, because, he said, the US armed forces were trained in a "tradition of restraint." Other officials of the armed forces also raised objections. And Chief of the Army Intelligence Law Division warned that stress positions and sensory deprivation "crossed the line of 'humane treatment'" that might "violate the torture statute."[16]

In 2002, revelations were emerging that al Qaeda operatives and Taliban commanders were going through harsh interrogation at Bagram in Afghanistan, where US occupation forces had turned the Soviet-era air base into one of their own, and the CIA was using it as a detention and interrogation center. The Washington Post reported that, deep inside the forbidden zone, suspects

---

[13] Senate Select Committee on Intelligence, "Declassified Narrative Describing the Department of Justice Office of Legal Council's Opinions on the CIA's detention and Interrogation Program," document released on April 22, 2009.
[14] "Getting Away With Torture," Human Rights Watch, July 12, 2011.
[15] Richard L. Abel, *Law's Wars: The Fate of the Rule of Law in the US "War on Terror,"* (Cambridge, UK: Cambridge University Press, 2018), 208–209.
[16] Ibid. For definition of torture, see "TORTURE (18 U.S.C. 2340A), US Department of Justice Archives.

were kept in metal shipping containers surrounded by wire. Those who refused to cooperate were sometimes "kept standing and kneeling for hours, in black hoods or spray-painted goggles."[17] They were held in "awkward, painful positions and deprived of sleep with a 24-h bombardment of lights." Some of those who still did not cooperate were turned over—"rendered"—to foreign intelligence services, as officially described, whose practice of torture had been documented by the US government, and human rights organizations. The George W. Bush presidency (January 2001—January 2009) will forever be known for his war on terror.

Although President Barack Obama avoided terms like the war on terror and the long war, he continued several of the same practices of the previous administration. Indeed, he significantly increased drone attacks, killing suspects as well as innocent civilians. In an article in Reason magazine, Eli Lake wrote that when it came to the legal framework for confronting terrorism, "Barack Obama is operating with the war powers granted George W. Bush three days after the 9/11 attacks."[18] Under the Obama presidency, the United States still reserved the right to hold suspected terrorists without charge, try them via military tribunal, keep them in prison even after they were acquitted, and kill them in foreign countries such as Yemen, Somalia, and Pakistan with which America was not formally at war. Lake also pointed out that when Obama closed the secret CIA prisons known as "black sites," he specifically allowed temporary detention facilities where suspects could be taken before being sent to a foreign or domestic prison.

The basis of this was the Congressional resolution after the attacks that authorized the President to "use all necessary and appropriate force against those nations, organizations, or persons he determines planned, authorized, committed, or aided the terrorist attacks that occurred on September 11, 2001, or harbored such organizations or persons, in order to prevent any future acts of international terrorism against the United States by such nations, organizations, or persons."[19] While the Obama administration avoided terms like the long war, he did speak of open-ended ambiguities of the war, saying: "Unlike the Civil War or World War II, we cannot count on a surrender ceremony to bring this journey to an end."[20] As for Obama's successor, President Donald Trump, despite his repeated declarations that he wanted to end forever wars, he signed an executive order to keep the Guantanamo Bay detention

---

[17] Dana Priest and Barton Gellman, "US Decries Abuse but Defends Interrogations," Washington Post, December 26, 2002.
[18] Eli Lake, "The 9/14 Presidency," Reason, April 6, 2010.
[19] Joint Resolution S.J.23 Authorization for Use of Military Force, September 14, 2001.
[20] "Remarks by the President on National Security," Obama White House Archives, May 21, 2009.

center open.²¹ In response to a Freedom of Information Act lawsuit filed by the American Civil Liberties Union (ACLU), the Biden administration on April 30, 2021, released President Trump's secret rules for use of force on terrorism suspects abroad—a document called "Principles, Standards, and Procedures for US Direct Action Against Terrorist Targets."²² Those rules gave details of Trump's principles governing direct action against targets outside the United States, capture of terrorists, and procedures for the disposition of individuals held by the United States.

3.1 Guantanamo Bay

Shortly after a detention center was opened on January 11, 2002, within the United States Naval Base at Guantanamo Bay in Cuba, we saw first pictures of hooded, goggled, and shackled men in orange jumpsuits kneeling before a wire mesh fence.²³ Some of them had been captured in Afghanistan. Others had been turned over to American forces from distant places. The American military acknowledged that many of the inmates should not be there. In October 2004, Brigadier General Martin Lucenti, deputy commander of the task force running the detention center, said that of the 550 detainees at Guantanamo, the majority would be released or transferred to their countries. He admitted that most of them were not fighting, but running away. A Guantanamo interrogator also said that the United States was holding dozens of prisoners who had no meaningful connection to al Qaeda and the Taliban, and the US was denying them access to legal representation. In January 2005, the Guantanamo Naval Base Commander, Brigadier General Jay Hood, admitted: "Sometimes we just didn't get the right folks." These comments were in direct contrast to those coming from President Bush and Defense Secretary Donald Rumsfeld, describing Guantanamo detainees the "worst of the worst."

Some early cases were illustrative of this contrast. Mohammed Nechla and five other Bosnians were captured by the Bosnian authorities in Fall 2001 at

---

²¹ "Trump signs order to keep Guantanamo Bay prison open," BBC, January 31, 2018.
²² "ACLU comment on release of Trump administration lethal force use," ACLU, May 1, 2021. For the document "Principles, Standards, and Procedures For US Direct Action Against Terrorist Targets," see New York Times data archive.
²³ "Report On Torture And Cruel, Inhuman and Degrading Treatment Of Prisoners At Guantanamo Bay, Cuba," July 2006 (New York: Center for Constitutional Rights). For a comprehensive account of America's prison system during the war on terror, read Clive Stafford Smith, *Bad Men: Guantanamo Bay and the Secret Prisons* (London: Phoenix, 2007), especially 229–251. Also see "Guantanamo by the Numbers," ACLU, May 2018.

the demand of the United States, based on unsubstantiated allegations by the US embassy that they were planning an attack on the embassy. At the time, Mohammed Nechla was a social worker helping orphans. His employer was the United Arab Emirates Red Crescent Society in the Bosnian city of Bihac. After a 3-month investigation, the Bosnian Supreme Court ordered the release of the six from arrest after extensive searches of their homes, computers, and documents. Nechla was given a document at Sarajevo prison, confirming that he was to be released. But he was not released, and instead handed over to security officers including an American soldier in riot gear. A hood was placed over Nechla's head, his wrists were bound tightly, and all six were taken to an airport, where they were handed over to Americans. Nechla's hood was removed, the Americans placed sensory deprivation goggles on his eyes, a mask on his mouth, and headphone-type coverings over his ears. After hours of sitting in sub-freezing temperatures on the ground, they were all put on a plane. Following a long journey during which soldiers were shouting insults at him and his family, and he was punched by a soldier, Nechla arrived at Guantanamo Bay.

Omar Khadr, aged 15, was taken prisoner in Afghanistan in July 2002. He was mistreated by military officers at Bagram despite his young age, and poor physical condition. He went through long sessions of interrogation and was carried into the interrogation room on a stretcher on many occasions. He was grabbed, pulled and fell, injuring his knee. His interrogators brought barking dogs into the room when his head was covered with a bag, and threw cold water on him. They tied his hands above the door frame and made him dangle painfully for hours. Interrogators made Khadr clean the floors on his hands and knees while his wounds were healing, and forced him to carry heavy buckets of water. He was not allowed to use the bathroom and was forced to urinate on himself. Around March 2003, Omar Khadr was taken out of his cell, told that his brother was at Guantanamo, and that he should "get ready for a miserable life." Khadr responded that he would answer the interrogator's questions if they produced his brother before him. Military police cuffed his hands, and made him sit in painful positions. Khadr urinated on the floor, military police poured pine oil on the floor, and then his hands and feet were cuffed together behind him. The military police dragged him back and forth on the floor through the mixture of urine and pine oil. Khadr was locked back in his cell without allowing him a shower and change of clothes.

As part of a deal, Khadr pleaded guilty to five terrorism charges against him at the US military tribunal at Guantanamo Bay in October 2010.[24] The charges included the murder of a US Army Sergeant, Christopher Speer, with a hand grenade in a battle in Afghanistan, and making bombs for use against US troops. Khadr's father was alleged to have been a financier and confidante of Osama bin Laden and was killed in a shootout with Pakistani security forces in 2003. Lawyers for Omar Khadr, a Canadian citizen born in Toronto, had reportedly discussed terms that would let him serve one more year at Guantanamo, followed by 7 years in Canada. In 2010, the Supreme Court of Canada ruled that Khadr's detention violated "the principles of fundamental justice," and "the most basic Canadian standards about the treatment of youth suspects." Khadr was transferred to Canadian custody in 2012 to serve the remainder of his sentence. In May 2015, he was released on bail after another Supreme Court ruling that he had been sentenced by a US military tribunal as a minor. In March 2019, a Canadian judge ruled that Khadr had completed his sentence, and he was a free man.

Another Guantanamo inmate, Mustafa Ait Idir, asked to speak with an officer when guards refused to turn down fans that were making prisoners cold. He was alone in his own cell when guards entered saying they wanted to search his cell. Idir sat on the floor as instructed with his hands tied behind him. Suddenly guards grabbed him and picked him up. They cursed him and his family. The bunk in that cell was a three-foot-high steel shelf. The guards banged Idir's head and body into the steel bunk.

These cases cited in the *Center for Constitutional Rights* report are among numerous examples of abductions, imprisonment, and torture at Guantanamo and around the world. The Bush administration's practices received widespread condemnation at home and abroad, and had to defend its policies in numerous lawsuits. The UN Commission on Human Rights, in its report, reminded the United States: "International human rights law is applicable to the analysis of the situation of detainees in the Guantanamo prison camp. Indeed, human rights law applies in all cases, even in situations of armed conflict and emergency."[25] Further, the UN report protested that the executive branch of the United States government operated as "judge, prosecutor and defense counsel" of the Guantanamo Bay detainees. This constituted "serious violations of guarantees of the right to a fair trial before an independent tribunal" provided for by Article 14 of the International Covenant on Civil and

---

[24] "Facts about Khadr and the Charges," Globe and Mail, October 10, 2010. Also see "Omar Khadr Case," Canadian Encyclopedia, July 30, 2015, last edited July 8, 2019.
[25] "Situation of detainees at Guantanamo Bay," UN Commission on Human Rights, February 27, 2006, available at UN Digital Library.

Political Rights. The UN Secretary-General, Kofi Annan, said that the United States should close the Guantanamo Bay prison as soon as possible.

Two years into his second term, President Bush was under growing pressure. He admitted that Guantanamo was a sensitive issue for people and that he would like to close the prison, but was waiting for a Supreme Court ruling.[26] At the end of June 2006, the court ruled that the military commissions system established by President Bush to try Guantanamo detainees was "unfair and illegal."[27] And in a further rebuke in June 2008, the Supreme Court rejected the administration's position of Guantanamo as a "law-free zone."[28] President Bush had asserted that the procedures established in the Detainee Treatment Act of 2005, and the Military Commissions Act of 2006, were an adequate substitute for habeas corpus. But that position was rejected.

Amid growing criticism, the Bush administration began to change its policy, which was to continue after his presidency. Of at least 780 detainees held in the prison since the first detainees were taken there in January 2002, about 540 men were transferred to their homes and third countries by the end of the Bush presidency; just under 200 during the administration of President Barack Obama; and one during the presidency of Donald Trump.[29] But this reduction in the number of detainees was no indication that the war on terror was ending, for the use of killer drones was intensified, as we shall see later. Meanwhile, it would be useful to look at some numbers, which put Guantanamo in perspective.

As the total number of prisoners at Guantanamo shrank, the US military admitted to as many as 14,000 prisoners being held elsewhere at Bagram and Kandahar in Afghanistan, and about 12,000 in Iraq and other secret prisons.[30] These and other numbers help us understand how expansive President Bush's program of hunting suspects in the war on terror was. Those held in the Guantanamo prison were citizens from 48 countries around the world, including Afghanistan (219), Saudi Arabia (134), Yemen (115), Pakistan (72), and Algeria (23).[31] Only 16 were ever charged with criminal offences. The detainees came from every continent. The youngest was 15-year-old Canadian

---

[26] "Bush says he wants to close Guantanamo," CBS News, May 8, 2006.

[27] "Supreme Court Says Guantanamo Bay Military Commissions Are Unconstitutional," ACLU, June 29, 2006.

[28] "US: Landmark Supreme Court Ruling on Detainees: Guantanamo Inmates Have Right to Challenge Detention," Human Rights Watch, June 12, 2008.

[29] Mohammed Haddad, "Guantanamo Bay explained in maps and charts," Al Jazeera, September 7, 2021.

[30] Clive Stafford Smith, *Bad Men* (London: Phoenix, 2007), 230.

[31] "The Guantanamo Docket," New York Times. Also, "Guantanamo Bay explained in maps and charts," Al Jazeera.

citizen, Omar Khadr, who spent 13 years in detention before being released in 2015. The Canadian government paid Khadr more than ten million Canadian dollars 2 years after his freedom and apologized for any role it played in the abuses he suffered as a prisoner. The oldest prisoner, 73-year-old Saifullah Paracha, was a Pakistani citizen, who spent 17 years without charge. Paracha was approved for release in May 2021 after the United States concluded that he was "not a continuing threat," and could be returned home.

As the number of prisoners at the camp reduced to about forty, the cost of holding each detainee at Guantanamo was estimated to be more than 13 million dollars per year, compared to 78,000 dollars for every prisoner in a maximum security federal prison in Colorado.[32] The annual cost of operating Guantanamo detention center was 540 million dollars in 2018. It made Guantanamo the most expensive detention center per prisoner.

3.2 Drones

Just 3 days into his presidency, President Barack Obama ordered his first drone attacks on January 23, 2009. Within hours, two remotely piloted unmanned aerial vehicles, as drones are called, killed a number of people in Waziristan tribal agency in Pakistan.[33] It soon became clear that the very first strike had hit the wrong target. Instead of hitting a Taliban hideout, the missile hit the home of a tribal leader and members of a pro-government peace committee.[34] Drones had been in use to target and kill suspects in the war on terror since the Bush administration, but advocates of drone warfare continued to insist that they saved American lives, and reduced the need for ground operations like the 2003 invasion of Iraq.[35] The extent to which drone warfare was intensified by President Obama was illustrated by numbers. During the Bush administration, a total of 47 drone attacks were launched in Pakistan, Somalia, and Yemen.[36] The number of attacks ordered during President Obama's two terms was 563.[37] Obama oversaw more drone strikes in his first

---

[32] Carol Rosenberg, "The Cost of Running Guantanamo Bay: $13 million Per Prisoner," New York Times, September 18, 2019, reproduced by Pulitzer Center.

[33] Micah Zenko, "Obama's Final Drone Strike Data," Council on Foreign Relations, January 20, 2017.

[34] Daniel Klaidman, "Drones: The Silent Killers," Newsweek, May 28, 2012.

[35] "History of Drone Warfare," Bureau of Investigative Journalism.

[36] "Obama's Covert Drone War in Numbers: Ten Times More Strikes in Numbers," Bureau of Investigative Journalism, January 17, 2017. Also, Alice Ross, "Drones may predate Obama, but his resolute use of them is unmatched," Guardian, November 18, 2015.

[37] Bureau of Investigative Journalism does not log drone attacks in active battlefields except Afghanistan. Strikes in Iraq, Syria, and Libya are not included. For the latest in these countries, see Airwars.org

year as president than the entire Bush presidency. For Obama, drones made it possible to continue the war on al Qaeda and affiliated groups, and extricate American forces from expensive ground wars. His administration described drones as "exceptionally surgical and precise" weapons, causing next to no collateral damage. The extent of civilian casualties told a different story.[38]

In 2013, the Obama administration put in place a framework for use of lethal weapons against terrorism suspects that applied to "areas outside of active hostilities."[39] The term had no basis in domestic or international law, but it was understood that it meant locations outside recognized battlefields, where the laws of war clearly applied. Afghanistan, Iraq, and Syria were armed conflict zones, where the United States asserted that it would obey its law-of-war obligations. It was also understood that the Obama administration's rules applied to the rest of the world, more specifically, at various points, to Pakistan, Yemen, Somalia, and Libya, "to safeguard individual life and international peace and security." Obama sought to impose policy limits based on locations inside and outside "areas of active hostility" to determine who could be killed, and what precautions were to be taken.

President Trump cast aside several of Obama's constraints in his rulebook "Principles, Standards, and Procedures for US Direct Action Against Terrorist Targets." Trump's rulebook stressed flexibility in taking "direct action"—in other words, kill and capture operations as a "critical component" of US counterterrorism policy. It signaled to heads of agencies that they had primary responsibility for proposing and taking direct action, and that the president was prepared to give them more flexibility if they asked for it. Trump made it clear that gloves were off to "further US national security interests." For instance, the first Policy Standard (Section 2A) authorized the use of force against any "terrorist group (1) against which the United States may lawfully use force; and (2) that are engaged in ongoing hostilities against the United States or pose a continuing, imminent threat to the United States."[40] As Charlie Savage of the *New York Times* reported, the Biden administration discovered that Trump's officials used latitude allowed under his rules to kill men in some countries by a lower standard: "While Trump kept that [near

---

[38] For the latest known numbers, see "Drone Warfare," Bureau of Investigative Journalism."

[39] For this discussion, see Hina Shamsi, "Trump's Secret Rules for Drone Strikes and Presidents' Licence to Kill," Just Security, May 3, 2021. Also, see Note 22.

[40] Trump's "Principles, Standards, and Procedures for Direct Actions Against Terrorist Targets," as in Footnote 22.

certainty] rule for women and children, he permitted a lower standard of merely 'reasonable certainty' when it came to civilian adult men."[41]

President Joe Biden's announcement of the withdrawal of American troops from Afghanistan, and its implementation, in 2021 had the effect of a quick return of the Taliban to power in Kabul two decades after they were ousted. Writing for the Modern War Institute At West Point Military Academy, Daniel Brunstetter, referred to Biden's description of it as the "end of the war in Afghanistan."[42] Brunstetter disagreed with Biden's portrayal, saying that it was an opportunity for a "recalibration in the use of force abroad" in the global war on terror. Brunstetter reminded that Biden, in fact, was poised to increase his reliance on "over-the-horizon" operations—in other words, a continuation of drone warfare and raids by special forces to try to make sure that Afghanistan did not become a heaven for international terrorism.

By asserting that the military withdrawal from Afghanistan was the end of the "forever war," Biden was suggesting that the alternative was "limited war"—a less risky, less expensive option. In fact, this option was exercised by the United States prior to the 9/11 attacks, and immediately after the Taliban were ousted from power by forces of the Northern Alliance. But, as the military situation became more challenging, and the Bush administration's ambition of nation-building required a seemingly indefinite stay, the United States sent massive troop reinforcements to Afghanistan. Consequently, American combat operations with ground troops and air power alienated and radicalized many in the Afghan population, and contributed to support for the Taliban. In particular, the use of drones by asserting made-up rules, and causing civilian casualties, attracted widespread condemnation in the United States and abroad. And they added to the damage that the war on terror was already causing to America's reputation.

3.3 Abu Ghraib

In the Saddam Hussein era, Abu Ghraib was a maximum security prison west of Baghdad, where tens of thousands of prisoners were kept, tortured, and executed. Not much was known about Abu Ghraib before the American invasion, and Saddam Hussein regime's overthrow in 2003. Abu Ghraib came to world attention after the invasion in 2004, when accounts with graphic

---

[41] Charlie Savage, "Trump's Secret Rules for Drone Strikes Outside War Zones Are Disclosed," New York Times, May 1, 2021.
[42] Daniel Brunstetter, "Over-the-Horizon Counterterrorism: New Name, Same Old Challenges," Modern War Institute At West Point, November 24, 2021.

images of naked Iraqis being abused and humiliated by US prison guards were published, and persistent evidence emerged in later years that among the interrogators and trainers were Israeli security personnel.[43] One of those speaking out was a senior US officer, Brigadier General Janis Karpinski, head of a military police unit at Abu Ghraib, who came under suspension after disclosures about Abu Ghraib, and other detention and intelligence centers in Iraq. In a BBC interview, General Karpinski said that she had met a man who spoke Arabic, and claimed to be from Israel doing some of the interrogations in Iraq. She said that a coalition general was with the man when they met. These disclosures about Israelis interrogating prisoners in Iraq were bound to cause anger in Arab countries.

Abu Ghraib had been transformed into a US military prison by the occupation forces. There were detainees that included women and teenagers, all civilians, many picked up at random in raids and at highway checkpoints. Some of the detainees were common criminals. Others were suspected of "crimes against the coalition," and those described as "high-value" leaders of the insurgency against the coalition forces. The officer in charge, General Karpinski, was an experienced intelligence officer, who had served with the Special Forces, and fought in the first Gulf War in 1991 to liberate Kuwait from Iraqi occupation. However, she had no experience of running prisons. Yet, she was named commander of a US military police brigade, given overall control of three large prisons including Abu Ghraib, and 30,000 army reservists who also had no training in handling prisoners. Amid mounting revelations about prisoner abuse and torture, Karpinski was suspended, and an investigation into the prison system was ordered by the senior commander in Iraq, Lieutenant General Ricardo Sanchez. The head of the inquiry was Major General Antonio Taguba.

Reacting to sickening photographs of American soldiers abusing Iraqi prisoners, President Bush was defensive. He insisted that the United States was a "nation of law," and the "disgraceful conduct" was the work of a "few bad apples."[44] He said that those responsible would be brought to justice, and promised that terrorism suspects and "unlawful enemy combatants" such as those in the Guantanamo detention center in Cuba would be treated according to domestic and international law. The United States, he declared, was

---

[43] "Israeli interrogators 'in Iraq'," BBC, July 3, 2004. Also, "Ex-Abu Ghraib Interrogator: Israelis Trained US to Use "Palestinian Chair" Torture Device," Democracy Now, April 7, 2016; and Seymour M. Hersh, "Torture At Abu Ghraib," New Yorker, April 30, 2004.

[44] "Just a few bad apples?," Economist, January 22, 2005. Also, Julia Michaels, "Understanding Abu Ghraib: Accountability, the United States, and the Continuity of Torture," 51–52, Thesis, Scholarly and Creative Work from DePauw University, 2020.

"committed to the worldwide elimination of torture, and we are leading this fight by example." The reality, however, was very different. It emerged that in 2005 the Bush administration had issued two memorandums redefining the concept of torture more narrowly. The implication was that accountability only meant punishment for some people for abusing prisoners. Bush continued to defend his policies on detention and interrogation, saying they were both successful and lawful, and the "government does not torture people."[45] He was responding to a *New York Times* report that revealed contents of secret memos which allowed extreme interrogation tactics against suspects. The memos were issued by Alberto Gonzales, the attorney general at the time, authorizing the use of head slaps, freezing temperatures, and simulated drownings known as waterboarding.

Bush continued: "When we find someone who may have information regarding a potential attack on America, you bet we are going to detain them, and you bet we are going to question them. The American people expect us to find out information, actionable intelligence so we can help protect them. That's our job." Furthermore, he said that techniques used by the United States had been "fully disclosed to appropriate members of Congress." He did not take questions. In the meantime, Major General Taguba delivered his report in May 2004, and his findings were devastating.[46] The report concluded that "numerous instances of detainee abuse occurred during October and December 2003," that the "perpetrators of the torture committed egregious crimes," and that "inadequate oversight on the part of their supervisors also contributed to the torture at Abu Ghraib."

Taguba found that the abuse of detainees by military police was intentional, and included the following acts[47]:

- Punching, slapping, and kicking detainees; jumping on their naked feet
- Videotaping and photographing naked male and female detainees
- Forcibly arranging detainees in various sexually explicit positions for photographing
- Forcing detainees to remove their clothing and keeping them naked for several days
- Forcing naked male detainees to wear women's underwear

---

[45] "Bush denies torture of terror suspects," NPR, October 5, 2007.
[46] "Taguba Report: AR 15–6 Investigation of the 800th Military Police Brigade – Certified Copy," May 27, 2004, Torture Database (New York: ACLU).
[47] "Taguba Report," 16–17.

- Forcing groups of male detainees to masturbate themselves while being photographed and videotaped
- Arranging naked male detainees in a pile and then jumping on them
- Positioning a naked male detainee on a MRE Box with a sandbag on his head, and attaching wires to his fingers, toes, and penis to simulate electric torture
- Writing "I am a Rapest" (sic) on the leg of a detainee alleged to have forcibly raped a 15-year-old fellow detainee, and then photographing him naked
- Placing a dog chain or strap around a naked detainee's neck and having a female soldier pose for a picture
- A male MP guard having sex with a female detainee
- Using military dogs (without muzzles) to intimidate and frighten detainees, and in at least one case biting and seriously injuring a detainee
- Taking photographs of a dead Iraqi detainee

These acts of dehumanization and torture are repulsive anywhere, but particularly so when they occurred under the American military's watch, and US army and intelligence personnel participated in the acts. For men to be naked in front of other men, and forced to have homosexual acts, are against Islamic law and culture. Iraqis enduring abuse by Israelis was extremely offensive. Taking photographs of dead bodies was against military rules. Such treatment of Arab men, women, and even minors was against all social norms. The serial abuses that occurred in the Abu Ghraib and Guantanamo detention centers left a stain on the image of the United States. The expanding long war was extracting a high cost in economic and military terms, as well as draining America's moral capital.

4

Afghan War

There is a tendency to depict America's war in Afghanistan as a 20-year war from 2001, when President George W. Bush ordered reprisal against al Qaeda and the Taliban after the 9/11 attacks, to 2021, when President Joe Biden withdrew US forces from the country. However, this is not a full and accurate account of America's military engagement in Afghanistan, because that engagement actually began on July 3, 1979, when President Jimmy Carter signed the first directive for secret aid to the opponents of the pro-Soviet communist government in Kabul. Robert Gates, then a career CIA officer, disclosed in his memoir nearly two decades later that the aim of President Carter's secret order was to support "insurgent propaganda and other psychological operations" in Afghanistan.[1] It opened the way for America's proxy war using Mujahideen fighters, first against the pro-Soviet regime in Kabul, then against the Soviets themselves after they invaded Afghanistan at the end of 1979.

4.1 War on Soviet Communism

Gates's memoir was an authoritative rejection of the official version that the United States began military assistance to the Mujahideen after the Soviet invasion of Afghanistan. According to Gates, the Carter administration started to consider providing secret aid to Afghan insurgents in early 1979—well before the Soviet military invasion of Afghanistan. Carter, a born-again

---

[1] Robert Gates, *From the Shadows: The Ultimate Insider's Story of Five Presidents and How They won the Cold War* (New York: Simon & Schuster, 1997), 143–149. Also, see Deepak Tripathi, *Breeding Ground: Afghanistan and the Origins of Islamist Terrorism* (Washington, DC: Potomac, 2011), 62–64.

Christian, came to the White House determined to make human rights a key part of his administration's policies. His National Security Advisor, Zbigniew Brzezinski, a Polish émigré, was a staunch anti-communist and a firm supporter of those policies. As part of Carter's policy to provide secret aid to Afghan insurgents, the CIA provided several options.

Under Brzezinski's chairmanship, a Special Coordinating Committee oversaw policy issues that cut across several government departments, including intelligence, evaluation of arms control, and crisis management. The CIA argued that the Afghan insurgents had achieved surprising successes against the pro-Soviet government in Kabul, citing rebellions in the countryside and in the army. The military government in neighboring Pakistan had indicated that it might be more willing and ready to help the insurgents than previously expected. Moreover, American intelligence officials had learned that Saudi Arabia could provide money and encourage Pakistan, and other countries could offer at least tacit support.[2] These developments influenced President Carter's decision to sign the first order to provide Mujahideen with secret aid.

Not long after Gates's disclosures were made, Brzezinski himself spoke in public in 1998. He revealed that, on the day Carter signed the order, he told the president that the "American action was going to induce a Soviet military invasion" in Afghanistan.[3] Brzezinski described Carter's intervention in July 1979 as an "excellent idea," because it drew the Soviet Union into "the Afghan trap." He said that, on the day the Soviet troops crossed into Afghanistan, he wrote a note to President Carter that the United States had "the opportunity to give the USSR its Vietnam War." The US plan quickly acquired momentum, with Pakistan's military regime, Saudi Arabia, a host of other Arab countries, and China joining in to help the Afghan Mujahideen.

After the defeat of Jimmy Carter by Ronald Reagan in the November 1980 presidential election came a major escalation in America's proxy war in Afghanistan. Carter had used largely covert actions against the Soviets, but the Reagan administration was more belligerent and bold. Reagan denounced the brutal invasion of Afghanistan and warned the Soviet Union against intervening in Poland, where the Solidarity trade union was challenging the communist system.[4] Afghanistan thus became the main strategic battleground for

---

[2] Gates, *From the Shadows*, 144.

[3] Zbigniew Brzezinski's interview in French in Le Nouvel Observateur (Paris), January 15–21, 1998, translated by William Blum and David N. Gibbs in "Afghanistan: The Soviet Invasion in Retrospect," International Politics 37, no 2, 2000, 241–242. Also, see Chalmers Johnson, "The Largest Covert Operation in CIA History," History News Network, George Washington University.

[4] See Ronald Reagan's speeches: welcoming the British Prime Minister, Margaret Thatcher, in the White House on February 26, 1981; the state banquet for President Ziaul Haq of Pakistan on December 7, 1982; radio address on defense spending on February 19, 1983; address on foreign policy on October 20, 1984; and welcoming King Fahd of Saudi Arabia in the White House on February 11, 1985—all available in the Ronald Reagan Presidential Library & Museum.

Reagan's fight against Soviet communism, and Pakistan was turned into a frontline base for the United States. In June 1981, Pakistan became a beneficiary of a three-billion-dollar military and economic assistance package from America over 6 years.[5] The Reagan offensive began to take shape at the same time when the Kremlin plunged into a political crisis toward the end of 1982.[6]

Meanwhile, in September 1981, President Anwar Sadat of Egypt revealed details of the CIA's Afghan operation involving his country.[7] In an interview with the American television network NBC, Sadat disclosed that the United States was buying Soviet-designed equipment from Egypt, and shipping it to Afghan insurgents. These weapons, "either originals or duplicates," included shoulder-fired antitank and antiaircraft missiles, guns, and ammunition. Sadat told NBC that the American administration originally contacted him. Thereafter, "the transport of arms started from Cairo on US planes." The NBC report also revealed that the operation had been going on for 21 months, suggesting that it clearly started in January 1980, a year before President Carter left the White House.[8] Carter himself did not comment on the report.

China condemned the Soviet invasion of Afghanistan, reflecting Beijing's fear that the Soviets were extending their influence in Asia with the aim of encircling China.[9] Soon after the invasion, China began sending military aid to Afghan Mujahideen. The Chinese leadership favored firm military force, and opposed any compromise which would have allowed the Soviet troops to withdraw, but still keeping the Kremlin-installed Afghan leader, Babrak Karmal, in office. For its part, the United States calculated that support from the Saudi royal family, the custodians of two of the holiest shrines in Islam, was essential.[10] With its enormous oil wealth, Saudi Arabia was in a position to make a significant contribution to America's war effort in Afghanistan. So, Brzezinski visited Riyadh, and secured agreement from Saudi rulers to "match

---

[5] "The United States has offered Pakistan a military and economic package," UPI, at the end of a visit by Undersecretary of State for Security Assistance James Buckley.

[6] The Soviet leadership was in a state of paralysis during the early 1980s. Three leaders died in less than three years: Leonid Brezhnev in November 1982; his successor, Yuri Andropov, in February 1984; and Konstantin Chernenko in March 1985. Chernenko's death led to the appointment of Mikhail Gorbachev, at 54 the youngest member of the Politburo, as the General-Secretary of the Soviet Communist Party in May that year.

[7] Sadat's remarks were broadcast on NBC on September 22, 1981. For details, see "Sadat on Arms to Afghan Freedom Fighters" (Washington, DC: Joint Chiefs of Staff Message Center, US Defense Department, September 23, 1981).

[8] For corroboration, see John Cooley, *Afghanistan, America and International Terrorism* (London: Pluto Press, 2002), 21.

[9] "China and the Afghan Resistance," Weekly summary of the US Defense Intelligence Agency, March 6, 1981.

[10] The two shrines are Mecca and Medina.

the US contribution to the Mujahideen."[11] It also suited General Zia of Pakistan, because it served to end the international isolation of his military regime.

With a massive war machine including Pakistan, Saudi Arabia and other Gulf states, China, and European allies, the Americans had clearly decided to draw more and more Soviet troops into Afghanistan. Within 6 months of the invasion, more than 80,000 Soviet troops were occupying Afghanistan.[12] The Soviets launched frequent offensives in areas where rebellions were building up in 1980.[13] Despite heavy reinforcements, however, the occupation army spread out too quickly, and its battleground challenges continued to multiply. Due to the insurgents' harassment tactics, Soviet troops were brought out of their garrisons before they could even settle down. The occupation army began to take an increasing number of casualties.[14] The Soviets could not seal off Afghanistan from the outside world. The rugged terrain, the limited manpower of the Soviet army, the hostile Afghan population, and the well-resourced and trained Mujahideen guerrillas—all conspired against any attempt to close the Afghan border. The United States and its allies could always supply the guerrillas fighting deep inside Afghanistan.

During the Reagan presidency, a more intensive phase of American proxy war against the Soviets began at the end of 1983. William Casey, the CIA director, had been in his post for about 3 years. In the first half of 1984, the number of Mujahideen guerrillas, trained and armed by the CIA in Pakistani camps, increased from 400 to about a thousand men a month. By 1987, the total number of training camps run by the ISI around the Pakistani border towns of Peshawar and Quetta had risen from two to seven.[15] Between 1983 and 1987, "at least 80,000 Mujahideen received training in Pakistan" and thousands more inside Afghan territory. The CIA provided training camps in Pakistan and guerrilla bases throughout Afghanistan with secure radio sets. The amount of arms and ammunition through the CIA pipeline to the Afghan resistance also increased dramatically from 10,000 tons in 1983 to 65,000

---

[11] Gates, *From the Shadows*, 148.
[12] Russian General Staff, *The Soviet Afghan War: How A Superpower Fought and Lost*, translated and edited by Lester Grau and Michael Gress (Lawrence: University Press of Kansas, 2002), 12.
[13] Gates, *From the Shadows*, 148.
[14] Casualty estimates were not available, but the Russian General Staff gave an account of what happened. See Russian General Staff, *The Soviet-Afghan War*, 20–24. The author also heard similar accounts in 1990–1991 during private briefings with senior military officers in the communist army of Afghanistan, General Mohammad Afzal Lodin and General Nabi Azimi.
[15] Mohammad Yousaf (Brigadier, retired) and Mark Adkin, *Afghanistan: The Bear Trap* (Barnsley, UK: Leo Cooper, 2001), 117. Brigadier Yousaf was head of the Afghan Bureau of Pakistan's ISI from 1983 to 1987.

tons in 1987.[16] Memories of the defeat in Vietnam, and its domino effect in Cambodia and Laos, were still fresh in American minds. Casey, the CIA director, was determined to "make the Soviets bleed," and administration officials thought a Soviet "Vietnam" would be just retribution.[17]

The US-led war against the Soviet and Afghan communist forces brought about dramatic social and economic changes in Afghanistan. One million Afghans died, and more than four million refugees fled to Pakistan.[18] Many districts in the Afghan countryside were all but emptied of people. Education and medical care suffered greatly. A whole generation of Afghans had little chance of getting secondary education. Mosques and madrassas were often all that was available for primary education. War disrupted agricultural production, and there were extreme shortages of goods in the markets. Infrastructure was either destroyed or fell into disrepair. A point came in November 1986 when Gorbachev gave a gloomy assessment of the Soviet occupation of Afghanistan at a Politburo meeting.[19] He said that the Soviet Union had already been involved in Afghanistan for 6 years, with some saying that "if we carry on like that, it is going to go on for another 20–30 years."

The Soviet leader admitted that the Afghan government's military position was weak, and President Najibullah's policy of national reconciliation had not worked. Gorbachev proposed withdrawing half of the Soviet troops from Afghanistan in 1987, and the rest in the following year.[20] By the Kremlin's own admission, the costs of occupation had been devastating. Officially, the war resulted in an estimated 55,000 Soviet casualties, including dead, wounded, and mentally ill, without achieving "the desired victory."[21] In its postmortem, the Russian General Staff admitted that the Soviet Union's goals in Afghanistan were extremely vague, and their time for military planning was limited. The Soviet army's style of warfare—that is fighting a conventional war with heavy ground weapons and airpower—was not suited for the mountainous terrain. And the Russian General Staff admitted that Afghan armed forces struggled to understand the resistance fighters' tactics.

---

[16] Ibid, 98. Although Robert Gates is less specific, he confirms that "the CIA covert program to the Mujahideen increased several times over." See *From the Shadows*, 321.

[17] Odd Arne Westad, *The Global Cold War* (Cambridge, UK: Cambridge University Press, 2005), 328. Also, Carter Malkasian, *The American War in Afghanistan: A History* (New York: Oxford University Press, 2021), 30.

[18] Malkasian, *The American War in Afghanistan*, 32.

[19] "Politburo on Afghanistan," November 13, 1986, in document collection *Soviet Invasion of Afghanistan* (History and Public Policy Program Digital Archive, Wilson Center, Washington, DC).

[20] Ibid. The timing of Gorbachev's remarks is worth noting. They were made just 2 months after the Afghan resistance began using heat-seeking Stinger missiles.

[21] The Russian General Staff, *The Soviet-Afghan War*, 1.

Some Afghan military planners on the Mujahideen side observed that the Soviet plan failed, because it was based on the experience in the East European countries—in particular, East Germany, Hungary, and Czechoslovakia—after 1945.[22] The explanation of this view is simple. The Soviets intervened in these countries with overwhelming force, as they did in Afghanistan. Tanks rolled in to impose the Kremlin's will. They removed counterrevolutionaries from the regime and replaced them with compliant officials. The situation was then stabilized before Soviet troops withdrew from the streets. Thereafter, the country's client regime was left to rule according to Soviet guidance. But Afghanistan's territory, demography and culture, and level of national development were all very different from Eastern Europe.

The Soviets finally began their military withdrawal in May 1988 under the Geneva Accords between Pakistan and Afghanistan, witnessed by the United States and the Soviet Union, signed on April 14 of the same year.[23] The final column of Soviet troops crossed the Hairatan Bridge into the USSR on May 15, 1989. The accords consisted of three main instruments: a bilateral agreement between Pakistan and Afghanistan on non-interference and non-intervention; a declaration of international guarantees signed by the United States and the Soviet Union; and an agreement between Pakistan and Afghanistan on the voluntary return of Afghan refugees. But documents released later showed that the US position changed from "the mutual withdrawal of all outside forces," as President Reagan told Gorbachev in Geneva in November 1985, to insistence on continued arms support to the Afghan Mujahideen in 1988, and further to the refusal of free election plans in 1990 if they allowed the Soviet-supported Afghan leader, Najibullah, to run.[24]

With the Soviet withdrawal from Afghanistan completed after a decade of occupation, the United States succeeded in giving the USSR its "Vietnam." The next step was to bring down Najibullah's government. Soviet help to Najibullah's government dried out, large-scale defections depleted his armed forces, and changing loyalties of officials greatly weakened the Kabul regime. In December 1991, the USSR itself was dissolved, and Mikhail Gorbachev resigned as president of the defunct state. Four months later, the Najibullah

---

[22] Ali Ahmad Jalali and Lester W. Grau, *The Other Side of the Mountain: Mujahideen Tactics in Soviet-Afghan War* (Quantico, VA: Military Press, 2000), 126.

[23] "The Geneva Accords of 1988 (Afghanistan)," signed on April 14, 1988, insidethecoldwar.org

[24] See "Memorandum of Conversation: Reagan-Gorbachev, Second Plenary Meeting, Geneva, November 19,1985"; "Powell letter to Shultz, April 15, 1988"; and "Memorandum of Conversation between Secretary Baker and Eduard Shevardnadze, March 20, 1990," in documents published on February 27, 2019, titled "The Soviet Withdrawal from Afghanistan 1989," National Security Archive, Washington, DC.

regime in Kabul collapsed, and with it Afghan communism.[25] What followed was internecine warfare among rival Mujahideen factions, and the rise of the Taliban.[26] America's interest in Afghanistan and Pakistan diminished, though did not cease completely.[27] The idea of opening trade routes through Afghanistan began to be actively considered. One of the options was to build pipelines between the Pakistani port of Karachi and Central Asia to carry fuel from oil and gas fields in the region.[28]

US corporation Unocal proposed a plan in partnership with Saudi Arabia's Delta Oil—an enterprise with an estimated cost of two billion dollars. American oil executives were in discreet contact with Pakistani and Saudi officials about the idea. The US-led enterprise won the bid, and the Turkmen president, Saparmurat Niyazov, signed an agreement with the consortium.[29] We also know that, for a period, US diplomats were in contact with the Taliban directly, or through Pakistan, to secure Osama bin Laden's extradition from late 1998 onward, without success.[30]

4.2 War on Al Qaeda and the Taliban

We know that the Taliban were evicted from their seat in Kabul with apparent ease due to America's overwhelming airpower, and Northern Alliance fighters on the ground, in December 2001, and Taliban and al Qaeda leaders melted away into the countryside. The atmosphere in Washington was triumphant at that initial success, with Defense Department officials telling Congress and the public in early 2002 that the Taliban had been destroyed, al Qaeda had

---

[25] The Najibullah regime fell in April 1992.

[26] For Taliban's rise, see Deepak Tripathi, *Breeding Ground: Afghanistan and the Origins of Islamist Terrorism* (Washington, DC: Potomac, 2011), 107–116.

[27] Ibid. For the "Taliban and the United States," see 112–114. US interest in Afghanistan could not have ended because of post-revolution Iran, interest in oil, and close ties with Saudi Arabia.

[28] Turkmenistan had vast gas and oil reserves, as well as a government eager to do business with the outside world.

[29] It was seen as a move by the Turkmen leader to encourage a big American company and the Clinton administration in his country. See Ahmed Rashid, *Taliban: Islam, Oil and the New Great Game in Central Asia, Revised Edition* (London: IB Tauris, 2008), 160. Rashid provides a detailed analysis of the battle for pipelines in chapters 12 and 13. Olivier Roy examines Pakistan's strategic objectives behind its support for the Taliban, and points out that the American political advisor to Unocal, Charles Santos, was close to the Clinton administration. See Roy's "Rivalries and Power Plays in Afghanistan: The Taliban, the Shari'a and the Pipeline," *Middle East Report* no. 202 (Winter 1996), 38–39.

[30] US Embassy cable, "Ambassador raises bin Laden with Foreign Secretary, Shamshad Ahmad," Islamabad, October 6, 1998; "Osama bin Laden: Charge reiterates U.S. concerns to key Taliban official, who sticks to well-known Taliban position," Islamabad, December 19, 2000, in *Update*: *The Taliban File Part IV* (Washington, DC: National Security Archive, August 18, 2005).

dispersed, and terrorist camps shut down.[31] From the Taliban's heartland, Kandahar, a member of a team of allied commandos, Roger Pardo-Maurer, wrote a lengthy letter of observations to his Pentagon colleagues that caught the attention of the Defense Secretary, Donald Rumsfeld.[32] Pardo-Maurer's letter had a blunt warning. Al Qaeda, he said, "have licked their wounds and are regrouping in the Southeast with the connivance of a few junior warlords and the double-dealing Pakistanis." And in somewhat colorful language, he went on: "Along the border provinces, you can't kick a stone over without Bad Guys swarming out like ants and snakes and scorpions. It is amazing how many are foreigners." Given Afghanistan's terrain, Pardo-Maurer's warning was: "The number one *military* mistake we could make here is to go 'conventional' in the war."[33]

American troops struggled to distinguish al Qaeda and the Taliban from other Afghans.[34] Taliban and al Qaeda fighters moved around wearing the same headgear and baggy trousers as locals, and blended into the population. Just because someone carried an AK-47 rifle did not automatically indicate that they were America's enemies. Weapons were in abundance since the Soviet invasion in 1979, and Afghans carried them for self-protection and pride. Removing the Taliban from power in Kabul was easy. Maintaining control in the country was hugely challenging, as events in the years to come would show.

Another mistake of the Bush administration was to blur the line between al Qaeda and the Taliban.[35] Both shared an extremist religious ideology. Al Qaeda and bin Laden moved to Afghanistan, because the Taliban gave them sanctuary. But their structure and objectives were not the same. Al Qaeda was a network of Arabs, with a global presence and ambitions, its focus on the United States. Bin Laden's objective was to overthrow the Saudi royal family and other Middle Eastern rulers allied to the United States. On the other hand, the Taliban were almost entirely made of Pashtun tribes in southern and eastern Afghanistan, from where they fought other ethnic groups, and in border areas of Pakistan, where they grew up, found support, and sustenance, and eventually took control of most of Afghanistan. Despite their alliance with al

---

[31] Craig Whitlock, "Who Are the Bad Guys?," *The Afghanistan Papers: A Secret History of the War* (New York: Simon and Schuster, 2021), 18. See the following pages for more on declassified government documents on the war obtained by Washington Post, and published in *The Afghanistan Papers*.

[32] "Greetings from scenic Kandahar," Roger Pardo-Maurer letter from Kandahar, August 11–15, 2002 (Washington, DC, National Security Archive, George Washington University). The letter was partially declassified by the Defense Department on September 22, 2010.

[33] Ibid, 9–10.

[34] Whitlock, *The Afghanistan Papers*, 18–19.

[35] Ibid, 19–20.

Qaeda, there was little evidence that the Taliban had prior knowledge of the 9/11 attacks on America. After the US-led invasion of Afghanistan, hundreds of al Qaeda fighters were killed or captured, but al Qaeda leaders, including bin Laden, escaped to Pakistan and other countries. President Bush's reprisal against the Taliban was due largely to the Taliban's refusal to hand over bin Laden after the 9/11 attacks. For the next 20 years, the United States fought the Taliban and other militants in the region, among them Uzbeks, Chechens, and Pakistanis, who had little or nothing to do with the 9/11 atrocities.

The letter by Roger Pardo-Maurer from Kandahar was among hundreds of confidential documents, transcripts of interviews with US and allied officials, notes, and audio recordings obtained by the *Washington Post* after a 3-year legal battle in what was a secret history of America's war in Afghanistan after the 9/11 attacks. The collection in the *Lessons Learned* project of the US agency called *Office of the Special Inspector General for Afghanistan Reconstruction* (SIGAR), discussed in *The Afghanistan Papers*, gave a deep insight into decisions that led to failures in the war between 2001 and 2021.[36] A US Navy SEAL, Jeffrey Eggers, who worked on the National Security Council under Bush and Obama, said in an interview: "Our entire post-9/11 response is all subject to question because of this increasing complexity. Why did we make the Taliban the enemy when we were attacked by al Qaeda? Why did we want to defeat the Taliban?"[37]

Accounts of how opportunities to get bin Laden were missed gradually emerged after December 2001. At an early stage of the American military operations, intelligence reports indicated that he had fled with several hundred of his fighters to a large complex of caves and tunnels called Tora Bora in the Safed Koh (White) mountain range on the Afghan-Pakistan border. Fewer than a hundred American commandos were on the scene with their Afghan allies, but calls for reinforcements to launch an assault on the Tora Bora complex were rejected, and US sniper teams and mobile divisions of the Marine Corps were kept on the sidelines.[38] Instead, the US command "chose to rely on airstrikes and untrained Afghan militias to attack bin Laden and on Pakistan's loosely organized Frontier Corps to seal his escape routes."

---

[36] Craig Whitlock, *The Afghanistan Papers* (New York: Simon & Schuster, 2021). Also, Saphora Smith, "US officials misled public on Afghan war, according to Washington Post," NBC, December 9, 2019. Also, Associated Press, "Confidential documents show failure of Bush, Obama administrations during Afghanistan war," December 9, 2019.

[37] Interview of Jeffrey Eggers in Lessons Learned Project, Special Inspector General for Afghanistan Reconstruction (SIGAR), August 25, 2015, cited in Craig Whitlock, *The Afghanistan Papers*, 20.

[38] "Tora Bora Revisited: How We Failed To Get bin Laden And Why It Matters Today," The US Senate Foreign Relations Committee Report, November 30, 2009, 1–13.

On or around December 16, 2001, "bin Laden and his bodyguards walked unmolested out of Tora Bora and disappeared into Pakistan's unregulated tribal area." The decision not to deploy American forces to go after bin Laden was made by the Secretary of Defense, Donald Rumsfeld, and General Tommy Franks. Rumsfeld said at the time that he was "concerned that too many US troops in Afghanistan would create an anti-American backlash and fuel a widespread insurgency." In time, the insurgency spread, American and allied forces had to be massively reinforced, and bin Laden was found and killed on President Obama's orders by US Special Forces in Abbottabad, Pakistan, on May 2, 2011.

Barnett Rubin, a US academic who served as an advisor to the United Nations, told government officials: "A major mistake we made was treating the Taliban the same as al Qaeda."[39] Rubin disclosed that "key Taliban officials were interested in giving the new system a chance, but we did not give them a chance." The United States made a serious miscalculation and concluded that the Taliban were a finished force, and could be ignored. In fact, they were still the largest group in the country, but were excluded from the Bonn talks and eventual agreements. James Dobbins, a veteran diplomat and among those guiding the Bonn process, acknowledged that Washington failed to realize the gravity of the error. He spoke of a "missed opportunity" when a number of Taliban leaders and influential figures did surrender or offered to surrender including, according to one account, Mullah Omar himself. Dobbins admitted that he was among those who erroneously assumed that the Taliban "had been heavily discredited," and unlikely to make a comeback. Such assumptions ignored the fact that the Taliban were part of the same society, and would not disappear.

Officials who served in the Bush and Obama administrations said that both leaders failed in the most important task to devise a clear strategy with attainable objectives.[40] Military commanders and diplomats could not answer simple questions like who is the enemy, and who can be counted as allies. While Bush expanded the mission soon after the initial successes, American, NATO, and Afghan officials all told government interviewers that Obama's strategy was also destined to fail, because he tried to achieve too much too quickly, and depended on an Afghan government that was corrupt and dysfunctional. Obama tried to set artificial dates for ending the war. All the Taliban had to do was wait. Richard Boucher, a career diplomat and chief State Department spokesman under President Bush, said that "we went in to get al Qaeda … we

---

[39] Whitlock, *The Afghanistan Papers*, 27–28.
[40] *Associated Press*, December 9, 2019.

did that." Then the Taliban began "shooting back at us, and they became the enemy ... we kept expanding the mission."

The Bush administration's decision to expand the Afghan mission within months of removing the Taliban from power, and forcing out al Qaeda leaders, to Afghan nation-building was criticized. However, there was a context that explained how that decision was reached. When US officials visited Kabul in late December 2001 for the inauguration of the interim administration, they found overflowing toilets in the Presidential Palace, and public amenities almost non-existent.[41] Kabul city airport was not functioning, so Ryan Crocker, a veteran diplomat who arrived in January 2002 to help reopen the US embassy, landed at Bagram air base thirty miles north of the capital. Plumbing in the embassy was broken, and a hundred Marine guards had to share a single toilet. In meetings with Hamid Karzai, Crocker realized that the occupying powers, and the new administration that was being installed, faced bigger challenges than the United States had imagined. Karzai, leader of the interim administration, had no real authority, nothing to work with, no military or police, and there was no functioning society.

It seemed that Afghanistan, and the new government the occupation forces were trying to install, would simply not survive without nation-building. The question was what kind of nation-building? An administrative system with a devolved structure that respected the centuries-old tribal and ethnic character of Afghanistan, or a centralized state system more like Western-style democracies. America, and its allies, went for the latter. So it was to be a presidential system with a bicameral legislature along the lines of the US system, with certain local adaptations.[42] In the period between 2002 and 2020, the United States allocated $143.27 billion for reconstruction, aid programs, and Afghan security forces, and the cost of war had risen to more than $815 billion.[43] But, instead of peace and stability, the United States built a corrupt and dysfunctional Afghan government that depended on US military power to survive.[44]

US officials estimated that even under the best-case scenarios, Afghanistan would need billions of dollars every year for decades. Bush was initially undecided whether he wanted to commit the United States to a long-term

---

[41] See Whitlock, "Afghan Nation-Building Project," *The Afghanistan Papers*, 29–39.
[42] The legislature, *Shura-e-Milli* (National Assembly), had two chambers: Meshrano Jirga or the House of Elders (upper house with 102 members) and *Wolesi Jirga* or the House of the People (lower house with 250 members).
[43] "Quarterly Report to US Congress (SIGAR: Special Inspector General for Afghanistan Reconstruction), January 30, 2021. Also, Whitlock, *The Afghanistan Papers*, 30.
[44] Whitlock, *The Afghanistan Papers*, 30.

nation-building program, or leave Afghanistan for others to deal with.[45] But US officials consistently gave a bleak assessment of Afghanistan's ability to stabilize the country without massive help, and Afghanistan's desperation for help became plain to see. Ultimately, in his State of the Union Address to Congress in January 2002, Bush praised "the spirit of the Afghan people" and promised: "We'll be partners in rebuilding that country."

The above context helps to explain the change in the Bush administration's thinking toward a long-term nation-building commitment to Afghanistan. In *Lessons Learned* interviews, American officials said that Bush and others in the White House feared "repeating the mistake Washington made during the 1990s, when it stopped paying attention to Afghanistan after US-backed rebels forced the Soviet Army to withdraw–leaving chaos in its wake." However, against such official explanations, we must not ignore that, on President Bush's instructions to develop a plan for Iraq, the Defense Secretary, Donald Rumsfeld, had already ordered the CENTCOM Commander General Tommy Franks in November 2001 to start planning for "decapitation" of Saddam Hussein's government, and install a "Provisional Government" in its place.[46] The Bush administration was embarking on nation-building in Afghanistan, and, at the same time, making preparations to invade Iraq.

From that point on, the Bush administration's decision about Afghanistan should be seen in a more expansive context, which included invading Iraq and overthrowing Saddam Hussein, and continuing the global war on terror, including the campaign against al Qaeda. Bush, therefore, refused to contribute American troops to the international peacekeeping force in Afghanistan, in case it diverted resources away from fighting al Qaeda and the Taliban, and the plan to invade Iraq.[47] Richard Haass, at the time the Bush administration's coordinator for Afghanistan, floated the idea of deploying 20,000–25,000 American troops, along with an equal number of allied forces, but he said "there was no enthusiasm," and his plan was "shot down."[48]

Instead, the Defense Department took responsibility for training a new Afghan army, but only as part of a joint effort with other countries in nation-building. Under the agreement, for example, Germany accepted the responsibility for creating a new Afghan police force, Italy agreed to help overhaul the justice system, and the United Kingdom would discourage Afghan farmers

---

[45] Ibid, 31–33.
[46] "US Sets "Decapitation of Government" As Early Goal of Combat," in the document collection *The Iraq War—Part I: The US Prepares for Conflict, 2001*, posted on September 22, 2010, National Security Archive.
[47] Whitlock, *The Afghanistan Papers*, 33.
[48] Ibid, 34. Also, see Associated Press, December 9, 2019.

from opium production to grow other crops for their livelihood. However, as the Taliban regrouped in subsequent years, and the occupation forces were unable to subdue them, the number of US troops grew steadily, and under President Obama it reached a hundred thousand in August 2010, remaining at that level until May 2011.[49]

As for Afghanistan's new government and institutional structure, it was a "rudimentary version of Washington," with power concentrated in the capital, Kabul.[50] From the early stages of development, a form of federal bureaucracy began to grow in all directions, cultivated by American money and foreign advisors. An important difference was that the Bush administration, with its own man Hamid Karzai installed in Kabul, pushed the Afghans to consolidate power in the presidency. There were few checks and balances of the kind in the US constitution. The objective was to curtail the influence of regional warlords. Numerous US and European officials admitted in *Lessons Learned* interviews that "to put so much power in the hands of one man was a disastrous miscalculation." That rigid constitutional system was contrary to Afghan tradition, typified by decentralized authority and tribal customs. An unnamed European Union official remarked that the "worst decision was to centralize power." Another senior US official supported that view, saying he was "astounded that the State Department thought an American-style presidency would work in Afghanistan." It was as if "they had never worked overseas."

In Army oral history interviews, even soldiers who were not familiar with Afghanistan said that "they found Afghans intrinsically hostile toward national power brokers, with little concept of what a bureaucracy in Kabul might actually do."[51] In the past, the central government had not been a provider to them in many locations, so they did not really understand what benefits of having a central government in Kabul were. They often said they had raised their sheep and goats, and grown vegetables on their small piece of land, for hundreds of years without a central government. So what was the point? Army officers said it often fell to them to try to explain to farmers what a government did, and how a bureaucracy worked. Colonel Paschal, an infantry officer who spent 6 months in the eastern province of Ghazni, told interviewers that his unit handed out posters of Hamid Karzai to villagers who had never seen the image of their president before. Colonel Paschal had previously served in

---

[49] "A timeline of US troop levels in Afghanistan since 2001," Associated Press, reproduced in Military Times, July 6, 2016.
[50] Whitlock, *The Afghanistan Papers*, 36–37.
[51] Ibid, 39.

the Balkans in the 1990s when the US military and NATO allies established democracy in Bosnia and Kosovo. The process was started with elections at the district and regional levels, finally reaching the national level. What happened in Afghanistan was the exact opposite, with the presidential election coming first. Most Afghans did not know what it meant to vote. At one time, people asked Colonel Paschal's unit: "What are the Russians doing back here?" They did not even know the Americans had been there for a couple of years.

Such detachment of the Afghan people from the government and state institutions created after the 2001 invasion, and removal of the Taliban from power, was a fundamental cause of failure of the state-building project in Afghanistan under President Hamid Karzai and his successor, Ashraf Ghani. Progress was evident in areas like education and health in Kabul, and other urban centers. However, bureaucratic branches that ran from the capital to provinces, towns, and villages in the countryside were alien for the masses, who recognized little gain from the new system. Afghans have had a centuries-old history of accepting foreign assistance, only to turn against foreigners who insist on their terms. This fierce independence often played a dominant role in conflicts between Afghans and foreign powers in the past. It ultimately led to the failure of America's 20-year project after the 9/11 attacks in 2001.

5

Iraq War

Just as there is a tendency to take a narrow view of the US war in Afghanistan as a 20-year war (2001–2021), often a narrow view is taken of America's war in Iraq. In Afghanistan, we know that the Carter administration began providing secret aid to the anti-communist Mujahideen guerrillas in July 1979, and thereafter the United States fought a proxy war against the Soviet occupation forces until their retreat in 1989. American interest in Afghanistan subsequently diminished, but did not end, as we have seen in the previous chapter. Then came the US reprisal against al Qaeda and the Taliban after the 9/11 attacks on America.

Similarly, the Iraq War is often viewed as two separate conflicts. One, the brief Operation Desert Storm, described as the First Gulf War (January–February 1991), to liberate Kuwait from Iraq's occupation; second, the 2003 invasion of Iraq, called the Second Gulf War, with the primary aim to overthrow President Saddam Hussein's regime.[1] Although Saddam Hussein was swiftly deposed, and the Ba'athist state dissolved in a short period of 3 weeks, Iraq descended into anarchy, and the United States fought a prolonged war to try to subdue insurgencies until 2011, before President Obama announced his first official withdrawal of US troops from the country. But the violence escalated again, and America had to reinforce its military presence. The period from the 1991 liberation of Kuwait to the 2003 invasion of Iraq often is not considered part of the conflict. Nevertheless, the fact was that, for more than a decade during this period, Saddam Hussein's regime was subject to an array

---

[1] "Operation DESERT STORM," US Army Center of Military History. For the US-led invasion of Iraq by President George W. Bush's coalition of the willing, and subsequent phase of war, without UN Security Council approval, see "The Iraq War: 2003–2011," Council on Foreign Relations.

of economic sanctions by the UN Security Council, and air-exclusion zones enforced by the United States and the United Kingdom to protect Kurds in Iraqi Kurdistan and Shi'a in the south from air attacks by the Iraqi government. It was war by other means.

5.1 Desert Storm

US involvement in Iraq had seen several ups and downs before Operation Desert Storm in the wake of Saddam Hussein's decision to invade Kuwait. Washington had friendly relations with Iraq's secular and nationalist Ba'ath Party since the 1950s, and supported the February 1963 coup that the State Department and the CIA viewed as considerably improving US-Iraq relations, and Iraq's internal situation.[2] Later in November 1963, factional divisions in the Ba'ath Party led to another military coup.[3] In years after that, Washington distanced itself as Iraq began to develop closer ties with the Soviet Union. The United States again supported Iraq during the Iran-Iraq War from 1980 to 1988.[4]

In the early hours of August 2, 1990, Saddam Hussein's forces invaded Kuwait, Iraq's tiny oil-rich neighbor.[5] Kuwaiti defense forces were no match for the invading Iraqis, so they retreated to Saudi Arabia along with the Emir of Kuwait, his family, and other government officials. Within hours, Iraq had occupied Kuwait, gained control of about one-fifth of the world's oil reserves, and a substantial coastline on the Persian Gulf. The United Nations Security Council denounced the invasion on the same day and demanded that Iraq immediately withdraw from Kuwait. Failing that, the Security Council imposed a worldwide ban on trade with Iraq on August 6, 1990. On November 29, the Security Council authorized the use of force if Saddam Hussein did not pull out his forces from Kuwait by January 15, 1991. The Iraqi leader refused.

---

[2] "Memorandum from Stephen O. Fuqua of the Bureau of International Security Affairs, Department of Defense to the Deputy Assistant Secretary of Defense for International Security Affairs," February 8, 1963, US Office of the Historian.

[3] Ibid, "Circular Telegram from the Department of State to Certain Posts," November 15, 1963. Also, John Ehrenberg, J. Patrick McSherry, Jose Ramon Sanchez, Caroleen Marji Sayej (editors), *The Iraq Papers* (New York: Oxford University Press, 2010), xxx.

[4] Washington's policy to support Iraq was prompted by the overthrow of the pro-US Shah in the Islamic revolution in Iran in 1979.

[5] "Iraq invades Kuwait," History.com

Saddam Hussein's decision to annex Kuwait was based on three claims.[6] First, that Kuwait was stealing oil by drilling non-vertical wells across the border into Iraqi oilfields, a technique called slant-drilling. Second, he demanded that the Kuwaitis cancel the more than forty billion dollar debt they were owed for financing Iraq's war against Iran. And third, as Kuwait was part of Iraq before it was carved off by Britain in the beginning of the twentieth century, it should be returned to Iraq. It was obvious that the idea of seizing an enormously wealthy oil-rich neighbor came at a time when Iraq's economy had been devastated by the war with Iran, and Saddam Hussein thought annexing Kuwait would be easy.

Following Saddam Hussein's refusal to end the occupation of Kuwait, President George H.W. Bush moved to build an international coalition, raising an army of nearly a million troops in the region to evict the Iraqi forces from Kuwait.[7] In previous years, the United States had given Iraq military assistance during the war with Iran, and Iraq had the fourth-largest army in the world at the time.[8] So, the threat to Saudi Arabia, a major oil exporter, was obvious. If Saudi Arabia had fallen, Iraq would gain control of one-fifth of the world's total oil supply, and threaten Western interests in the Middle East. Saddam Hussein was in defiance of United Nation resolutions, so the US-led coalition of more than 35 countries, including Arab nations, had UN backing.[9]

The war to liberate Kuwait was initially called Operation Desert Shield, led by General Norman Schwarzkopf. Most allied forces were stationed in Saudi Arabia. Soon after the UN deadline of January 15, 1991, passed without Iraq withdrawing its occupation forces, coalition forces began a 6-week bombing campaign against Iraqi command and control targets. There were fears that Saddam Hussein might use chemical weapons. Nonetheless, a ground invasion began in February 1991, and Desert Shield became Operation Desert Storm. The 6-week bombing of Iraqi targets included 116,000 air combat sorties, and more than 80,000 tons of bombs were dropped. Notwithstanding other coalition members, the United States deployed more than half a million troops to Saudi Arabia alone, in case Iraq attacked Saudi Arabia—almost as many as the highest number of American troops deployed in the Vietnam War.

Saddam Hussein tried to divide the coalition by firing Scud missiles at Israel, but the George H.W. Bush administration persuaded Israel not to retaliate against Iraq, and the coalition held together. For the first time, Patriot

---

[6] Ehrenberg et al., *Iraq Papers*, xxx–xxxi.
[7] Alan Taylor, "Operation Desert Storm: 25 Years Since the First Gulf War," Atlantic magazine, January 14, 2016.
[8] Shannon Collins, "Desert Storm: A Look Back," January 11, 2019, US Department of Defense.
[9] Among Arab members of the coalition were Saudi Arabia, Egypt, Syria, Oman, UAE and Qatar.

missiles were used in war to intercept Scud missiles. In all, about 697,000 American troops took part in the war. The lives of nearly 300 Americans were lost. Once the ground assault started, it took a 100 h to drive the Iraqi occupation forces from Kuwait, and Bush declared ceasefire.[10]

The brief occupation of Kuwait ended, but the Saddam Hussein regime was left in place in Baghdad. The UN Security Council had given approval for use of force to free Kuwait from occupation, and nothing more. The first Bush administration wanted to avoid chaos and disintegration and wanted to have a central authority with which it could come to an agreement at some stage. A much weakened Saddam Hussein survived as Iraq's leader. In his State of the Union Address to the American Congress on January 29, 1991, a triumphant President George H.W. Bush said: "What is at stake is more than one small country. It is a big idea: a new world order, where diverse nations are drawn together in common cause to achieve the universal aspirations of mankind—peace and security, freedom, and the rule of law."[11] That was the moment when American power was at its peak, and the restoration of Kuwait's independence was the beginning of America dominating in the Middle East.[12] The collapse of the Soviet Union had left the United States as the only superpower in the world. America had demonstrated that its precision weapons made military resistance pointless.

This level of military dominance, essentially based on the accuracy of air power, was the main reason for triumphalism in Washington. Bush Senior spoke of a "defining hour" for the nation, and the promise of renewed America.[13] Fifteen years after the shocking outcome of the war in Indochina, the United States had triumphed over its most powerful adversary, the USSR, and subsequently Saddam Hussein of Iraq. In a moment of euphoria, George H.W. Bush recalled America's political and military failures in the Vietnam War, and proclaimed: "We've kicked the Vietnam Syndrome once and for all." A day after, he repeated the sentiment in a radio address: "The specter of Vietnam has been buried forever in the desert sands of the Arabian Peninsula."

The financial cost of the Gulf War was estimated at 61 billion dollars for the United States alone, while other countries contributed about 50 billion

---

[10] On February 28, 1991.

[11] President George H.W. Bush, "Address Before a Joint Session of the Congress on the State of the Union," January 29, 1991, American Presidency Project.

[12] Lexington, "The Kuwait war plus 20," Economist, February 12, 2011.

[13] President George H.W. Bush, "Remarks to the American Legislative Exchange Council," March 1, 1991, American Presidency Project, University of California Santa Barbara.

dollars.[14] The conflict did not improve the American economy that had been on a downward spiral since the Vietnam War. It was the effectiveness of America's war machine that was celebrated, and it changed the national mood. In a state of hubris, the United States risked living in a world of its own imagination. But a country in such a state renders itself oblivious of failure lurking around, ignores early warning signs, and long-term costs in the years to come. America was entering that phase as future events would demonstrate. Great powers seek reasons to rationalize their status in the world. For the United States, it was about containment of communism after WWII. In the 1990s decade of the post-Soviet world, it was expansion of democracy, freedom, and a new world order. After the events of 9/11, it would be war against Islamist terrorism. It was a recipe for perpetual conflict.

As part of America's push for democracy and freedom in the post-Soviet 1990s decade, the US Congress passed, and President Clinton signed into law, the 1998 Iraq Liberation Act, which declared that "it should be the policy of the United States to support efforts to remove the regime headed by Saddam Hussein from power in Iraq and to promote the emergence of a democratic government to replace that regime."[15] The Act authorized the President to provide the democratic opposition in Iraq with help, including military training, humanitarian assistance, and information and broadcasting. Although Clinton expressed support for the Congressionally inspired legislation, he was unenthusiastic in its implementation.[16] The administration was reluctant to make a commitment it could not fulfill. Clinton was aware that, during the 1991 Gulf War, Bush Senior had urged the Iraqi people to rise up against Saddam Hussein, raising expectations that America would support them—only to abandon them when they did against the regime, which crushed the uprisings.

Those mass revolts by Kurds in the north, and Shi'a in the south, erupted barely a month after the Iraqi army's retreat from Kuwait. Saddam Hussein's military units turned on both rebellions with all their fury.[17] First, the military restored control over cities where uprisings had broken out. After consolidating control, his forces killed thousands of civilians by firing indiscriminately in residential areas; executing young people on the streets, in homes, and in hospitals; rounding up suspects, especially young people, during

---

[14] Stephen Daggett, "Costs of Major US Wars," June 29, 2010, Congressional Research Service. Also, Erik Mustermann, "The First Gulf War: Ten Fast Facts," August 21, 2016, War History Online.
[15] "Iraq Liberation Act of 1998," October 31, 1998.
[16] David Isenberg, "Imperial Overreach: Washington's Dubious Strategy to Overthrow Saddam Hussein," November 17, 1999, Policy Analysis No 360, Cato Institute, Washington, DC.
[17] "Endless Torment: The 1991 Uprising in Iraq And Its Aftermath," June 1992, Human Rights Watch.

house-to-house searches, arresting them without charge, shooting them en masse; and using helicopters to attack civilians as they fled the cities. The fate of thousands of Kurds and Shi'a remained unknown long after. Rebels also committed atrocities, summarily killing suspected members of the Iraqi security forces. The internal challenge to Saddam Hussein was suppressed at a high cost.

5.2 Containment

After the brutal suppression of Iraqi uprisings, a bipartisan agreement to contain Saddam Hussein developed in Washington.[18] That policy continued from 1992 to 2001. Containment was not about ground war, but about restraining Saddam Hussein by other means. To that end, Presidents George H.W. Bush and Bill Clinton worked with the United Nations to organize a range of restrictive measures—economic sanctions, oil embargoes, weapons inspections, and enforcement of air-exclusion zones over Iraq to prevent Saddam Hussein using air power against opponents. The United States ringed Iraq by military bases and forces in the region, strengthened Kuwait, ran intelligence and harassment operations in the Kurdish north, punished Saddam Hussein's forces from time to time, and supported Iraq's opposition. The US policy did contain Saddam Hussein, but the Iraqi leader found ways to undermine it. Washington claimed that containment was relatively inexpensive in terms of American lives, money, and political capital. However, that claim ignored the humanitarian price Iraqis paid in terms of extreme hardships, including shortages of food and medicines.

Iraq was no longer an active threat to regional security, but more of an irritant to Washington. Iraq was a significant power in the Gulf that still refused to accept US hegemony. The Saddam Hussein regime maintained its hostility to Israel, and challenged the Washington consensus on globalization, open markets and free trade, and sought to counter US plans for the region.[19] The challenge to America's hegemony was taken particularly seriously in Washington because of Iraq's large oil reserves, and Saddam Hussein's status as one of the last Arab nationalists in the region. The Gulf War and the sanctions regime seriously degraded Iraqi power, so the portrayal by American policymakers that Baghdad was a continuous threat to international peace and stability was weak at best. Containment was intended to serve broad US

---
[18] John Ehrenberg et al., *Iraq Papers*, 1–2.
[19] "Washington Consensus," Britannica.com

strategic interests rather than meet a particular threat at a huge cost to Iraqi civilians and infrastructure. A UNICEF report in 1999 documented "a 75 percent reduction in Iraq's gross national product, a doubling of the child mortality rate, and significant increases in malnutrition and mental illness since the embargo had begun."[20] But Saddam Hussein's government continued to resist inspection and monitoring, circumvent weapons embargoes, undermine UN Oil-for-Food Program, and defy air-exclusion zones.[21]

The Iraqi tactics to frustrate the sanctions regime, and the Oil-for-Food Program, caused international and domestic controversy in the United States. In January 2004, Iraq's al-Mada newspaper published a list of 270 names from forty countries, including UN officials and politicians who may have profited from the Iraqi oil while the program was running, and companies in receipt of oil vouchers in exchange for helping Saddam Hussein.[22] The disclosures triggered a scandal, and in its wake, the General Accountability Office, a Congressional watchdog, said that it believed the Iraqi leader had made ten billion dollars from the program between 1997 and 2002. Then, a Central Intelligence Agency investigation found that Saddam Hussein's abuse of the program earned him about eleven billion dollars through oil smuggling, and nearly two billion through kickbacks and surcharges. These revelations involved countries as diverse as Australia, China, Indonesia, India, Iran, Jordan, Russia, Switzerland, the United Kingdom, and the United States.[23]

The Oil-for-Food Program ended after the fall of Saddam Hussein's regime in 2003. But the scandal cast a troubling shadow not only on the United Nations, which set up its own inquiry headed by Paul Volcker, former chairman of the US Federal Reserve, but on the countries involved as well. The Volcker Commission's report cited "poor judgement by the UN Secretary-General Kofi Annan in failing to pursue inquiries involving his son, Kojo, and companies involved in the Oil-for-Food Program, lax oversight by the UN Security Council, and shoddy UN procurement practices."[24] It accused the former head of the program, Benon Sevan, of a "conflict of interest for

---

[20] John Ehrenberg et al., *Iraq Papers*, 2.
[21] Oil-for-Food Program, established by the United Nations under Security Council Resolution 986 in 1995, and implemented a year after, was designed to allow Iraq to sell oil on the world market in exchange for food, medicine, and other humanitarian needs for ordinary citizens of Iraq, without allowing the Iraqi regime to boost its military capability. See "Oil-for-Food," UN Office for Iraq Program.
[22] "Timeline: Oil-for-Food Scandal," BBC News, September 7, 2005; Robert McMahon, "The Impact of the Oil-for-Food Scandal," Council on Foreign Relations, May 11, 2006; Sharon Otterman, "Iraq: Oil-for-Food Scandal," Council on Foreign Relations, October 28, 2005.
[23] Kenneth Katzman and Christopher M. Blanchard, "Iraq: Oil-for-Food Program, Illicit Trade and Investigations," Congressional Research Service Report, June 14, 2005.
[24] McMahon, "The Impact of Oil-for-Food Scandal."

helping a friend obtain contracts to sell Iraqi oil"—a charge Sevan denied. Further, more than 2000 companies were accused of "paying bribes and receiving kickbacks to participate in the program."

In Washington, critics of the United Nations seized on the scandal, and demanded reforms. The Chairman of the House International Committee, Henry Hyde, described the scandal as a "symptom of a larger contagion that infects both procurement and oversight within the UN." The General Accountability Office, in its 2006 report, said: "The UN lacks an effective organizational structure for managing procurement, has not demonstrated a commitment to improving its procurement workforce, and has not adopted specific ethics guidance." At the time of the report's publication, Volcker Commission officials said that only about one-fourth of the 40 countries, whose citizens or companies were implicated in their inquiry, had requested further evidence for use in prosecutions.

The decision of the George H.W. Bush administration to not go beyond liberating Kuwait, but to resort to containment of Saddam Hussein's regime, prompted criticism from neoconservatives. After Bush Senior's defeat in 1992, those critical voices became louder during the Clinton administration, leading to the establishment of the neoconservative Project for the New American Century (PNAC) in 1997. It was to become the platform for George W. Bush's presidential campaign, and his presidency. One-time speechwriter of President Reagan's Secretary of State, George Shultz, and a cofounder of PNAC, Robert Kagan, made an argument for unilateralism in organizing a US-led world order.[25] In a commentary, Kagan wrote that a more general approach was essential in foreign policy that took America to the international pinnacle in the first place. In his view, it was about maintaining American military superiority, "not only to deter aggression, but to discourage other powers from trying to achieve parity" with the United States. This was the "recommendation, unfortunately rejected, of the Pentagon's best policy planners" during the George H.W. Bush administration. In a warning about America's policy in the 1990s, Kagan said that military strength alone would not be enough if "we do not use it to maintain a world order which both supports and rests upon American hegemony."

This advocacy by neoconservatives for an aggressive unilateralist world posture came despite early warnings from prominent figures who had served in previous Republican administrations. Henry Kissinger, national security advisor and secretary of state in the Nixon and Ford administrations, warned

---

[25] Robert Kagan, "American Power—A Guide for the Perplexed, Commentary, April 1996 (Excerpt), in Ehrenberg et al., *Iraq Papers*, 14–15.

against George H.W. Bush's optimism that a "new world order" was at hand.[26] In a concurrent warning to his neoconservative critics, Kissinger suggested that a messianic desire to remake the world was no substitute for a sober and careful assessment of each situation. Despite his previous record of supporting covert action during the Vietnam War, Kissinger seemed to defend caution and acceptance of limits which underlay containment in the wake of the Gulf War. "The new world order," he said, "cannot possibly fulfill the idealistic expectations." He underlined George H.W. Bush's personal relations with world leaders and coalition-building during the conflict. But Kissinger warned that America's preeminence could not last. He thought that had Kuwait been invaded 2 years later, the "American defense budget would have declined so as to preclude a massive overseas deployment." He said it was not possible for the American economy to "indefinitely sustain a policy of global unilateral interventionism," pointing out that it had to seek a "foreign subsidy of at least $50 billion" to prevail in the Gulf crisis. Despite his view of calculated realism, Kissinger acknowledged the limits of power and warned against overstretching three decades before it became a compelling reality.

5.3   Operation Iraqi Freedom

The US-led invasion of Iraq to overthrow Saddam Hussein's regime began with massive air attacks on March 19, 2003, and a ground invasion the following day.[27] We know that the Bush administration had begun planning to invade Iraq soon after Afghanistan, and starting the war on terror in late 2001. However, two important points need to be made before we take a closer look at the invasion, and its consequences. First, the invasion of Iraq was illegal under international law, and breached the UN Charter.[28] Article 39, Chap. 7 of the charter says: "The Security Council shall determine the existence of any threat to the peace, breach of the peace, or act of aggression and shall make recommendations, or decide what measures shall be taken in accordance with Articles 41 and 42, to maintain or restore international peace and security."

So President Bush and British Prime Minister Tony Blair, two leading advocates of regime change in Iraq, were unable to obtain the Security

---

[26] Henry Kissinger, "A False Dream," Los Angeles Times, February 24, 1991 (Excerpt), in Ehrenberg et al., *Iraq Papers*, 5–8.
[27] "Iraq Timeline: Since the 2003 War," United States Institute of Peace, last updated May 29, 2020.
[28] Juan Cole, "The Real Problem with the Iraq War: It was illegal," Informed Comment, July 7, 2016. Also, Ewen MacAskill and Julian Borger, "Iraq war was illegal and breached UN Charter," Guardian, September 16, 2004.

Council's approval for the war against Iraq. They blamed France for this failure, though Germany and Russia also resisted the push for war. All three members made it clear in a joint statement that they would oppose any Security Council resolution authorizing preemptive war.[29] The second point to be made is that there was no immediate threat to the peace. Iraq had been under a sanctions regime since after the First Gulf War. The UN chief weapons inspector in Iraq, Hans Blix, was continuing his inspections of Iraqi sites and was satisfied with the progress. There was no consensus in NATO on attacking Iraq either. Bush and Blair could only find support from Spain and Portugal in Europe before launching the war. When it was too late, the UN Secretary-General, Kofi Annan, declared unequivocally in September 2004 that the US-led war on Iraq was illegal.[30]

Having failed to get the Security Council's authorization, Bush began assembling a "coalition of the willing"—an international force of countries willing to join him.[31] And his mission of regime change in Baghdad moved ahead regardless of the UN chief weapons inspector, Hans Blix, briefing the Security Council on the progress of weapons inspections and disarmament ordered by the Security Council in Resolution 1441. When Blix briefed the council just 12 days before the invasion, his message was markedly different to claims by officials in Washington. The Bush administration used three main arguments for going to war—allegations that Saddam Hussein had links to al Qaeda, he had acquired weapons of mass destruction, and it was Washington's duty to spread democracy to countries ruled by dictators. Blix could not say anything about Baghdad's links with al Qaeda, and Washington's duty to establish a democratic system in Iraq. However, his conclusion about the weapons inspection process was that it was progressing, and "it would not take years, nor weeks, but months."[32]

The report by Hans Blix was an overwhelming repudiation of Washington's claims. In its wake, opposition to the administration's plans began to harden, and domestic critics became more vocal. Nonetheless, President Bush unilaterally issued an ultimatum in which he said that the Iraqi government had used "diplomacy as a ploy to gain time and advantage," and had "defied

---

[29] "Declaration of France, Germany, and Russia on War with Iraq," March 5, 2003, Ehrenberg et al., *Iraq Papers*, 142–143.

[30] MacAskill and Borger, "Iraq war was illegal and breached UN Charter," Guardian, September 16, 2004.

[31] "Q&A: What is the Coalition of the Willing," from the Council on Foreign Relations, cited in the New York Times, March 28, 2003.

[32] Hans Blix, "Briefing to the United Nations Security Council," March 7, 2003. Ehrenberg et al., *Iraq Papers*, 106–110. The official name for Iraq weapons inspectors was the United Nations Monitoring, Verification and Inspection Commission (UNMOVIC).

Security Council resolutions demanding full disarmament."³³ He went on to say that the Security Council had "not lived up to its responsibilities, so we will rise to ours." And addressing the Iraqi people, Bush said: "The tyrant will soon be gone. The day of your liberation is near." With those words, the job of the UN weapons inspectors was over. With his coalition of the willing, President George W. Bush went ahead to invade Iraq, and change the regime in Baghdad—a step his father, Bush Senior, had decided against in 1991.

After the ground invasion was launched on March 19, 2003, Iraqi forces were overwhelmed quickly.³⁴ Coalition troops faced less resistance from the Iraqi army than they expected, but there were a surprising number of attacks from irregular forces using guerrilla tactics, and hostile reaction from Iraqi people.³⁵ The Bush administration also faced criticisms at home and abroad. The Iraqi capital fell to coalition troops on April 9. Its fall was symbolized by the toppling of a large statue of Saddam Hussein in Firdos Square. Over the next week, coalition forces went on to capture Mosul and Tikrit in northern Iraq, and the southern city of Basra. On May 1, 2003, President Bush proclaimed from the deck of the USS Abraham Lincoln: "Major combat operations have ended. In the battle of Iraq, the United States and our allies have prevailed. And now our coalition is engaged in securing and reconstructing that country."³⁶ His victory speech was far too early, and premature.

Even before the invasion, millions of people in major cities around the world had been demonstrating against the imminent war. In Britain and Spain, where leaders aligned themselves with Bush, there were huge protests—two million in Barcelona, one million in Madrid, and as many as two million in Britain.³⁷ The European Parliament passed a resolution in "opposition to any unilateral action." The strongest warning came from the South African President, Nelson Mandela, who said that a US invasion of Iraq would plunge the world into a "holocaust." On the day of ground invasion, China condemned the United States, and other countries, for bypassing the UN Security Council and launching the invasion of Iraq.³⁸ And, in a separate statement, the Russian President, Vladimir Putin, while expressing his commitment to control weapons of mass destruction, nevertheless emphasized the importance of international law and institutions in resolving global conflicts. Referring to President Bush's defiance of the Security Council, the Russian

---

[33] George W. Bush, "Ultimatum to Iraq," March 17, 2003, in Ehrenberg et al., *Iraq Papers*, 110–113.
[34] "Operation Iraqi Freedom," US Naval History and Heritage Command.
[35] "The Fall of Baghdad," Encyclopedia.com, April 2003.
[36] "Text of Bush Speech," May 1, 2003, CBS News.
[37] Ehrenberg et al., *Iraq Papers*, 116.
[38] Ibid, "Foreign Ministry of China, Statement on War with Iraq," March 20, 2003, 157.

leader said that Russia was for "solving such conflicts through the United Nations."[39]

The ease with which Saddam Hussein's regime collapsed took America by surprise, leaving a power vacuum. As soon as his statue was toppled in the capital's main square, Iraqi opposition parties started arguing about the future shape of the country. An early attempt to call a meeting of exiled groups in the southern city of Nasiriyah to form an interim government ended in failure.[40] In Washington, the State Department and the Pentagon disagreed over when such a meeting should take place, and who should be in the new Iraqi government. The State Department advocated a gradual process of "de-Saddamification"—purging the Ba'ath Party and the state of officials at the top of the command structure but leaving most of the institutions intact.[41] The Pentagon, on the other hand, wanted a more radical purge, because it wanted to install Ahmed Chalabi, founder of the Iraqi National Congress, and other exiled Iraqis.[42]

The CIA agreed with the State Department, but Vice President Dick Cheney's office supported the Pentagon's recommendation. Meanwhile, the occupation forces found themselves thinly stretched, and anarchy spread as a consequence. The Iraqi army disintegrated, and its troops dispersed. Saddam Hussein went underground. Paul Bremer, the man the Bush administration appointed as head of Iraq's Coalition Provisional Authority (CPA), arrived in Baghdad on May 12, 2003, and immediately made it clear that he was in charge. Bremer started his tenure by signing Orders 1 and 2, which dissolved the Ba'ath Party, the Iraqi government, the armed forces, and a host of other institutions—a project which was dear to Chalabi.[43]

---

[39] Ibid, "Vladimir Putin, "Press Statement on Iraq," April 3, 2003 (Excerpt), 159.

[40] Ewen MacAskill and Oliver Burkeman, "Power vacuum that has taken US by surprise," Guardian, April 11, 2003.

[41] Ehrenberg et al., *Iraq Papers*, 182.

[42] From September 2003 to January 2006, Chalabi served first briefly as President of the Governing Council of Iraq, then as Deputy Prime Minister and Minister of oil.

[43] Ehrenberg et al., *Iraq Papers*. Bremer's Order No 1 "De-Ba'athification of Iraqi Society" was signed on May 16, 2003; Order No 2, signed on May 23, 2003, was "Dissolution of Entities" and signed on May 23, 2003. Together, the two orders amounted to complete dismantling of the Iraqi state structure under Saddam Hussein.

5.4 Uprisings

These orders exacerbated the power vacuum in the country, and, within months, US forces and allies faced a growing challenge from insurgents. Iraq's Sunni minority was dominant during the previous regime of Saddam Hussein, who himself belonged to the Sunni sect. The Provisional Authority's focus on empowering the Shi'a majority made Sunnis fear that they would lose their privileges in the new Iraqi state. It was one of the factors why many Sunnis joined the insurgency.[44] Initially, the US administration insisted that the resistance was limited to criminals, diehards, and terrorists, and the Defense Secretary, Donald Rumsfeld, repeatedly asserted that the vast majority of Iraqis saw US forces as liberators, and the preemptive war and occupation were proceeding smoothly.[45] Rumsfeld admitted that in the first 6 weeks since major combat was officially declared over on May 1, about 50 American troops were killed in attacks and accidents, and between the start of the war in March and the end of April, 130 Americans had died from accidents and hostile fire; but pockets of "dead-enders" were being rooted out. He maintained that while the loss of American troops was a matter of "deep sorrow," the American people felt the sacrifices were "worthwhile."

The insurgency continued to grow throughout 2003. But in the following year, major uprisings broke out in Najaf and Anbar Provinces, centered around the cities of Najaf and Fallujah, and covering large parts of southcentral and western Iraq. Washington described the rebellion as a hodgepodge of different groups, including Ba'athists, secular nationalists, religious extremists, and foreign groups such as al Qaeda.[46] The rebels were not all Sunni. Shi'a groups such as the Mahdi Army of Muqtada al-Sadr, a cleric with a large following, rose up against coalition forces in Najaf Province, using guerrilla tactics in the urban environment such as remote-controlled land mines, rocket-propelled grenades, and suicide bombers. Supply convoys were particularly targeted.

The fusion of different groups behind these uprisings was complex, and should be seen in context. On the one hand, there was evidence of sectarian collaboration when it came to rising up against the occupation forces, and the government installed by them. On the other, there was Shi'a-Sunni sectarian violence. Although the Sunni minority that had a privileged status under

---

[44] "Part I: The Iraqi Insurgency, 2004–2007, United States Marine Corps, 13.
[45] "Rumsfeld Blames Iraq Problems on Packets of 'Dead-Enders,'" Associate Press, June 18, 2003, in Ehrenberg et al., *Iraq Papers*, 188–190.
[46] "Part I: The Iraqi Insurgency, 2004–2007," United States Marine Corps, 13.

Saddam Hussein was fearful and uncertain about its future in the new Iraqi state, it did not always mean that relations between the Sunni and Shi'a communities were irreconcilable. After the US occupation started, but before the outbreak of violence, Muqtada al-Sadr issued communiques calling on Sunnis and Shi'a to work together against the occupation.[47] Grand Ayatollah Ali al-Sistani, and other Shi'a and Sunni religious leaders, also called for cooperation. In the dialogue among local Iraqis, none of the groups called for dismantling or partitioning of the state. At other times, however, there was widespread Shi'a-Sunni violence as we will see below.

In 2004, a spokesman of one of the insurgent groups, Jaish Muhammad (the Army of Muhammed), denied any ties with al Qaeda in Mesopotamia, a Sunni group.[48] When asked whether there was any relationship between Jaish Muhammed and al Qaeda, the spokesman said: "No, there is no relationship between us and al Qaeda network, which has no role in our jihad." However, al Qaeda in Iraq or al Qaeda in Mesopotamia, an Iraqi Sunni group affiliated with al Qaeda's core leadership, was a reality. It operated between 2004 and 2006, but was severely weakened after its Jordanian-born leader, Abu Mus'ab al-Zarqawi, was killed in a US attack.[49] The group was known for suicide bombings, targeting security forces, government institutions, and officials. Its objective was to deepen the sectarian divide in the Iraqi population, so it especially targeted Iraqi Shi'a, sometimes during religious processions, or at Shi'a mosques and shrines. The most serious was the destruction of al Askari shrine in the city of Samarra on February 22, 2006, that led to retaliatory violence.[50] In a deadly sectarian attack in Baghdad on November 22, a series of car bombs and a mortar attack killed more than 200 people and wounded many more in the Shi'a district of Sadr city. The following day, gunmen from the Mahdi Army of Muqtada al-Sadr retaliated with attacks on Sunni mosques, including the Abu Hanifa mosque in central Bagdad, killing many people.

As is often the case, when a group on the extreme splits or suffers heavy setbacks, a more radical fringe emerges. It happened after the decline of al Qaeda in Iraq following al-Zarqawi's death. The remnants of al Qaeda in Iraq rebranded themselves as an even more violent Islamic State of Iraq, later

---

[47] Ehrenberg et el., *Iraq Papers*, 249.

[48] For the interview of Jaish Muhammed's spokesman with the Institute of Peace and War Reporting (IWPR) in the town of Bacuba, see Ibid, 251. For full interview, see 250–252.

[49] "al Qaeda in Iraq," Britannica.com

[50] Ahmed S. Hashim, "Iraq's Civil War," in *Current History* Vol 106, No 696, January 2007, University of California Press, 3–10.

known as the Islamic State of Iraq and Syria (ISIS).[51] These names referred to the territory corresponding with the Levant, or eastern Mediterranean, reflecting the group's broader ambitions since the beginning of the 2011 uprising in Syria. The group was mainly composed of foreign fighters, including from Western countries, and remained a threat in northeastern Syria. On splitting from al Qaeda, the Islamic State became its rival. While al Qaeda focused on attacking American and Western allies, ISIS concentrated on capturing territory, and establishing its own state. At its height, ISIS controlled approximately one-third of Syrian and 40% of Iraqi territory, including Mosul, Iraq's second-largest city, and the northern Syrian city of Raqqa. By the end of 2017, it had lost almost 95% of that territory.

The fall of ISIS was primarily due to two reasons. First, its fighters spread over a large area across Iraq and Syria. Second, air attacks by US-dominated forces beginning in August 2014, and expanding to Syria the following month.[52] The ISIS leader, Abu Bakr al-Baghdadi, was killed in one such attack on October 29, 2019. Despite losing most of the territory it controlled in 2017, Islamic State insurgents remained active in rural Iraq and other parts of the Middle East. However, ISIS was generally unable to hold territory since the fall of the Baghouz close to Iraq in March 2019 but remained most active in Syria.[53]

5.5 New Iraqi State

Saddam Hussein's regime was dominated by Sunnis in a Shi'a majority country. After his overthrow, and amid sectarian violence, things began to change. The Bush administration was under sustained domestic and international criticism for the manner in which Iraq was invaded, was being run by the Coalition Provisional Authority (CPA), and the state of human rights in the country. American lives were being lost in Iraq and Afghanistan. And the US annual military expenditure was rising steadily, with America fighting its most expensive foreign wars in Iraq and the Afghanistan-Pakistan theater. A comparison between the 1990s and 2000s decades was revealing. According to the respected Stockholm International Peace Research Institute (SIPRI), the US defense budget during the Bill Clinton presidency (January 1993–January

---

[51] Zachary Laub, "Backgrounder: The Islamic State," last updated August 10, 2016, Council on Foreign Relations.
[52] "Timeline: The Rise, Spread and Fall of the Islamic State," Wilson Center, October 28, 2019.
[53] Cole Bunzel, "Explainer: The Islamic State in 2021," December 10, 2021, Wilson Center.

2001) dropped from 4.7% in 1992, the last year of the Ronald Reagan-George H.W. Bush presidency, to 2.9% of the gross domestic product in 2001, the final year of President Clinton in office.[54]

The defense expenditure was higher as a proportion to the GDP in previous years of Presidents Reagan and Bush Senior, as high as 5.7% in 1988. But as George W. Bush began his presidency, and started his war on terror, the defense expenditure increased again—from 3.6% of the GDP in 2003 to 3.8% annually between 2004 and 2007, and was 4.6% in 2009. It began to drop again during the Obama presidency after the first 2 years. These comparisons in terms of the GDP tell us more than absolute numbers in billion dollars, because the GDP percentages indicate how much of America's economic capacity was being consumed by foreign wars. The decision of the George H.W. Bush administration to embark on state-building in Iraq was hasty and suffered from a lack of planning. The process of consultation, drafting of the new 2005 constitution, and implementation was far from perfect. And some of the worst sectarian violence took place during and after the new constitution was implemented. Nonetheless, Iraq's transition was possible, because it was a wealthy country with vast oil resources, and an educated population, unlike Afghanistan, one of the poorest countries in the world.

Under the 2005 constitution, Iraq became a single federal state with a strong parliamentary system. It had an elected, largely symbolic, President.[55] The country's history of suppression of the Shi'a population in the past, sectarian violence, the Shi'a majority over Sunnis in southern Iraq, and demands for autonomy in the northern Kurdistan region—all influenced the making of the constitution. Under the new arrangement, the Shi'a majority in the south would ensure a strong Shi'a representation in the Iraqi Parliament. The constitution proclaimed religious freedom, but its identity was Islamic and Arab. The national government was granted exclusive authority over foreign, defense, and fiscal policies, with the governing powers divided among the executive, legislative, and judicial branches.

Iraqi Kurdistan, in northern Iraq, was recognized as an autonomous region by the new constitution, with Erbil its capital.[56] The Iraqi Kurdistan region was to have a directly elected President, and a Council of Ministers headed by

---

[54] "Military expenditure by country as percentage of gross domestic product," SIPRI 2018.

[55] For the 2005 Constitution of Iraq, Ehrenberg et al., *Iraq Papers*, 306–313; also, "Constitutional history of Iraq," ConstitutionNet.

[56] Ehrenberg et al., *Iraq Papers*, 2005 Constitution of Iraq Article 113: First. See page 312. Greater Kurdistan, where Kurdish people form a majority, is divided into four countries—Iraq, Iran, Syria, and Turkey.

a Prime Minister.⁵⁷ The region's administrative system would be responsible for the provinces of Erbil, Sulaymaniyah, Duhok, and Halabja, which was split from Sulaymaniyah in 2014. Both Kurdish and Arabic became the official languages of Iraq.

5.6 Obama's Withdrawal and Reentry

President Barack Obama inherited the Bush administration's foreign wars in January 2009. The previous 2 years had seen intense sectarian violence between Iraq's government forces along with American-dominated coalition forces on one side, and armed groups, mainly al Qaeda and the Mahdi Army of Muqtada Al-Sadr, on the other. In early January 2007, President Bush admitted that the 2005 constitution, and subsequent elections, in Iraq had not brought peace.⁵⁸ Violence, particularly in Baghdad, overwhelmed the political gains made in the country. Bush said that "al Qaeda terrorists and Sunni insurgents recognized the mortal danger that Iraq's elections posed for their cause, and they responded with outrageous acts of murder aimed at innocent Iraqis." He said that 80% of Iraq's sectarian violence occurred within 30 miles of the capital, and had shaken the confidence of the Iraqi people. One US intelligence assessment in February 2007 described certain aspects of the conflict as "civil war."⁵⁹ The outbreak of violence coincided with the trial and execution of Saddam Hussein in December 2006.⁶⁰ At the time, the number of American troops in the country stood at around 130,000, but was raised to nearly 165,000 in 2007 in an attempt to suppress the violence.

In November 2009, Obama announced after his inauguration that he would withdraw most of US combat troops from Iraq.⁶¹ Over the next 2 years, US troop numbers were reduced, and, in October 2011, Obama proclaimed that "America's war in Iraq will be over" by the end of the year.⁶² Accordingly, only about eleven-and-a-half thousand troops were left in Iraq in January 2012. In 2014, however, Obama was forced to reverse his withdrawal

---

⁵⁷ "Kurdistan Region Presidency."
⁵⁸ "President's Address to the Nation," White House Archives, January 10, 2007.
⁵⁹ "Elements of civil war in Iraq," BBC News, February 2, 2007.
⁶⁰ Saddam Hussein was captured by American troops near the Iraqi city of Tikrit in December 2003, and handed over to the Iraqi authorities, who put him on trial in June 2006. He was found guilty, and executed by hanging on December 30, 2006.
⁶¹ "Obama Announces Iraq Exit Plan," VOA News, November 2, 2009. Also, see "US ends Iraq combat mission," Graphic News.
⁶² "Barack Obama announces total withdrawal of US troops from Iraq," Associated Press cited in Guardian, October 21, 2011.

pledge, and send nearly 5000 troops after ISIS captured large areas of Iraqi territory, including the cities of Mosul and Tikrit along with much of northern Syria, and declared the creation of an Islamic State.[63] Obama acknowledged that the United States had underestimated the rise of the Islamic State of Iraq and Syria, and overestimated the ability of the Iraqi military to deal with the group.[64] The war against ISIS by Iraqi government troops, backed by US air support, continued for 3 years before the US-Iraqi coalition prevailed over the insurgent group. Obama's successor, Donald Trump, intensified the military campaign against ISIS in Iraq and Syria, and US-backed Kurdish forces captured Raqqa, which had been the ISIS capital just inside Syria.[65]

5.7   Retreat

Big demonstrations against the presence of American troops were held in Baghdad in response to a call by the Shi'a cleric, Muqtada Al-Sadr in January 2020.[66] The city's heavily fortified International Zone, commonly known as the Green Zone, had been the scene of rocket attacks after the US-targeted killing of one of Iran's most powerful general, Qasem Soleimani, and the Iran-backed Iraqi commander, Abu Mahdi al-Muhandis. The killings triggered angry protests against what many Iraqis saw as a violation of their country's sovereignty. The Iraqi Parliament voted to expel American troops, though the Trump administration said it did not intend to pull troops out. Iran also responded to the killing of General Soleimani by firing ballistic missiles at US positions in Iraq. After taking office, President Biden announced in July 2021 that he would end America's combat mission in Iraq by the end of the year, and only about two-and-a-half thousand troops would stay as advisors.[67] The US combat role duly ended in December 2021.[68]

---

[63] "How ISIS Is Filling A Government Vacuum in Syria with An Islamic State," Huffington Post, November 4, 2014.
[64] "Obama: US underestimated rise of ISIS in Iraq and Syria," 60 Minutes, CBS News, September 28, 2014.
[65] Jane C. Timm, "Factcheck: Trump is right, ISIS did lose almost all its territory in Iraq and Syria," NBC News.
[66] Mohammed Tawfeeq, "Hundreds of thousands protest US troop presence in Iraq," CNN, January 24, 2020.
[67] Kevin Liptak and Maegan Vazquez, "Biden announces end of combat mission in Iraq as he shifts US foreign policy focus," CNN, July 26, 2021.
[68] "US-led combat mission in Iraq ends, shifting to advisory role," AL Jazeera, December 9, 2021.

6

Arab Spring

On December 17, 2010, Mohamed Bouazizi, a vendor selling fruit and vegetables, set himself on fire outside a government office in the town of Sidi Bouzid in Tunisia. He was protesting against harassment by corrupt municipal officials, who had been frequently confiscating his goods, claiming that he did not have the necessary permit.[1] He died less than 3 weeks later on January 4, 2011. Bouazizi's ultimate sacrifice triggered a popular uprising against corruption, poverty, and repression in Tunisia. The authorities responded with force against the protests, and dozens of people were killed in clashes with the police. The unrest spread to other parts of Tunisia, including the capital, Tunis, where troops were deployed to control the situation. Amid accusations of excessive force being used, the government attracted international criticism.[2] The failure to control the violence led the Tunisian President, Zine al-Abidine Ben Ali, to announce a series of concessions, including a promise not to seek reelection at the end of his term in 2014. He expressed regret at the deaths of demonstrators and pledged to order that the security forces stop using live ammunition, to reduce prices and ease restrictions on Internet use. Ben Ali also dismissed the Interior Minister, Rafik Belhaj Kacem, and said he would set up an investigation.

All these concessions were not enough, and demonstrations continued. A state of emergency was declared in Tunisia. The state media announced that the government had been dissolved, and that legislative elections would be held in the next 6 months. That, too, failed to end the violence. Ben Ali was

---

[1] "Remembering Mohamed Bouazizi: The man who sparked the Arab Spring," Al Jazeera, December 17, 2020. Also, "Mohamed Bouazizi: Tunisian street vendor and protester," Britannica.
[2] "Jasmine Revolution: Tunisian History," Britannica.

forced to resign, and left the country, finally arriving in Saudi Arabia. The Prime Minister, Mohamed Ghannouchi, took over. A day later, Ghannouchi was himself replaced by the former speaker of the lower house of the Tunisian parliament, Fouad Mebazaa, as interim president. Both men were from Ben Ali's party, the Democratic Constitutional Rally (RCD). Unrest continued in the country for days after Ben Ali left. Incidents of sporadic violence were attributed to people loyal to the ousted president. Finally, the ban on opposition parties was lifted, the interim government granted amnesty to political prisoners, and all activities of Ben Ali's party, RCD, were suspended. The transition from decades of repression to a democratic government in Tunisia was long and difficult. In January 2014, the proclamation of a new constitution was greeted as a compromise by Islamists and secularists in Tunisia, as well as by international observers. In 2019, Tunisia completed its first peaceful transfer of power from one democratically elected government to another. The popular uprising leading to change in Tunisia came to be known as the Jasmine Revolution.

The Tunisian uprising was spontaneous, sparked by a very public self-sacrifice of a poor young man protesting against government corruption and repression. It spread so quickly because the social conditions were right—poverty, unemployment, daily struggles, and shattered expectations of many young and educated people.[3] With the help of social media, cell phones, and satellite television, expressions of mass anger against a dictatorial regime, and demands for freedom and democracy, went viral. There were similar conditions in other countries in the Arab world as well. They included some wealthy authoritarian regimes, particularly in the Gulf region. In a social media environment with news traveling fast, how would the events in Tunisia affect the Greater Middle East? Would regimes elsewhere in the region be as brittle as the regime in Tunisia? If not, how would they face the specter of popular uprisings? It was not possible to answer these questions immediately.

The United States had been on the offensive with its expansion of democracy agenda in the Greater Middle East for a number of years, mainly in Iraq and Afghanistan. Helped by its overwhelming military presence in the region, America's posture was also uncompromising toward Syria, Libya, and Iran. Still bogged down in Iraq and Afghanistan, the US administration was seeking to stabilize both countries, and a way out. In one sense, Washington seemed to be sending mixed messages. In another, its military venture appeared to have achieved key objectives of the neoconservatives. Saddam Hussein was

---

[3] Ragul Assaad, "How will Tunisia's Jasmine Revolution Affect the Arab World?," Brookings op-ed, January 24, 2011.

eliminated in Iraq, the Ba'athist state was dismantled, and the new state created to replace it was a much weaker entity, neutralizing a major challenge to America's supremacy in the Middle East.

In Afghanistan, the Taliban were removed from power, and a compliant government was installed in Kabul. Several years of US-dominated military occupation enabled the coalition forces to raise, train, and supply Afghanistan's national army and police force. An indigenous version of democracy was in place. In Washington, these were seen as comforting achievements since the 2001 invasion of Afghanistan. Against this mirage was a very different reality. The Iraqi population was split along sectarian lines between the Shi'a, Sunni, and Kurdish communities. Iran's influence in Iraq, a Shi'a majority state, was greater than before. Al Qaeda and the ISIS had secured a foothold in both Iraq and Afghanistan. Uprisings against the central government could be suppressed with the help of American-led allied forces. However, the Afghan government in Kabul was weak on its own, and its ability to withstand the insurgents was in doubt.

Significantly, the message of America's democracy promotion was reaching other parts of the Arab world, and hopes and expectations it generated could not be underestimated. If social media and IT tools like cell phones and the Internet were not available, people would not receive news, communicate with each other, organize, or fundraise, making it far more difficult to complain about their grievances, and demand change. That was the case before information technology became widely available, and the causes of protest remained confined within smaller areas. But the world had changed due to the technology revolution. In June 2009, in one of the first known cases that came to international attention, tech-savvy protesters were reported using Twitter, and other news media in Iran, in what was described as the Twitter Revolution.[4] At the time, only just over 8000 people were registered with Twitter in Iran, but it signified a trend that grew year by year. The uprisings in Tunisia, and the rest of the Arab world, happened once the Twitter Revolution had started.

The Tunisian Revolution beginning in December 2010 triggered a wave of democracy uprisings—including both peaceful protests and armed resistance—against authoritarian regimes across the Arab world. As well as Tunisia's Ben Ali, Muammar Gaddafi of Libya, Hosni Mubarak of Egypt, and Abdullah Saleh of Yemen were toppled. Street protests swept from Algeria and Morocco in North Africa across the Middle East to Saudi Arabia and smaller emirates

---
[4] Gadi Wolfsfeld, Elad Segev, and Tamir Sheafer, "Social Media and the Arab Spring: Politics Comes First," International Journal of Press/Politics Vol 18 Issue 2 (Sage, 2013), 117.

in the Gulf region.⁵ The speed with which the uprisings spread took the world by surprise. Within a few weeks, significant countries such as Algeria, Morocco, Sudan, Libya, Egypt, Syria, and Saudi Arabia were affected. Also affected were smaller states like Bahrain, Kuwait, and Oman, as well as the Palestinian National Authority.⁶

6.1 Egypt

The uprising in Egypt, also known as the January 25th Revolution, was inspired by the Jasmine Revolution in Tunisia. Organized by groups of young Egyptians mostly independent of political parties against the 30-year rule of President Hosni Mubarak, its focal point was Tahrir (Liberation) Square in Cairo, from where demonstrations spread to other cities in Egypt.⁷ The Mubarak regime had declared a national holiday to honor the police on January 25, 2011.⁸ In turn, it became a day of rage against police brutality, and what was supposed to be a 1-day protest turned into an 18-day peaceful sit-in at Tahrir Square, embodying a movement that eventually deposed Hosni Mubarak from power. Like in Tunisia, big crowds filled the capital's main square and city streets every day, chanting slogans against corruption, political repression, and poverty. Amid growing unrest, the Mubarak regime came down hard on protesters, but failed to control them, and Egypt's established opposition parties increased their participation. Former director general of the International Atomic Energy Agency (IAEA) and Nobel Prize winner, Mohamed ElBaradei, who had become leader of the opposition coalition, National Association for Change, arrived in Cairo to take part in the demonstrations within days. And Muslim Brotherhood, which had the greatest popular support in the country, also announced that it would take part.

After Friday prayers on January 28, 2011, demonstrators clashed with the police who used tear gas, water cannons, and rubber bullets to control the crowds. The regime declared a curfew, and cut off Internet and telephone services to disrupt communication. Many people were beaten by uniformed

---

⁵ See Malise Ruthven's book review article, "How to Understand ISIS," reviewing Marc Lynch, "The New Arab Wars" and Fawaz Gerges, "ISIS: A History," in New York Review of Books, June 23, 2016.
⁶ "The Arab Spring—a timeline," PEN/Opp magazine, published by Swedish PEN. Also, "Timeline: The Major Events of the Arab Spring," NPR, January 2, 2012; and "Timeline: How the Arab Spring Unfolded," Al Jazeera, January 14, 2021.
⁷ "Egypt uprising of 2011," Britannica. Also, "Unrest in 2011: January 25 Revolution," Britannica.
⁸ For the first day's events and more, see digital archive "Politics, Popular Culture and the 2011 Egyptian Revolution," (Coventry, UK: University of Warwick).

or plainclothes security forces. But the unrest continued, and many buildings of the ruling National Democratic Party, and police stations, throughout Egypt were set on fire. Protesters fought running battles with security forces, so the army was deployed in the city center of Cairo to protect official buildings. The Mubarak regime was shaken. He went on television to insist that he would remain president, but said that he had asked his cabinet to resign. He acknowledged protesters' grievances, and promised social reforms. However, Mubarak's speech was dismissed as a desperate attempt to cling to power, and disturbances continued. Over the next 2 weeks, Mubarak made more announcements to pacify angry crowds, appointed Omar Suleiman as vice president, and gave him some of his powers.[9]

Reports of the number of dead varied, but the United Nations reported about 300 dead. As the protesting crowds at Tahrir Square increased, it became a tent city. The US President, Barack Obama, told Mubarak to begin transition to democracy immediately.[10] And the Obama administration was reportedly in talks with Egyptian government officials about Mubarak's immediate resignation. On February 9, trade unions joined the protest movement, and strikes took place all over the country. Egyptian Foreign Minister, Ahmed Aboul Gheit, warned that the army could intervene to protect the country. After demonstrations spread to other parts of Cairo, big crowds assembled outside the Presidential Palace, and state television. At that point, the army said it would guarantee free and fair elections, and called on Egyptians to return to normalcy. Later, reports came that President Mubarak had left Cairo, and was resigning.

The role of the armed forces was central in both Tunisia and Egypt for the outcome of revolutions. In Tunisia, President Ben Ali fled when the chief of staff ordered the army not to fire on protesters.[11] The Egyptian army not only refused to fire live rounds on demonstrators, it ousted 83-year-old Hosni Mubarak in the end. The army took note of President Obama's message to Mubarak to leave and begin transition to democracy at once. The armed forces had a firm grip in Egypt since the 1952 Free Officers' coup that overthrew the monarchy, and brought Gamal Abdel Nasser as President of a Republic. Since then, only three presidents—Nasser, Anwar Sadat, and Hosni Mubarak—had ruled the country in nearly 60 years. They were all military

---

[9] "Timeline of the revolution in Egypt," DW.
[10] Ibid, February 2–4, 2011.
[11] James L. Gelvin, *The Arab Uprisings: What Everyone Needs to Know* 2nd ed. (New York, NY: Oxford University Press, 2015), 67–68.

men. The new generation of officers had acquired a taste for power and was unwilling to lose its privileged position.

Another significant development was a change of tone in the US administration's pronouncements. Democracy promotion was pursued aggressively by President George W. Bush, and the Project for the New American Century. Obama was less enthusiastic about that policy and was inclined toward stability in the region. Relations between Washington and Cairo had been close since President Anwar Sadat switched Egypt's Cold War allegiance from the Soviet Union to the United States in 1972, made a historic visit to Israel 5 years later, and signed the Camp David Accords in 1978, leading to normalization with Israel.[12] As a reward, Egypt received billions of dollars in American aid that benefited the ruling army establishment. Why lose it all by going against what appeared to be America's priority?

The revolution in Egypt was a historic event, but the euphoria of victory did not last long. A constitutional referendum was held in March, and the first parliamentary elections since Mubarak was deposed took place in November 2011. They were followed by the presidential election in May and June 2012. Mohamed Morsi of the Muslim Brotherhood defeated Mubarak's last prime minister, Ahmed Shafik, by a narrow margin.[13] President Morsi and the Muslim Brotherhood moved quickly to consolidate their hold on power. The military chief, Mohamed Hussein Tantawi, who was de facto head of state after Mubarak's ouster, was replaced by Lt-General Abdel Fattah al-Sisi. Morsi then unilaterally assumed greater powers, giving himself immunity from judicial review, and barring the courts from dissolving a panel that was drafting a new constitution. In December 2012, the constitution hastily drafted and passed by the Islamists was approved in a referendum despite protests and boycott by other groups. The vote in favor was over 63%, but the turnout was only about one-third of the total electorate.

On March 12, 2013, President Morsi's government rejected a rescue plan worth 750-million dollars from the International Monetary Fund. Fuel and electricity shortages caused widespread public anger during the next several months. A signature campaign was launched calling for Morsi's removal, and a new presidential election. On Morsi's first anniversary in office on June 30, millions of people began demonstrations demanding his resignation. Despite

---

[12] For Anwar Sadat's switch of allegiance to the United States, see Edward R.F. Sheehan, "Why Sadat packed off the Russians," New York Times, April 6, 1972. For Sadat's visit to Israel, see "Egypt's President Sadat visit in Israel, November 1977," IDF Archives. For Egypt and Israel normalization of relations, see "Egypt and Israel Treaty of Peace," March 26, 1979, UN Peacemaker.org

[13] Morsi got 51.7% of the vote in the second round. See "A timeline of key events in Egypt since the 2011 uprising," Associated Press, March 25, 2018.

the military giving him an ultimatum to reach an agreement within 48 h, Morsi insisted he would stay on. On July 3, 2013, General al-Sisi announced that President Morsi had been removed, and the Constitutional Court Chief Justice, Adly Mansour, was the new interim president. Resistance from Islamist supporters brought retaliation from the army. In a presidential election in May 2014, General al-Sisi won nearly 97% of the vote. A year later, Morsi was tried and sentenced to 20 years in prison on charges related to the killing of protesters in 2012. Thus, Egypt's brief experiment in democracy came to an end, and the army was back in power.

6.2 Libya

Libya and Syria were among the rejectionist Arab states that had long refused to be part of the diplomatic efforts encouraged by the United States to normalize relations with Israel since the 1970s, when Egypt's President Anwar Sadat took the lead to make peace with the main foe of the Arabs.[14] Due to their close ties to Moscow, and large oil and gas wealth, the rejectionist Arab states represented a formidable front in opposition to the United States and allies, who found the rejectionist leaders particularly tenacious to deal with. But following the Soviet Union's dissolution, the rejectionists lost their most powerful backer and were under pressure to adjust in the new post-Soviet world. Saddam Hussein of Iraq was first to fall, but Libya's Muammar Ghaddafi, and Syria's al-Assad dynasty, remained in power.[15] Both were left vulnerable in the face of America's advances in the Greater Middle East.[16]

On February 15, 2011, anti-government protests broke out in Libya's second largest city, Benghazi, and spread to Beyda and Zintan overnight.[17] Located between Tunisia and Egypt, Libya had been ruled by Muammar Gaddafi, who had no official status, but held absolute power. The demonstrations were against the arrest of a human rights activist, Fathi Terbil. Angry

---

[14] Prominent Arab rejectionist states were Iraq, Libya, Syria, Algeria, and the People's Democratic Republic of Yemen (South Yemen) before unification with the Yemen Arab Republic (North Yemen) to form a single state Yemen in 1990.

[15] President Hafez al-Assad ruled Syria from 1971 till his death in 2000, when his son, Bashar al-Assad, became president of Syria.

[16] A loosely defined region to which countries are added or removed sometimes according to individual preferences, occasionally including Afghanistan, Pakistan, Central Asia, and South Caucasus. Generally speaking, the region includes countries of West Asia, in addition to the Arabian Peninsula, and most of North Africa.

[17] "Violent Protests rock Libyan city of Benghazi," France 24, February 16, 2011. Also, "Libyan police stations torched," Al Jazeera, February 16, 2011.

crowds demanded the end of the Gaddafi regime, and protesters in Zintan set up tents in the city center reminiscent of Tahrir Square in the Egyptian capital, Cairo. Police stations and security offices were set on fire. As the unrest spread, there were dozens of casualties in clashes in which anti-government demonstrators fought with security forces, and government supporters, across the country. Social media showed videos of crowds shouting "Muammar is the enemy of Allah." Something unthinkable was happening in Libya—a country Gaddafi had ruled with an iron fist for four decades.

On February 17, 2011, a "Day of Rage" was called in an attempt to emulate uprisings in Tunisia and Egypt. As demonstrations grew, relatives of inmates killed in a prison massacre 15 years before joined the protests. Demonstrators took control of Benghazi, and the unrest spread to the Libyan capital, Tripoli.[18] At that point, security forces, and squads of mercenaries recruited by the regime, began using live ammunition on protesters. Tanks, helicopter gunships, and artillery fire were also used. On February 21, Muammar Gaddafi's powerful son, Saif al-Islam, insisting that the regime fight "to the last bullet," blamed outside agitators for the unrest.

Muammar Gaddafi seized power in Libya in 1969 when, as a young military officer of 27, he led a group of "Free Officers" in a coup that abolished the monarchy. Initially, Gaddafi modeled his regime on Gamal Abdel Nasser's Egypt, but abandoned the experiment with Nasser-style institutions, and formed what were called "people's congresses." He proclaimed that such congresses would make direct democracy possible at various levels, and he dismantled representative institutions.[19] There was also an informal layer where real power was concentrated. It was controlled by Gaddafi, his family, and trusted loyalists in his tribe. Instead of president, Gaddafi adopted titles like "Guide of the First of September Great Revolution" and "Brotherly Leader and Guide." He had absolute power. But, in reality, Libya was a weak state that did not have a functioning government and bureaucracy, which normal states have. A much smaller country than Egypt and Tunisia, Libya is all desert with a Mediterranean coast to the north. Its cities are separated by vast distances along a strip of land by the sea. As much as 85% of its population lived in urban areas at the time of the uprising. There were no trade unions, political parties, or independent media. Gaddafi also dismantled the country's economic structures, arguing that they would create inequalities.

---

[18] "Libya revolt of 2011," Britannica.
[19] James L. Gelvin, *The Arab Uprising* (NY: New York, Oxford University Press, 2015), 89–90. For detailed analysis, see chapter "Uprisings in weak states: Yemen and Libya," 86–114.

How did Libya survive as a weak state? The answer lies in the fact that it earned about 95% of its revenues from oil. Gaddafi's son, Saif al-Islam, disbursed the money directly to loyal clients until the uprising.[20] Factors such as corruption, brutality of Gaddafi's rule, and undoubted inequalities that he professed not to exist in his country served as powerful ammunition for the uprising. By February 20, 2011, the revolt had spread to the capital, Tripoli, and, a week later, the regime's opponents formed a transitional council to run the areas under rebel control. France became the first country to recognize the council as Libya's legitimate government.[21] But other European Union members held back, cautioning against "rushing" into decisions.

It is not surprising that the trail of the Libyan uprising against Gaddafi began from Benghazi in the east to Tripoli in the west. Gaddafi's control in eastern Libya was weaker, and popular resentment over lower investment and higher employment was strong. The speed with which violence spread to the capital, and government forces lost large areas of the country, took the regime by surprise. Gaddafi's forces used brutal force to suppress the demonstrations and recover the areas lost.[22] Amid the government offensive resulting in large numbers of casualties, international pressure to intervene in the conflict mounted. The UN Security Council adopted Resolution 1973, proposed by France, the United Kingdom, and Lebanon, that formed a basis for military intervention in the Libyan civil war.[23] The resolution called for an immediate ceasefire, a complete end to violence and all attacks against, and abuse of, civilians, and an air-exclusion zone over Libya, to protect the civilian population. It also strengthened the arms embargo, and asset freeze, under the earlier Security Council resolution 1970. The United States voted for the resolution, but was not among the proposers. The Obama administration was resistant to getting involved in another Middle East conflict of indefinite duration like in Iraq and Afghanistan.[24] Unlike George W. Bush's unilateral action in Iraq, President Obama made sure that Washington was not seen as the originator of any intervention in Libya, and that the coalition intervening on the side of

---

[20] Ibid, 95.
[21] "Libya: France recognises rebels as government," BBC News, March 10, 2011.
[22] "Libya: Pro-Gaddafi forces attack rebel-held Ras Lanuf," BBC News, March 7, 2011. Also, Chris McGreal, "Libyan rebels in retreat as Gaddafi attacks by air, land and sea," Guardian, March 10, 2011; Liz Sly and Tara Bahrampour, "Libya gains control of more rebel territory," Washington Post, March 13, 2011; and Liz Sly and Joby Warrick, "Gaddafi's forces push back rebels in key town; world leaders call for his ouster," Washington Post, March 29, 2011.
[23] UN Security Council Resolution 1973 was passed under Chapter VII of the UN Charter, which empowers the Security Council to take steps to maintain peace. Also see, UN Security Council Resolution 1970, February 26, 2011.
[24] James Kitfield, "Obama: The Reluctant Warrior on Libya," Atlantic magazine, March 18, 2011.

rebels against Gaddafi included Arab countries. He let the Europeans, France, and the United Kingdom in particular, take the lead—a stand for which his administration was ridiculed when an unnamed official was quoted in *The New Yorker* magazine saying that the United States would be "leading from behind."[25]

Two leading advocates for intervention against Gaddafi were President Nicolas Sarkozy of France and Prime Minister David Cameron of the United Kingdom. Both had their own domestic reasons for doing so. Sarkozy had been slow to support the uprising in Tunisia, where France had a long-standing interest. He did not want to repeat that omission, especially as he was entering a campaign for reelection only a year away. Prime Minister David Cameron had been in power since the 2010 general election and looked confident. Memories of two terrorist incidents were still alive in British minds. One was the 1988 bombing of Pan Am Flight 103 over the Scottish town of Lockerbie, resulting in the deaths of 270 people, for which Libyan intelligence was implicated. The other was the 1984 killing of Policewoman Yvonne Fletcher outside the Libyan embassy in London from a shot fired from inside the embassy. There was no love lost between Britain and Gaddafi.

Overall, the European Union's dependence on Libyan oil was higher. Before the mass revolt, the EU imported about 10% of its oil from Libya.[26] Italy was the largest importer with about 25% of its oil coming from Libya against less than 1% of US oil imports. Immigration was also an issue. Europeans feared not only a massive wave from Libya if Gaddafi continued his campaign of violence, but also from sub-Saharan Africa if his regime lost control over Libya's coastline. As the situation deteriorated, the International Contact Group on Libya, which consisted of about 30 countries including the United States, recognized Libya's main opposition group, the National Transitional Council (NTC), as the country's government.[27] At the end of a meeting in the Turkish city of Istanbul, the NTC said that the Gaddafi regime no longer had any legitimate authority, and Gaddafi and certain members of his family must go. Diplomatic recognition was a significant boost for the Libyan opposition. It meant that America could fund the opposition from about thirty billion dollars of assets of the Gaddafi regime frozen in US banks. The Secretary of State, Hillary Clinton, announced that until an interim authority was

---

[25] Ryan Lizza, "Leading From Behind," New Yorker, April 26, 2011.
[26] James L Gelvin, *The Arab Uprising* (New York: NY, Oxford University Press, 2015), 104.
[27] "Libya Profile—Timeline," BBC News, March 15, 2021. Also, "US recognizes Libyan opposition group," Al Jazeera, July 15, 2011.

established in Libya, the United States would deal with the TNC as the government of Libya.

Gaddafi was fast losing his grip. The NATO air-exclusion zone over Libya severely reduced his ability to control rebels. Recognition to the TNC by the United States, European, and Arab countries increased his isolation. In August and September 2011, African Union members also joined in recognizing the opposition council as Libya's legitimate government.[28] Gaddafi went into hiding when rebels stormed his fortress compound in Tripoli. After 8 months of intense conflict and NATO military intervention, Gaddafi and members of his inner circle were cornered and isolated in his hometown, the coastal city of Sirte.[29] The city had been besieged by armed militias from Benghazi, Misrata, and elsewhere. On October 20, 2011, the Libyan dictator's son, Mutassim, leading the defense of Sirte, ordered loyalists to abandon their hideout, and tried to escape in a convoy of about 50 armed vehicles. NATO drones and warplanes carried out heavy bombardment of the convoy in which dozens of Gaddafi loyalists were burnt to death. Gaddafi and other survivors tried to escape through the fields and drainage pipes underneath a major road, where the Misrata militia caught them. Members of the Gaddafi convoy were captured, disarmed, and subjected to brutal beatings. Gaddafi himself was dragged, tortured, and put to death.[30]

So, the Libyan uprising came to an end insofar as the Gaddafi era was concerned. For the United States, Western allies, and many countries in the Middle East and North Africa, a difficult and obdurate ruler had gone. Gaddafi had few friends. France and the United Kingdom were euphoric about the Libyan ruler's demise. The UK Defence Secretary, Philip Hammond, even urged British companies to "pack their suitcases" and head for Libya to secure contracts.[31] Overcome with excitement, little did the optimists realize what was to come. They ignored the most fundamental lesson of Iraq and Afghanistan that it is easy to intervene in a weak state, and overthrow the dictator, but much more difficult to deal with the aftermath of chaos and power vacuum. In an interview in 2016, President Obama admitted that the failure in Libya was the worst mistake of his presidency. And in a rare rebuke,

---

[28] Ibid.
[29] "Death of a Dictator: Bloody Vengeance in Sirte," Human Rights Watch, October 16, 2012.
[30] "The Death of Gaddafi," Al Jazeera, October 20, 2011.
[31] Jo Adetunji, "British firms urged to "pack suitcases" in rush for Libya business," Guardian, October 21, 2011.

Obama criticized France and the United Kingdom, saying that the British Prime Minister, David Cameron, became "distracted" and described Libya as a "mess."[32]

6.3 Yemen

Abdullah Saleh was a military man who ruled Yemen, another weak state, with absolute power over his people. Saleh had been in power since 1978, when Yemen was still divided into two independent states, and he was president of the Yemen Arab Republic (North Yemen).[33] The other was the People's Democratic Republic of Yemen (South Yemen). When the two states merged into one in 1990, Abdullah Saleh became president of the unified Republic of Yemen. He was reelected in 1999. Although he announced in 2005 that he would not seek another term as president, he changed his mind, claiming to bow to "popular will," and was reelected in 2006. In 2010, Yemen's parliament announced a plan to amend the constitution, and eliminate presidential term limits, thus making Saleh president for life. He had already started sidelining allies and potential rivals, and begun promoting his son, Ali Ahmed Saleh, the commander of the Republican Guard and Special Forces, to succeed him. Other family members held important positions in various ministries. Beyond his immediate family, he believed in buying the loyalty of others.

In January 2011, a coalition of opposition parties called the Joint Meeting Parties (JMP) began a series of protests in the Yemeni capital, Sana'a, against the parliament's decision to remove presidential term limits, and Abdullah Saleh's plan for his son to succeed him.[34] The protests were called the Pink Revolution after the color the JMP chose to identify itself. The evolving movement had two main components. Saleh's political opponents, and outsiders who wanted to get back in. There were also social-networking Yemeni youths in the movement, though their role was peripheral, and their demand more radical—the immediate exit of Abdullah Saleh. On January 27, a large street demonstration in Sana'a was held calling for the ouster of Saleh.[35] As discontent grew, he announced that he would not run for reelection in 2013, and that his son would not succeed him. However, that did not calm the protesters, and there was an even bigger demonstration in the capital on February 3, marking a "Day of Rage" demanding President Saleh's resignation. Protests

---

[32] Catherine Treyz, "European distraction led to Libya mess," CNN, March 11, 2016.
[33] Gelvin, *The Arab Uprisings*, 87–89.
[34] Ibid, 97.
[35] "Timeline: Yemen's Uprising," Al Jazeera, March 21, 2011.

continued in Sana'a, and across the country. There were reports of deaths and injuries among detainees, who had gathered in a prison courtyard in the capital. More protesters were killed when security forces and unidentified armed men fired on agitators. President Saleh imposed a state of emergency and dismissed his entire cabinet. Yemen's ambassadors to the United Nations and Syria resigned, and several top military officers defected.

The Saleh regime had survived due to compliance or acquiescence of tribal, political, and military leaders. Once influential figures started defecting, his days were numbered. As the protests grew, security forces loyal to him used ever-increasing force to suppress protests. But the more violence was used by government forces, the greater was the resistance to him.[36] Sana'a was a divided city by late March between armed supporters loyal to the Saleh regime, and military units and armed people opposed to him. In a bomb explosion at the presidential palace, several people were killed or wounded, including Saleh. He was taken to Saudi Arabia for treatment, from where he returned. But his support in Yemen had collapsed by then, and the international community had had enough of the Saleh regime.

The United States, the Gulf Cooperation Council (GCC), and the United Nations negotiated a deal under which Abdullah Saleh would step down, and get immunity, Vice President Abd Rabbu Mansour Hadi would take over as president. Mansour Hadi later ran unopposed for president, and won. On December 4, 2017, Abdullah Saleh was killed by Houthi forces in Sana'a.[37]

6.4 Syria

Syria is a small, poor, and heavily populated country. It had a population of more than 21 million in 2010.[38] Only about a quarter of its area of seventy-one-and-a-half thousand square miles is arable land. Most of it is desert. Some is suitable for grazing, but only about 10% is suitable for growing crops. Prior to the uprising against President Bashar al-Assad's regime, Syria had a devastating drought for 4 years. At least 800,000 farmers lost their livelihood, and about 200,000 abandoned their lands. Many farmers fled to urban Syria in search of jobs that were nonexistent. As much as 85% of the livestock died of hunger or thirst. Syrians paid a terrible human and economic price when the

---

[36] Gelvin, *The Arab Uprisings*, 99–100.
[37] "Ali Abdullah Saleh," Britannica.
[38] William R. Polk, "Understanding Syria: From Pre-Civil War to Post Assad," Atlantic magazine, December 10, 2013. Also, Francesco Femia and Caitlin Werrell, "Syria: Climate Change, Drought and Social Unrest," February 29, 2012, Center for Climate and Security, Washington, DC.

uprising broke out. In towns and cities, they found themselves competing with hundreds of thousands of Palestinian and Iraqi refugees. According to UN experts, between two and three million of Syria's ten million rural inhabitants were reduced to "extreme poverty." Displaced farmers, once relatively prosperous, were forced to work as hawkers and street sweepers.

The history of state violence and repression of dissent in Syria was such that many people thought that Syrians would be too afraid to take on the regime. President Bashar al-Assad's father, Hafez al-Assad, had been part of the ruling clique since the 1963 coup that brought the Arab Socialist Ba'ath Party in Syria to power. For 37 years till his death in 2000, Hafez ran a brutal secular regime, and turned Syria into an important regional player in the Arab world. He kept his country firmly aligned to Russia even after the Soviet Union was dissolved. Syria allowed Russian naval and air bases in its territory, and the two countries negotiated an expansion of Russian facilities.[39] Al-Assad family's absolute control meant that the Alawite sect, a branch of Shi'a Islam, took dominant positions in the Syrian military and government.[40] Syria developed close ties with Iran and China over the years. It lost much of the Golan Heights in the 1967 Arab-Israeli War, but consistently rejected any rapprochement with Israel. For these reasons, Syria was isolated on the international stage, and relations with the United States and Europe were strained.

Although social-networking Syrian youths organized small protests beginning in January 2011 like Egyptian protests, they were feeble and failed to capture the public's imagination.[41] On March 15 of that year, a group calling itself "Syrian Revolution 2011 against Bashar al-Assad" held one such demonstration in the capital, Damascus, demanding that the government withdraw the emergency law and release political prisoners. It attracted no more than 200 or 300 people. Security forces easily broke up that protest. Only a few days later, the first big anti-regime demonstrations took place in the southern city of Deraa in reaction to an incident in early March. Fifteen boys, aged between 10 and 15, were arrested, detained, and tortured for painting slogans saying "the people want to topple this government."[42] The boys were taken to one of the cells of the Political Security branch under the supervision of General Atef Najeeb, a cousin of President Bashar al-Assad. Accounts of their torture said they were "beaten and bloodied, burned and had their finger nails

---

[39] Maxim A. Suchkov, "Why is Russia seeking to expand its military bases in Syria?," Middle East Institute, Washington, DC, June 1, 2020.
[40] Alawite Muslims are only about 15% in Syria. Other ethnic groups are Arab (50%), Kurd (10%), Levantine (10%), and others 15%.
[41] Gelvin, *The Arab Uprising*, 126.
[42] Hugh Macleod, "Inside Deraa," Al Jazeera, April 19, 2011.

pulled out." On March 18 began a series of demonstrations in Deraa calling for an end to corruption, release of the teenagers, and political freedom. It all escalated into a nationwide rebellion and became a multi-layered conflict, which would last for years with devastating consequences.

On the same day that demonstrations broke out in Deraa, protests erupted in the northern coastal city of Banias over local concerns, then spread to Latakia and Duma, north of the capital, Damascus, where protesters were again met with force. From village after village and town after town, people came out in the streets as news of trouble, and the regime's brutal response, spread.[43] The conflict intensified, and quickly became a full-scale war between the Syrian government supported by Russia and Iran, on the one hand, and anti-regime rebel groups backed by the United States, Saudi Arabia, Turkey, and other countries in the region.[44] In spaces vacated by other groups in the fighting, the Islamic State moved in and began to capture territory in 2013. What looked like a Hobbesian war of all against all in Syria, there appeared three identifiable layers of conflict: coalition drive against the Islamic State, fighting between the Syrian government and opposition forces, and operations against Syrian Kurds by Turkey that had entered the war. As part of their operations against the Islamic State in Iraq, the United States, the United Kingdom, France, Turkey, Saudi Arabia, and other Arab countries expanded their air attacks in Syria.

6.5 United States in Syria

America's intervention in the Syrian war happened in two ways after the uprising against the regime began during the Arab Spring. In the early phase, the US objective was to help regime change. To this end, the Obama administration provided aid to rebels and used its airpower and troops.[45] However, once the ISIS had established itself, Washington helped the Syrian Democratic Forces (SDF) to destroy the Islamic State's self-declared caliphate. How America's policy changed is worth examining. Syria ruled by the House of Assad was no friend of the United States. After attending a conference on Syria in April 2012, the US Secretary of State, Hilary Clinton, said that

---

[43] Gelvin, *The Arab Spring*, 127.
[44] "Global Conflict Tracker: Civil War in Syria," Council on Foreign Relations, Updated January 18, 2022.
[45] Benjamin H. Friedman and Justin Logan, "Disentangling from Syria's Civil War," Defense Priorities, Washington, DC, May 2019.

President Bashar al-Assad's days were numbered, and "we think Assad must go."[46] And so, "Assad must go" became Washington's slogan.

On a visit to Israel in March 2013, President Obama said that Bashar al-Assad had lost his legitimacy and "must go."[47] Reports of chemical attacks by Syrian government forces, and the Islamic State, had started to emerge at the time. Obama warned that the Syrian regime "will be held accountable for the use of chemical weapons or their transfer to terrorists." But he was cautious, and said that more investigation was necessary to determine whether chemical weapons were used. He said that he preferred to work within an international framework to bring about change in Syria, rather than taking unilateral military action. Visiting Jordan a few days later, Obama expressed concern that Syria could become an "enclave for extremism." He went on to say: "The United States continues to work with allies and friends, and the Syrian opposition, to hasten the end of Assad's rule, to stop the violence against the Syrian people, and begin a transition toward a new government that respects the rights of all its people."

Also in March 2013, Jordanian security officials were quoted as saying that Western training of Syrian rebel forces was going on in Jordan to strengthen secular groups as a bulwark against the Islamic extremists, and to build security forces in the event of Bashar al-Assad's fall.[48] The training effort was led by the United States, but also included French and British instructors. The United Kingdom government denied that any British soldiers were directly training the rebels, but said that military personnel, including special forces, were in the country training the Jordanian military. According to European and Jordanian sources, Western training had been going on for a year and was focused on senior officers who had defected from the Syrian army. In June 2013, the White House announced that it would arm rebels and impose an air-exclusion zone, because there was evidence the Syrian government had used nerve gas against them.[49] A day before, there were reports in western news outlets, with photographic evidence, that Syrian warplanes had used chemical agents, including nerve gas.[50]

---

[46] Rina Ninan and Marisa Taylor, "Secretary Clinton says Syrian President Assad 'Must Go.'" ABC News, April 1, 2012.

[47] "Obama on Syria: Assad must go." Wilson Center, March 24, 2013. Obama first spoke at a joint news conference with the Prime Minister of Israel, Benjamin Netanyahu, on March 20, 2013. Two days later, on March 22, Obama spoke at a news conference with King Abdullah in Jordan.

[48] Julian Borger and Nick Hopkins, "West training Syrian rebels in Jordan," Guardian, March 8, 2013.

[49] Parisa Hafezi and Erica Solomon, "US considers no-fly zone after Syria crosses nerve gas "red line,"" Reuters, June 15, 2013.

[50] Barbara Starr, Jessica Yellin, and Chelsea J. Carter, "White House: Syria crosses 'red line' with use of chemical weapons on its people," CNN, June 14, 2013.

Two months later, a chemical attack in the Ghouta district of Damascus killed more than 1500 people, including children.[51] Gruesome pictures of the victims were circulated around the world. In a speech after the attack, President Obama said that "the United States should take military action against Syrian regime targets."[52] But he refrained from a major commitment, making clear "this should not be an open-ended intervention. We would not put boots on the ground. Instead, our action would be designed to be limited in duration and scope." And he announced that he was seeking a Congressional authorization for any action.[53]

Obama was actually testing the mood in Congress and the country. But, over the next month, there was little Congressional or public support. In the end, the United States supported a Russian-backed plan to remove stocks of chemical weapons in Syria. In August 2014, the Obama administration announced that all of Syria's chemical weapons stockpiles had been destroyed.[54] Obama hailed it as an important step in preventing the spread of weapons of mass destruction, but added that President Bashar al-Assad must act on pledges to destroy his other weapons production facilities.

On April 4, 2017, another chemical attack was reported on Khan Sheikhoun, a rebel-held town in northeastern Syria.[55] More than eighty people were reported killed, and pictures of adults gasping for air, and babies on respirators, drew international attention. The UN-supported Organization for the Prohibition of Chemical Weapons (OPCW) concluded in June 2017 that sarin gas was used in that attack. Several months later, a UN panel concluded that it was confident the attack was launched by the Syrian government. Amid the Syrian regime's heavy bombardment of the Damascus suburb of Duma, dozens of civilians died in a strike that pro-opposition activists and rescue workers said was a chemical attack, The Syrian government denied launching the attack. Soon after, President Donald Trump ordered a retaliatory attack on the Shayrat airbase, from where the chemical attack was launched.[56] Fifty-nine Tomahawk missiles were launched from the USS Porter and USS Ross, destroying aircraft, aircraft shelters, ammunition, air defense systems, and radars. Russian personnel were deployed at the base. Moscow was warned in advance that the Syrian base was about to be bombed.

---

[51] Larry Kaplow, "History of US Responses to Chemical Weapons Attacks in Syria," NPR, April 13, 2018.
[52] "President Obama Turns to Congress on Syria," NPR, August 31, 2013.
[53] "Obama to Seek Congressional Approval for Action Against Syria," NPR, August 31, 2013.
[54] L. Carol Ritchie, "US Says Syria's Chemical Weapons Stockpile Is Destroyed," NPR, August 18, 2014.
[55] Kaplow, "History of US Responses To Chemical Attacks In Syria," NPR, April 13, 2018.
[56] Shayrat is home to the Syrian Air Force 50th Air Brigade in the west of the country.

Both Obama and Trump focused their anger at Bashar al-Assad and his regime over the use of chemical and nerve agents in the Syrian civil war. But the Syrian government was not solely responsible for using these weapons. A timeline of chemical weapons activity showed that the Islamic State also launched chemical and gas attacks during the conflict.[57] The Arms Control Association, a US-based non-partisan organization in Washington, gathered evidence of several chemical attacks by the ISIS. Specific incidents included the use of sulfur mustard in Marae, northern Syria in August 2015—an attack for which the Organization for the Prohibition of Chemical Weapons (OPCW) held the Islamic State responsible with "the utmost confidence." Allegations were made about the use of chemical weapons in the Islamic State-controlled territory northwest of Palmyra in December 2016. And a joint OPCW-UN investigation report, published in October 2017, held the ISIS responsible for using sulfur mustard at Umm Hawsh, northern Aleppo in September 2016.

Despite a decade of intervention, the professed policy of the United States to achieve regime change in Syria was a failure. Several factors were responsible for this. Bashar al-Assad's grip on power was far stronger, and Syrian opposition groups were far weaker, than had been estimated in Washington. Russia's political and military support for the Syrian regime played an important role in Assad's success in holding on to power, but his country was destroyed in the process. As the Islamic State captured more Syrian territory, and became a greater threat, the United States and other intervenors turned their attention to attacking the ISIS. Paradoxically, American weapons supplied to Syrian rebels to fight the regime ended up in the hands of the Islamic State in Iraq and Syria.[58] The situation had changed radically, and Bashar al-Assad had become a useful actor in the fight against the ISIS.

---

[57] "Timeline of Chemical Weapons Activity, 2012–2021," The Arms Control Association, last reviewed in May 2021.

[58] Zackery Cohen, "Amnesty Report: ISIS armed with US weapons," CNN, December 9, 2015. Also, Mallory Shelbourne, "Study shows US weapons given to Syrian rebels ended up in ISIS hands," The Hill, December 14, 2017. "ISIL weapons traced to US and Saudi Arabia," Al Jazeera, December 14, 2017.

7

Return to Kabul

The Taliban seemed to be utterly defeated by the United States and allies in 2001, and dispersed in the remote villages in Afghanistan and Pakistan. The network of the Taliban and al Qaeda was destroyed by relentless air bombardment and ground offensive by American-supported Afghan proxies, dominated by the Northern Alliance in the first few weeks of the invasion. The Taliban were no match for their opponents, took their small weapons, and melted away in the countryside across the Afghan-Pakistan border. Their leadership was in disarray. It took several months for them to begin to recover their morale and build a new network. Despite the Taliban's collapse, Hamid Karzai's administration installed by the United States began to show limitations that would only magnify the crisis over time. The Taliban were kept out of the Bonn process after their removal from power, delivering an early setback to prospects of reconciliation and rebuilding in Afghanistan.[1] They were defeated, yet remained the most significant single group in the country. Looking back, their exclusion at the Bush administration's insistence was a mistake, setting the scene for the Taliban to look elsewhere, and for the hostilities to continue. It did not have to happen, for the Taliban had approached Hamid Karzai in the final days of their rule in November 2001, and indicated that they wanted a deal.[2]

A leading Afghanistan expert, Barnett Rubin, who worked with the United Nations' political team at the time, recalled in an interview 20 years later: "The Taliban were completely defeated, they had no demands, except

---

[1] On the Bonn conference and how the Taliban were kept out, see William Maley, *The Afghanistan Wars* (London, UK: Macmillan/Red Globe, 2021), 215–221.
[2] Alissa J. Rubin, "Did the War in Afghanistan Have to Happen," New York Times, August 23, 2021.

amnesty." Emissaries shuttled back and forth between Karzai and the Taliban leader, Mullah Omar, based in Kandahar. Karzai could see a Taliban surrender, which would keep them from playing any significant role in Afghanistan's future. But the Bush administration was confident that the militants would be wiped out, and wanted no deal. The Defense Secretary, Donald Rumsfeld, insisted that the Americans had no interest in leaving Mullah Omar to live out his days anywhere in Afghanistan.[3] The United States wanted him captured, or dead.

The Taliban's recovery from what the Americans prematurely saw as their complete destruction was one of the most extraordinary military victories in modern guerrilla warfare. Not only did it require tenacity, but also a complex military plan, tactical competence not expected from them, and simple but highly effective messages over two decades.[4] The insurgents first wore down the US-led International Security Assistance Force (ISAF) and sent foreign troops home or back to their barracks in Afghanistan between 2001 and 2014. Then, against well-funded and well-armed Afghan security forces almost five times larger than the Taliban's estimated strength of between 40,000 and 60,000, the insurgents defeated the Afghan National Army. By the end of 2021, the Americans had withdrawn, the Afghan National Army had collapsed, and the Taliban seized power again. As those dramatic events unfolded, a leading academic on the Afghan conflict, and a former advisor to the international security force command in Kabul, Theo Farrell, offered his perspective on the way the Taliban advanced to power.[5] Farrell cited what he described as "four cores of success" for the insurgents. Before examining how the Taliban recovered their morale, then developed and executed their military plan, let us look at the "four cores of success" mentioned above.

The first was the Doha agreement between the United States and the Taliban, excluding the Afghan government. Ostensibly to bring peace to Afghanistan, Washington agreed to withdraw all foreign forces. Second, and more significantly, it required the US air attacks to stop. Air support was crucial for the defense of the Afghan security forces when they came under pressure from the rebels around the country. With the threat of air attacks gone, the Taliban had more freedom to engage the Afghan forces, and overran government-controlled areas. The fragility of the Afghan National Security Forces (ANSF) was the second source of the Taliban's victory, according to

---

[3] "Text: Pentagon Briefing with Secretary Rumsfeld," Washington Post, November 19, 2001.
[4] Ben Barry, "Understanding the Taliban's Military Victory," International Institute of Strategic Studies, August 19, 2021.
[5] Theo Farrell, "How the Taliban won," Australian Institute of International Affairs, October 10, 2021.

Farrell. For all the money spent, primarily by the Americans, weapons and equipment supplied, and training, their leadership and performance in the battlefield was poor. Recruits were largely illiterate and did not show the necessary commitment to fighting and obeying their officers. Unauthorized absence and desertions marred their effectiveness. An army lacking discipline cannot prevail over the enemy.

Third, the actual numbers of troops in the army and police force were not even close to the strength claimed, giving a false picture of their capability. Corruption inside the armed forces and government agencies was widespread. Officers routinely sold supplies they received to whoever would buy them for profit. They showed fake recruits to boost the army and police strength and pocketed the money assigned for their salaries. Finally, the US-trained special forces, which constituted just 7% of the Afghan National Security Forces, did 80% of the fighting and were exhausted. When they could no longer call on the US air support when in trouble, their morale collapsed, and the game was up.

7.1 Taliban Regroup

The Taliban represent a Deobandi-Pashtun Islamic fundamentalist movement. It is important to understand the role Pashtuns have traditionally played in Afghanistan, a sparsely populated country, with vast distances separating communities across a mountainous terrain. Pashtuns, the largest ethnic group, have had a dominant role socially and politically in a country of weak institutions, including institutions of justice.[6] Their population includes nomads of no fixed address who move with their animals, and farmers who cultivate their land through irrigation. So, tribes emphasize their ethnicity and kinship to national identity instead of location.

The Taliban began to recover about 6 months after their fall from power.[7] First, the amnesty that the new Afghan leader Hamid Karzai promised was granted only partially. Having failed to secure firm control over the new government, Karzai allied himself with local armed groups funded by the United States to fight the Taliban and al Qaeda. Those same allies of Karzai went for revenge against former Taliban at the behest of the Americans, determined to eliminate all traces of them. A similar power structure existed under Afghan

---

[6] Barnett Rubin, *Afghanistan: What Everyone Needs to Know* (New York, NY: Oxford University Press, 2020), 18–22.

[7] Ibid, Antonio Giustozzi, principal author of chapter "More War, Insurgency, and Counterinsurgency," 230–254.

kings, with local warlords ruling their areas in the name of the king. Under Karzai, the effect was very different, resulting in growing alienation and hostility. Pressure from the Americans and Karzai's government prompted many Taliban to go to Pakistan, where many of their leaders had already moved. While leading figures in the new regime favored their own tribes as they took control of their areas, rival communities were excluded, and the consequence was a wider social divide.

Across the border in Pakistan, the Taliban had a more welcoming environment, even though President Musharraf's government had declared its support for America's war on terror. Taliban leaders in Pakistan began to reconnect with each other while al Qaeda and groups linked to Pakistani Taliban launched raids to harass the evolving administration in Afghanistan. Having initially been deprived of resources after their defeat, the Taliban gradually found support from private donors linked to al Qaeda, and some intelligence agencies, mainly Saudi and Pakistani.[8] The first to benefit was the Haqqani network; other Taliban leaders based around Quetta in Pakistan's Balochistan province began to raise funding in the following year. With their efforts, the Quetta Shura (Council) was born in 2002. The Quetta Shura became the most powerful center of exiled Taliban, not least because their supreme leader, Mullah Omar, escaped there after their removal from power.[9] Initially, it consisted of a ten-man Rahbari Shura (Leadership Council), including eight old-guard military commanders from southern Afghanistan, and one each from Paktika and Paktia provinces. In March 2003, Mullah Omar expanded the Rahbari Shura to a total of 33 commanders, and in October 2006, created the majlis al-shura (Consultative Council) that had 13 members and some advisors. An Islamist government in exile was in the making.

The Quetta Shura became more complex in the next few years. As the Taliban's influence spread, and they began to reassert control in some rural areas, the Quetta Shura started to appoint members of a shadow administration for various areas with heavy Taliban presence and support. In time, the Quetta Shura increased in size as its organization became more efficient, and coordination improved between its constituents, which were loosely linked tribal and communal networks, to form an increasingly effective force. By May 2009, the Taliban had created more councils to perform specific tasks to be managed under the supreme leadership of Mullah Omar.

---

[8] Ibid, 231.
[9] *World Almanac of Islamism 2014*, American Foreign Policy Council (New York, NY: Rowman & Littlefield, 2014), 1043.

The reasons for the Taliban forming their leadership council in Quetta were to do with its location. Wedged between Afghanistan and Iran, Balochistan is the largest but poorest and least-populated province in Pakistan.[10] Communities of hardy tribesmen living by ancient laws are scattered in remote villages in a vast expanse of rocky deserts, occupying four-fifths of Pakistan's territory. Mining companies are interested in Balochistan for its vast reserves of copper, natural gas, and oil. It is also the world's heroin superhighway. A network of smuggling trails cutting through its frontiers is ideal ground for making easy money. From there, the Quetta Shura led by Mullah Omar, his deputy Mullah Baradar, and chief military commander Abdullah Zakir directed the war, conducting a review each winter.

The Pakistani government, a US ally in the war on terror, denied the presence of Taliban leaders and the Quetta Shura for several years despite persistent reports of their presence, and that they were receiving funding, training, and sanctuary from Pakistan's Inter-Services Intelligence.[11] In 2010, the London School of Economics published a report about the ISI's deep involvement with the Taliban, and that ISI agents even attended Taliban supreme council meetings.[12] The study concluded that "the ISI and elements of the Pakistani military may not actually *control* the Afghan insurgency." However, "as the provider of sanctuary, and very substantial financial, military, and logistical support, to the insurgency, the ISI appears to have strong strategic and operational influence—reinforced by coercion. There is thus a strong case that the ISI and elements of the military are deeply involved in the insurgent campaign, and have powerful influence over the Haqqani network." The LSE report warned that Pakistan's "double-game" on this scale could have major geopolitical implications.

---

[10] Declan Walsh, "Strategic Balochistan becomes a target in war against Taliban," Guardian, December 21, 2009.
[11] "Quetta Shura Taliban (QST)," Afghan War News.
[12] See Matt Waldman, "The Sun in the Sky: The relationship between Pakistan's ISI and Afghan insurgents," Crisis States Research Centre, London School of Economics, June 2010. Also, "Pakistani agents 'funding and training' Afghan Taliban," BBC, June 13, 2010.

7.2 Haqqani Network

The Haqqani network was a Sunni Islamist militant group operating in the southeastern region of Afghanistan and northwestern tribal areas of Pakistan.[13] It was founded by Jalaluddin Haqqani in the 1970s. The Haqqani family and clan originated from the eastern province of Khost in Afghanistan and belonged to Zadran tribe, across the border from North Waziristan in Pakistan. Haqqani first declared war in the summer of 1973 after Daud Khan overthrew his cousin, King Zahir Shah, and abolished the monarchy in Afghanistan. Haqqani went to Pakistan with other Islamist leaders for training and support to fight the new Afghan regime. In the 1980s, the Haqqani network was one of the most formidable insurgent groups, with a military organization and political ties in Pakistan to conduct a sustained war against the Soviet occupation forces, and the regime they installed in Afghanistan. Jalaluddin Haqqani was one of the Reagan administration's most favored Mujahideen commanders. Later, he formed close ties with foreign Islamists, including Osama bin Laden.[14] In 1995, Haqqani pledged allegiance to the Taliban as they advanced toward Kabul. Jalaluddin Haqqani died in 2018, when his son Sirajuddin succeeded him as the leader of the network.

During the period between 1996 and 2001, when the Taliban ruled most of Afghanistan, the Haqqani network developed a close personal relationship with Osama bin Laden, even organizing al Qaeda and Mujahideen training camps across the region under Haqqani's control.[15] His forces played a central role in a campaign of violence across Afghanistan, and victory in Kabul in 1996. In 2001, the network facilitated Osama bin Laden's escape from Afghanistan to Pakistan. For two decades after that, it conducted an increasingly violent campaign to evict NATO forces from Afghanistan. Over their years in exile, its members began to learn some important lessons, most significantly not only how to seek but also to hold on to power.[16] They learned to engage and to not repeat some of the most notorious practices on display in their earlier rule. They took steps to devolve. From Quetta, they expanded across Pakistan, establishing four centers of leadership.[17]

---

[13] "Haqqani Network," Mapping Militant Organizations, Stanford University, updated November 8, 2017.

[14] Joe Sommerlad, "What is the Haqqani network linked to the Taliban and al-Qaeda?," Independent, September 7, 2021.

[15] "Haqqani Network," Mapping Militant Organizations, Stanford University.

[16] See Anand Gopal and Alex Strick van Linschoten, "Ideology in the Afghan Taliban," Afghan-Analyst.org

[17] Giustozzi (principal author), "More War, Insurgency, and Counterinsurgency," in Rubin, *Afghanistan: What Everyone Needs to Know*," 234–235.

7.3 Miran Shah Shura

Although officially part of the larger Taliban umbrella and the Quetta Shura, the Haqqani network maintained distinct lines of operations, and command and control.[18] Parallel to Quetta, another center was formed around Miran Shah in the North Waziristan tribal belt in the Pakistani province of Khyber Pakhtunkhwa, known as the Miran Shah Shura, the hub of the Haqqani network. In 2007, it began to drift away from the Quetta Shura. The main complaint held against the Quetta Shura was that power was concentrated in the hands of southern Afghan Taliban while the Haqqani network's activity was concentrated in southeastern Afghanistan and the northern province of Kunduz. Key military, strategic, and financial decisions were made at Haqqani's family compounds and training camps in North Waziristan.[19] After Jalaluddin Haqqani's death in 2018, his son Sirajuddin, the new leader, masterminded military activities, managed relations with the Quetta Shura, and oversaw the network's business operations. In addition to private donations, the Miran Shah Shura received logistical and financial support from the Pakistani military and continued to maintain close ties with the ISI.

7.4 Peshawar Shura

The existence of the Miran Shah Shura, separate from the main leadership council in Quetta, was indicative of how fragmented the Taliban movement was. From 2005, a third command and logistics center emerged in Peshawar, known as the Peshawar Shura.[20] With more funding coming in, Taliban groups began to set up a wide array of commissions and offices in Pakistan to manage recruitment, finance, and governance. These offices were staffed by Taliban members with past experience and skills. Their military organization continued to improve, with attempts to improve their command system and discipline. The acceptance of Quetta by other shuras diminished; its men

---

[18] Ibid, 234. Also, Sarmad Ishfaq, "South Asia's Most Notorious Militant Groups," Diplomat, December 31, 2019.

[19] Gretchen Peters, "Haqqani Network Financing: The Evolution of an Industry," Combating Terrorism Center, West Point. This study gives an account of sources of the network's income, protection money from shop owners, and medium to large firms operating in Haqqani-dominated areas of North Waziristan, bank robbery, drug trafficking, and kidnapping for ransom.

[20] Antonia Giustozzi, "The Taliban and the 2014 Presidential Elections in Afghanistan," Conflict, Security and Development, 16(6), 557–573.

operated in southern, western, and some areas of northern, central, and southeastern Afghanistan. The Miran Shah Shura declared its autonomy from Quetta in 2008, operating mainly in the southeast and parts of central Afghanistan. And the Peshawar Shura, composed mostly of men who were not Taliban before 2001, declared its autonomy in 2009. Their areas of activity were in eastern, central, northeastern, and parts of northern Afghanistan. The structure of the Taliban took the form of a loosely federated movement.

The Peshawar Shura was initially weak because of lack of recruitment when it was formed in 2005.[21] The reason why it declared autonomy 4 years later was because a number of Hizb-i-Islami networks joined the war and became part of the Taliban. Peshawar had been a stronghold of Gulbuddin Hikmatyar's group since the war against the Soviet occupation forces in the 1980s, so competition for power was inevitable. While Quetta consisted of clerical and traditional leadership-wielding political power, Peshawar attracted young, more educated people. Peshawar also benefited from its closer links with Pakistan's military intelligence. It evolved into a more centralized command and control structure.[22] With the Haqqani network at Miran Shah, the two centers increasingly became more powerful at the expense of Quetta. Consequently, while the old Taliban structure remained active in the southern heartland, factions aligned to the Peshawar Shura, and the Haqqani network, became more active in the east and north of Afghanistan. They were successful in encircling Kabul, and other Pashtun-dominated pockets in the north—Balkh, Sar-e-Pul, and Samangan in the west, and Badakhshan in the east.

7.5 Karachi Shura

Karachi, with one of the largest Pashtun communities in a Pakistani city, became the fourth hub of Afghan resistance. The Karachi Shura was closely linked to Quetta, and "turned into the rear of the Taliban military machine, partly because it was more secure."[23] Minor satellite centers grew throughout Pakistan, where Afghans had settled. There were probably over 200 local Taliban shuras in the country. From 2005, the Iranian Revolutionary Guards developed close ties with the Taliban. The Iranians were interested in obtaining intelligence about American activities, and the Taliban commanders and

---

[21] Giustozzi (principal author), "More War, Insurgency, and Counterinsurgency," in Rubin, *Afghanistan: What Everyone Needs to Know*," 234.
[22] Shanthie Mariet D'Souza, "Afghan Peace Talks and the Changing Character of Taliban Insurgency," ISAS Brief No 291, Institute of South Asian Studies, Singapore, July 26, 2013.
[23] Giustozzi, "More war, Insurgency, and Counterinsurgency," 234.

leaders were not averse to developing relations with Iran if that led to significant support in return. The Revolutionary Guards were helping the Taliban to develop networks in western Afghanistan, near Iran, from where Taliban activities could be monitored. The Iranians also had a wider strategic interest in putting pressure on the Americans, whose presence in Afghanistan was not welcome in Tehran. In 2013, what was initially known as the Mashhad Office was set up as a wing of the Quetta Shura.

7.6 Political Crisis

The conduct and outcome of the 2014 presidential election set off a political crisis which had far-reaching consequences. The contest was between Ashraf Ghani, a Pashtun and ex-finance minister, and Abdullah Abdullah, a close associate of late Ahmad Shah Massoud, to choose a successor of President Hamid Karzai. Abdullah was foreign minister under President Karzai between 2001 and 2005, and contested the 2009 presidential election against him. In the first round in 2014, Abdullah got 45% against Ghani's 31.56%.[24] In the run-off, Ghani's vote saw a dramatic rise to 56.44% while Abdullah's vote actually went down to 43.56%. Abdullah's team felt he had been a victim of electoral fraud for the second time. Afghanistan was on the brink of a major constitutional crisis. President Obama intervened, and the Secretary of State, John Kerry, brokered a deal between the two candidates leading to a "National Unity Government." Ghani became president, and Abdullah the "Chief Executive Officer"—a position that did not exist under the constitution. Final result of the 2014 election was not declared until 2016, when the Election Commission announced that Ghani had secured 55.27% and Abdullah 44.73%.

While the formation of the "National Unity Government" appeared to avoid the most immediate crisis for the US-installed system in Afghanistan, the reality was very different. Most significantly, the Taliban had no part in it and were at war with the American-supported groups. The government was a coalition between Ghani, the declared winner, and the candidate he defeated, Abdullah, in an election widely seen as fraudulent. For Abdullah, it was a second defeat in a presidential election, for he had lost before to Karzai in 2009.[25] Many Afghans saw Abdullah as Tajik, despite his mixed Tajik-Pashtun ethnicity. The basic structure of the 2014 deal was circulated by the US embassy, and details of the powers and responsibilities of the Chief Executive

---

[24] William Maley, *The Afghanistan Wars* (London, UK: Macmillan/Red Globe, 2021), 269–270.

[25] Ben Farmer, "Afghan election: Hamid Karzai's rival crosses ethnic divide," Telegraph, August 13, 2009.

Officer were announced in a decree signed by President Ghani.[26] The agreement was signed by Ghani and Abdullah on September 21, and witnessed by the US ambassador and the Special Representative of the United Nations Secretary-General. There was little doubt that the deal was crafted by the Americans to save what they had created after 2001. It faced a credibility problem from the beginning.

The working relationship between Ghani and Abdullah was not a happy one. Ghani was not given to power-sharing. The agreement provided for holding a traditional Afghan assembly, Loya Jirga, to amend the constitution, and create the post of an executive prime minister, but it was never held. Ghani was to issue a decree to form a special commission for electoral reform, and the President and the CEO were to agree on its members. Attempts to introduce electoral reform collapsed when proposals put forward by the special commission were rejected by Wolesi Jirga (the National Assembly). Worse, little interest was shown by the international actors to ensure that the provisions of the agreement were respected. The gaps between the rival camps that made up Afghanistan's institutions were symptomatic of deep-rooted historical problems in the country. Since the days of monarchy through the communist era and after, governing Afghanistan had always been complex and turbulent due to different factions competing for power based on local, tribal, and ethnic divisions, and personal rivalries. The last king, Zahir Shah, held a coalition of local and regional warlords for almost 40 years before he was deposed in 1973. Afghanistan's history after that period was much more turbulent and violent. The Ghani-Abdullah coalition was an American-inspired experiment that met a similar fate.

Afghans have a tendency to want foreign aid, which the country badly needs. But when foreigners dictate terms of behavior to them, the result is conflict. This has been one aspect of the Afghan character through history—first against imperial Britain, then the Soviet Union, and lately the United States. Another is often shifting loyalties in Afghan society, with the balance of power moving toward whoever appears more powerful, can impose peace, and enforce order to deliver local services such as they are. These factors were decisive in the Taliban's ability to impose their rule in the late 1990s, and again in 2021, when the Americans withdrew, leading to the collapse of the government they had installed two decades before.

---

[26] Maley, *The Afghanistan Wars*, 271.

7.7 Toward the End Game

The end game in Afghanistan came in late 2021, but the process had started several years ago. While the Taliban regrouped, and the crisis deepened for the Afghan government in Kabul, the Obama administration's narrative in Washington was very different. In 2011, the American-led military occupation of Afghanistan was a decade old. President Obama was increasingly inclined to end the US involvement in the war, and the 2012 presidential election was coming. Obama was keen to demonstrate that he was ready to draw down the military presence in Afghanistan. The secret operation to find and kill bin Laden in the Pakistani city of Abbottabad, in May 2011, was a turning point, for the main purpose had been to eliminate al Qaeda leader and his network.[27] As long as bin Laden remained free, no president could claim that America's war was over. After bin Laden's killing, Obama could claim that the United States had finally got the retribution for the 9/11 attacks. Leon Panetta, the CIA director at the time, and soon to be defense secretary, and other leading figures hailed bin Landen's killing. On his move to the Pentagon 2 months later, Panetta described bin Laden's death as the beginning of the end of the war on terror. He asserted that, thanks to the CIA's unrelenting drone attacks, al Qaeda had only 10–20 "key leaders" alive in Pakistan, Somalia, North Africa, and the Arabian Peninsula, and that "We're within reach of strategically defeating al Qaeda."[28] As events would demonstrate, al Qaeda remained alive throughout the region, and parts of it morphed into ISIS.

In advance of President Obama's reelection in 2012, it was expedient to convey to the American people that his policies in Afghanistan were working. During his first presidential campaign 4 years before, Obama had promised to turn around the war. Now he had to demonstrate that it was happening. In June 2011, America's war in Afghanistan had been going on for nearly a decade, but Obama reminded the American people that, in the meantime, "a second war was launched in Iraq."[29] He was critical of losing the focus from al Qaeda's leaders who had fled to Pakistan, and pointed out that "the Taliban had regrouped and gone on the offensive." That is why, he said that he had ordered reinforcements. Now, he said he was meeting "our goals," and, starting in a month, the United States would be able to remove 10,000 troops in

---

[27] Craig Whitlock, *The Afghanistan Papers* (New York, Simon & Schuster, 2021), 200.
[28] Whitlock, *Afghanistan Papers*, 200–201. Also, Andrew Buncombe, Omar Waraich, and David Usborne, "US on alert as it hails success of mission to kill terrorist chief," *Independent*, May 3, 2011.
[29] Juan Cole, "Obama: The Tides of War are Receding," Informed Comment, June 23, 2011.

2011, bringing home a total of 33,000 by next summer. Thereafter, the withdrawal process would continue. The information recovered from Osama bin Laden's compound after his killing showed "al Qaeda under enormous strain." President Obama further claimed that America had "inflicted serious losses to the Taliban and taken a number of strongholds." And he declared that America's long wars would "come to a responsible end" and it was time to "focus on nation-building at home."

America's military commanders were in conformity with Obama's narrative. Having sold their counterinsurgency strategy to the president and the people, they continued to predict success. Chairman of the Joint Chiefs of Staff, Admiral Mike Mullen, said in an interview on the Charlie Rose Talk Show that the status on the ground in Afghanistan before the planned withdrawal was continuing to improve.[30] Since President Obama sent more reinforcements, Mullen said, "security had changed for the better dramatically in the south in particular." He claimed that the Taliban were not there, especially after the arrival of the Afghan army and the police. Such assertions, however, obscured the true picture. While the Obama administration made huge investments in the training and deployment of the Afghan security forces, their ability to stop the Taliban remained untested, as the insurgents simply had returned to their sanctuaries in Pakistan, and waited for the time until the foreign forces left.[31] Corruption rose in the Afghan government, alienating the people. The US administration wanted to pull out, but officials feared that the Afghan state would collapse if they did.

The Obama administration's drive to maintain the illusion of success continued even when the situation deteriorated on the ground. In September 2011, the Defense Secretary, Leon Panetta, told the Senate Armed Services Committee that things were "headed in the right direction" even though he acknowledged that after "the Taliban lost control of territory," they had "shifted away from large attacks on our forces to greater reliance on headline-grabbing attacks."[32] This optimistic assessment from Panetta came despite the assassination of former President Burhanuddin Rabbani in Kabul just 2 days before. On Panetta's next visit to Afghanistan in March 2012, as his aircraft landed at a NATO base in Helmand, an Afghan assailant drove a stolen truck on the tarmac, trying to run over the welcoming party that had gathered.[33] The attacker set himself on fire, and crashed his vehicle. He later died. Panetta

---

[30] "Admiral Mike Mullen interview," Charlie Rose Show, June 14, 2011.
[31] Whitlock, *Afghanistan Papers*, 203.
[32] Defense Secretary Leo Panetta's statement, "Hearing to Receive Testimony of the US Strategy in Afghanistan and Iraq," Senate Armed Services Committee, September 22, 2011.
[33] Whitlock, *Afghanistan Papers*, 202.

had not disembarked from the aircraft when the attack was launched. For several hours, American military officials withheld news of the incident from journalists traveling with the Defense Secretary and released sketchy details only when British news outlets had reported the incident.

Also in June 2011, as President Obama announced the withdrawal of more than 30,000 troops, the Secretary of State, Hillary Clinton, said that "we have broken the Taliban's momentum. So we begin this drawdown from a position of strength."[34] She made a number of assertions as evidence of Afghanistan's return to normality: schools had admitted seven million students, infant mortality had decreased by 23%, opium production was down, hundreds of thousands of Afghan farmers had been trained and equipped with new seeds and other techniques, and over a hundred thousand women had received microfinance loans. It was a rosy picture of Afghanistan's transformation since the Taliban were overthrown. However, in February 2012, the Director of the Defense Intelligence Agency, Lt. General Ronald Burgess, gave a gloomy assessment of the situation to the Senate Armed Services Committee, admitting that Obama's war strategy had done little to deter the insurgency.[35] Burgess said the Afghan army was plagued by "pervasive corruption and popular perceptions that it is unable to extend security in many areas." For the army and police, "persistent qualitative challenges continue to impede their development into an independent, self-sustaining security apparatus." In comparison, his assessment was that the Taliban were "resilient" and able to withstand losses inflicted by American troops.

Burgess's conclusion was that from their Pakistani safe havens, the Taliban leadership remained "confident of eventual victory." At the same hearing, members of the Senate Armed Services Committee asked James Clapper, director of National Intelligence, why the assessment of US intelligence agencies was so negative, and at odds with the optimistic scenario created by military commanders. Clapper tried to answer by saying that a similar gap existed during the Vietnam War. While intelligence knew that the US military was stuck in a quagmire, the generals did not want to admit it.

Like Vietnam, the United States was creating a grand illusion of its own making. Clapper's remarks laid bare the reality of the Afghan situation. Months before President Obama's reelection, the White House, supported by America's senior military commanders, was engaged in a drive to convince the electorate that the war aims in Afghanistan were being achieved, and the end

---

[34] "Secretary Hillary Rodham Clinton Testimony to the Senate Foreign Relations Committee," June 23, 2011. Also "Taliban momentum broken in Afghanistan, says Clinton," BBC News, June 23, 2011.

[35] Lt. General Ronald Burgess, "Annual Threat Assessment: Statement Before the Armed Services Committee," February 16, 2012. Also, Whitlock, *Afghanistan Papers*, 209.

was near. Obama won the November 2012 election against his Republican opponent, Mitt Romney, but control of the two Congressional chambers was split, with the Republicans retaining their majority in the House of Representatives, and the Democrats in the Senate. Obama focused on his foreign policy successes, highlighting the killing of Osama bin Laden, and withdrawal of most troops from Iraq.[36] Obama had promised to end the US war in Afghanistan. So, on December 28, 2014, American and NATO officials held a ceremony at their headquarters in the Afghan capital, Kabul.[37] In a statement released by the White House Press Secretary, President Obama called the ceremony "a milestone for our country."[38] Obama praised the military and intelligence services for "devastating the core of al Qaeda, delivering justice to Osama bin Laden, disrupting terrorist plots, and saving countless American lives." He said that the United States was safer, and more secure after 13 years of war, that "some 90% of our troops are home" from Afghanistan and Iraq, and "with growing prosperity here at home, we enter a new year with new confidence."

Yet, the new year brought bad news. In April 2015, an army medic, John Dowson, was killed in Jalalabad when an Afghan soldier opened fire on coalition troops at a government compound.[39] Two months later, a rocket attack killed a civilian, Krissie Davis, working for the Defense Logistics Agency. In August, Taliban fighters attacked a Special Operations forces camp in Kabul; Sgt. Andrew McKenna, and several Afghan guards, died in the incident. Nearly 3 weeks later, another insider attack at a police checkpoint in Helmand province killed Air Force Capt. Matthew Roland and Staff Sgt. Forrest Sibley. One of the biggest cities, Kunduz, in northern Afghanistan had been under a long siege by Taliban forces. The fall of Kunduz to the insurgents shocked the country, and US forces rushed there to help the Afghan army to recapture the city. On October 3, 2015, there was a US Air Force gunship attack on a Kunduz hospital run by the humanitarian agency, Doctors Without Borders. Forty-two people were killed. By the end of 2015, the myth that American troops were not engaged in combat was truly shattered. President Obama apologized for the attack on the hospital, and a US military inquiry concluded

---

[36] In Iraq, the withdrawal of US combat troops in December 2011 still left thousands of soldiers to protect the US embassy in Baghdad, and consulates in Basra, Mosul, and Kirkuk. See James Denselow, "The US departure from Iraq is an illusion," Guardian, October 25, 2011. Also, "Last US troops withdraw from Iraq," BBC News, December 19, 2011.

[37] Whitlock, *Afghanistan Papers*, 227.

[38] "Statement by the President on the End of Combat Mission in Afghanistan," White House Press office, Washington, DC, December 28, 2014.

[39] For an account of repeated military setbacks to the US-led forces in 2015–2016, see Whitlock, *Afghanistan Papers*, 232–239.

that the "fog of war," human error, and equipment failure were responsible. Within days, Obama ordered a stop to the troop withdrawal and extended their mission indefinitely. Nonetheless, Taliban forces continued to gain, capturing most of Helmand province in 2016. Fears grew in Washington that the Afghan government was on the verge of complete breakdown. Obama reversed his promise to end the war in Afghanistan and announced that at least five-and-a-half-thousand troops would remain after he left the office in January 2017. When Obama left the White house, there were about 8400 American troops in Afghanistan.

7.8 Trump and Afghanistan

The bitterly fought presidential election in 2016 between Hillary Clinton, secretary of state in President Obama's first term, and billionaire tycoon Donald Trump resulted in Trump's victory, starting an unpredictable era in the United States, and its behavior in international politics. Most important matters of the country, from appointments in the Trump administration to domestic and foreign policy decisions, were taken by Trump himself, or a few close aides, including his daughter, Ivanka Trump, his son, Donald Trump Jr., and Ivanka's husband, Jared Kushner. President Trump demanded absolute loyalty, and anyone who did not play according to his ever-changing wishes had their career cut short in the administration.

In 2011, 2012, and 2013, well before he began his official campaign, Donald Trump had posted a number of tweets calling for an end to the US involvement in Afghanistan.[40] Describing it as a matter of priorities, he said in 2011: "When will we stop wasting our money on rebuilding Afghanistan? We must rebuild our country first." In 2012, he described the war as "a total disaster," saying further: "We don't know what we are doing." Criticizing the Afghan forces he said: "They are, in addition to everything else, robbing us blind." Five months later, he wrote: "Why are we continuing to train these Afghanis who then shoot our soldiers in the back? Afghanistan is a complete waste. Time to come home!" And in January 2013, he echoed his earlier comments: "Let's get out of Afghanistan. Our troops are being killed by the Afghanis we train and we waste billions there. Nonsense! Rebuild the USA." Later in the same year, Trump looked dismayed by the prospect of keeping 20,000 troops "for many years," adding the next day "We have wasted an enormous amount of blood and treasure in Afghanistan." On November 21,

---

[40] Meghan Keneally, "What Trump has said about Afghanistan," ABC News, August 21, 2017.

2013, Trump wrote: "Do not allow our very stupid leaders to sign a deal that keeps Afghanistan through 2024—with all costs by U.S.A. MAKE AMERICA GREAT." By this time, Trump's election slogan had taken shape. After an insider attack in December 2015, one of his tweets was: "A suicide bomber has just killed U.S. troops in Afghanistan. When will our leaders get tough and smart? We are being led to slaughter?"[41]

Once in office in January 2017, Trump made an about-turn. He was commander-in-chief of the most powerful nation, and averse to creating any impression of weakness. He also encountered resistance from his own cabinet, and Pentagon officials warned him that a sudden withdrawal could have disastrous consequences.[42] The Afghan government could collapse, war could spill over into Pakistan, a nuclear-armed country, and he would have problems of his own on the domestic front at the very beginning of his term as president. The Defense Secretary, James Mattis, told the Senate Armed Services Committee that "we are not winning the war in Afghanistan right now." And the Chairman of the Joint Chiefs of Staff, General Joseph Dunford, said at an event at the National Press Club in Washington that "Afghanistan is not where we want to be." Trump did not like being told by subordinates, but he wanted to win.

In a speech at Fort Mayer, Trump announced a new strategy: "My original instinct was to pull out. And historically, I like following my instincts. But one way or another, these problems will be solved. I am a problem-solver. And in the end, we will win." It was a strange mix of skepticism and boast. He would not reveal how many more troops he was going to deploy. But anonymous US officials leaked that about 4000 or more troops would be sent. Trump's war became more secretive. And as part of that strategy, he authorized the military to intensify the bombing campaign.

Trump's secret bombing made America's war less visible. He also hoped that the pressure would force the Taliban to negotiate. In 2017, the number of air attacks more than doubled, and the amount of munitions dropped was three times greater. A year later, US bombers released more than 7300 bombs and missiles—a third more than any previous year. In 2019 and 2020, the bombing continued at a blistering pace. American, NATO, and Afghan air attacks killed more than a thousand civilians each year.[43] Anti-government

---

[41] Daniel L. Davis, "Trump Came This Close to Getting Afghanistan Right," American Conservative, October 25, 2018.
[42] Whitlock, *Afghanistan Papers*, 242–246.
[43] Neta C. Crawford, "Afghanistan's Rising Death Toll Due to Airstrikes, 2017–2020," Costs of War Project, Watson Institute, Brown University, December 7, 2020.

militant groups, including the Taliban and ISIS, also escalated their attacks, killing an average of 2000 people between 2017 and 2019.

In September 2018, the Trump administration named Zalmay Khalilzad as the Special Representative for Afghanistan Reconciliation, a newly created diplomatic post. Two months later in November 2018, negotiations began with the Taliban in Doha, the capital of Qatar, at the instigation of Trump, who had promised to finish "endless wars."[44] After nine rounds of talks, an agreement was signed in February 2020 by Khalilzad for the United States, and Mullah Abdul Ghani Baradar, the Taliban political chief, with the Secretary of State, Mike Pompeo, as a witness.[45] The Afghan government was kept out of the Doha process. The agreement came only months from the US presidential election in November that year. Its timing was calculated to help the Trump campaign against his Democratic opponent, Joe Biden. It addressed four issues: reducing violence, withdrawing foreign troops, starting intra-Afghan negotiations, and guaranteeing Afghanistan would not again become a refuge for terrorists.[46] While the US-Taliban agreement suited the Trump campaign, it was only the first step toward ending the war. A bigger challenge would be in negotiations between the Afghan government and the various factions making up the Taliban, and how earnestly the Doha accord was implemented. The United States agreed to reduce its troops from about 12,000 to 8600 in just over 4 months. If the Taliban fulfilled their commitment, then all US and foreign troops would leave Afghanistan within 14 months. However, three major questions remained, creating uncertainty. How productive the intra-Afghan negotiations were going to be? Would the Taliban observe their promise to reduce violence while the intra-Afghan negotiations aim at achieving a lasting ceasefire? And how stable would be the Afghan government as foreign forces withdraw?

While US-led international forces were being reduced, and those that were there mainly stayed in their barracks, coming out when Afghan troops got into difficulty, the recruitment drive by the Taliban was increasingly successful.[47] The US military estimated that the Taliban strength had risen to 60,000 fighters by 2018, and they were still recruiting while Afghan government

---

[44] Andy Gregory, "Taliban peace deal: what is the Doha agreement signed by the Trump administration?," Independent, August 19, 2021.

[45] "Agreement for Bringing Peace to Afghanistan between the Islamic Emirate of Afghanistan, which is not recognized by the United States as a state and is known as the Taliban and the United States of America," US State Department, February 29, 2020.

[46] Lindsay Maizland, "US-Taliban Peace Deal: What to Know," Council on Foreign Relations, Washington, DC, updated March 2, 2020.

[47] Whitlock, *Afghanistan Papers*, 247.

troops were deserting. The Taliban knew the momentum was with them. They had to gradually expand until the Americans with their allies left, and the victory would be theirs. On the other hand, President Trump was determined on withdrawal amid a blaze of publicity before the November 2020 presidential election. His initial attempt unraveled spectacularly. In September 2019, he secretly invited Taliban leaders to sign an accord at Camp David with President Ghani as a mere witness.[48] Both the Taliban and Ghani balked on the idea of going to Washington for a photo op. When news leaked that Trump had invited Taliban leaders to Washington, members of Congress expressed shock and disbelief. The invitation was immediately canceled, and Trump declared that the talks were "dead."

However, Trump had not given up. When the uproar subsided, Trump's envoy Khalilzad resumed negotiations with the Taliban in Doha, and the two sides eventually signed an agreement. The Afghan state which the United States created after 2001, and President Ghani's government, were left to be on their own. Direct talks, which were supposed to take place between the Taliban and the Kabul government, got nowhere. The Taliban advance continued. What American guarantees for the Afghan government had remained began to whittle away. Despite public optimism of top government officials in Kabul and abroad that Afghanistan's security forces, trained and heavily armed by the United States, were capable of resisting pressures from the Taliban, events on the ground told a very different story. Desertions were on the increase, influential Afghans began to make new accommodations, and a realization grew that while Pashtun-dominated nationalist forces had their supporters, days of western disposition were at an end.

Trump lost his reelection bid in November 2020, defeated by Joe Biden, who was skeptical of America's continued war since his days as Obama's vice president. Biden decided to stay the course and withdraw. He retained Khalilzad as his special representative for Afghanistan. On taking office in January 2021, President Biden, reiterating his promise to bring US troops home, said: "My administration strongly supports the diplomatic process that is underway and to bring to an end this war that is closing out 20 years. We remain committed to ensuring that Afghanistan never again provides a base for terrorist attacks on the United States and our partners and our interests."[49] Although the original deadline of May 1, 2021, for withdrawal was delayed

---

[48] Ibid, 272–273.
[49] Eugene Kiely and Robert Farley, "Timeline of US Withdrawal from Afghanistan," FactCheck. Org, August 17, 2021.

for "tactical reasons," Biden announced that America's "forever war" would end with the final withdrawal on September 11.[50]

Taliban fighters entered the Afghan capital, Kabul, on August 15, 2021, and President Ghani fled the country. The United States evacuated its diplomats from its embassy by helicopter, as hundreds of thousands of Afghans and foreign nationals tried to escape. Television pictures of desperate crowds, including women and children, around Kabul airport shown around the world were reminiscent of America's withdrawal from Vietnam after the fall of Saigon to North Vietnamese troops on April 30, 1975. As Taliban fighters watched, US troops, with smaller contingents from allied countries, processed those able to escape to board evacuation flights. Countless others were left behind to live under Taliban rule.

---

[50] "'It's Time To End This Forever War.' Biden Says Forces to Leave Afghanistan By 9/11," NPR, April 15, 2021.

8

Conclusion

Examples of great powers fighting long wars, but exhausting their ability to continue, can be found throughout the history of warfare. Symptoms of the Vietnam Syndrome were evident long before American commentators coined the term after the US withdrawal from Vietnam in 1975. The criticism in this book of the way the Vietnam Syndrome was originally defined by those commentators is made for two reasons. Chapter 2 explains, first of all, that the definition is too US-centric and narrow, seeking to explain away America's failure as something due to the lack of will and support at home. Second, it does not take account of external factors such as Indochina's history, geography, the fighting skills, and the will of the people who ultimately prevailed. The works of Paul Kennedy and Dennis Florig discussed in this book can be applied globally. They are more relevant to my attempt to explore parallels between the Afghan and Vietnam conflicts, and to examine factors that proved decisive in the Soviet-Afghan War (1979–1989) and the US-Afghan War (2001–2021). The reasons for the particular outcomes of these conflicts are not dissimilar to those which brought the war in Vietnam to its conclusion. Lessons from it can be applied to understand wars of the past.

Chapter 3, which focused on America's war on terror, began with an explanation of how a great power with the mindset of invincibility can be trapped in the belief that it is possible to ignore local and historical factors, and its own moral foundations. It shows, once again, that military superiority and economic resources are exhaustible after all. Furthermore, when a big power becomes oblivious of exhausting its moral capital—the basis of human values that it espouses—the damage to its reputation as a law-abiding member of the community of nations is difficult to repair. This theme continues through the book. Chapter 4 illustrates the limits of the Soviet Union and the US-led alliance in endless wars.

It is also worth recalling previous Anglo-Afghan Wars in the nineteenth and twentieth centuries, when the British Empire intervened in Afghanistan thrice, but failed each time. The First Anglo-Afghan War (1839–1842) was fought during a period when Great Britain and Russia were involved in a race for influence in Afghanistan, and the Afghan ruler, Dost Mohammad Khan, tried to balance between the two imperial powers.[1] Over time, the British became increasingly distrustful of Dost, believing that either he was hostile to them, or unable to resist the Russians. After trying to negotiate with the Afghan king and failing, the Governor-General of British India, Lord Auckland, ordered an invasion of Afghanistan, with the aim of restoring exiled ruler Shah Shuja to the throne. But Afghans resisted, as they would neither accept British occupation nor a ruler installed by a foreign power. Faced with relentless hostility, the British eventually found their occupation unsustainable. Attempts to negotiate withdrawal terms were foiled, and the British political agent, Sir William Hay Macnaghten, who had gone for talks, was assassinated. On January 6, 1842, an attempt to march out of Kabul by about four-and-half-thousand British and Indian troops, and thousands of followers, ended in a massacre when bands of armed Afghans attacked them. British control after that bloodbath became impossible, and the new Governor-General of India, Lord Ellenborough, decided to evacuate.

The Second Anglo-Afghan War (1878–1880) also took place in the context of imperial rivalries between Britain and Russia. Three years before, Prime Minister Benjamin Disraeli had appointed Lord Lytton as governor-general of British India with orders to counter growing Russian influence in Afghanistan, either by diplomatic means or securing the Afghan-India border by force. Soon after taking up his post, Governor-General Lytton informed Afghanistan's ruler, Sher Ali Khan, that he was sending a British mission to Kabul, but the British were refused permission. Feeling offended, Lord Lytton described Afghanistan as "an earthen pipkin between two metal pots." He waited until 1878, when a Russian mission led by General Nikolai Stoletov was allowed to visit the Afghan capital while Lytton's emissary, Sir Neville Chamberlain, was turned back by Afghan troops at the border. That was too much for Lytton, who launched the Second Anglo-Afghan War on November 21, 1878. King Sher Ali fled Kabul, and died a year later. His son, Yaqub Ali, who succeeded as king, agreed to allow a permanent British embassy in Kabul, and to conduct Afghanistan's foreign relations according to the wishes and advice of the

---

[1] See "Anglo-Afghan Wars," Britannica.com

British government. The British victory was, however, short-lived, because the British envoy, Sir Louis Cavagnari, and his son were assassinated in Kabul on September 3, 1879. British forces were sent again and occupied the Afghan capital. King Yaqub Ali Khan abdicated and was succeeded by Abdur Rahman on the throne. It was during his reign that the boundaries of Afghanistan were drawn by the British and Russian empires.

The Third Anglo-Afghan War (1919) was fought just after WWI. Although King Habibullah Khan pursued a policy of noninvolvement in the war, there was widespread support for the Ottoman Turkey against the British. Relations with the British Empire had been good during Habibullah's reign. Afghanistan followed British guidance in foreign affairs in return for an annual subsidy of 160,000 pounds, but Habibullah retained control of internal affairs. His neutrality was particularly unpopular with young anti-British Afghans. In February 1919, Habibullah was assassinated, and his son Amanullah Khan succeeded him on the throne. That is when Anglo-Afghan relations deteriorated rapidly. In his coronation address, Amanullah declared total independence from Britain—a declaration which led to the Third Anglo-Afghan War (May–August 1919). Heavy demands during WWI had drained the British Indian army. The war with Afghanistan ended with a peace treaty, which was signed at Rawalpindi on August 8, 1919. The document was later amended in 1921, when Afghanistan concluded a friendship treaty with the Soviet Union. Afghanistan recognized the Soviet Union, and the two countries established diplomatic relations. Their "special relationship" lasted until 1979, when the Soviets invaded Afghanistan.

Characteristics of the Vietnam Syndrome, the term introduced in the United States in the 1970s, were evident in the examples mentioned above. Citing Paul Kennedy and Dennis Florig, a modified definition of the Vietnam Syndrome is developed in Chap. 2. That definition is widely applicable and can be helpful to study the behavior of powers with exceptional military and economic capabilities. Such powers use their strength to intervene in weaker states based on their own assertions, irrespective of whether or not they are justifiable. In reality, Britain's interventions in Afghanistan in the nineteenth and twentieth centuries were part of the imperial race with Russia. So was the Soviet invasion of Afghanistan in December 1979, when the USSR intervened to protect its influence in that country.

Chapter 4 looks at how the Soviet invading forces killed the Afghan leader, Hafizullah Amin, and installed a puppet regime led by Babrak Karmal in Kabul. To justify its actions, the Kremlin falsely asserted that the Soviet forces were not invaders, but invited to protect the legitimate government of Afghanistan from the Mujahideen, who had started receiving support from the United States. Against this background, the Afghan conflicts between 1979 and 1989, and then again between 2001 and 2021, should be seen in the context of Vietnam, where the US war had punctured the myth of American invincibility. The United States was so hurt that it became driven by a desire to give the Soviet Union its Vietnam and restore America's global supremacy. Consequently, what began as a covert operation during the Carter administration to tempt the Soviets into launching an invasion of Afghanistan became a full-scale proxy war against the Soviet Union under the Reagan presidency.

In the Vietnam War, the Americans went in with force. They used a variety of overt and covert tactics against nationalists in what was previously French Indochina comprising Vietnam, Cambodia, and Laos. They failed to achieve a quick victory despite their vast military superiority. As the war continued year after year, it was evident that the Americans and their Indochinese allies could not win, and the nationalist forces showed no signs of giving up. Governments that the United States was propping up were corrupt, dysfunctional, and unable to survive without massive American support. The turning point came with the 1973 Paris Peace Accords—an agreement signed by the United States, South Vietnam, Viet Cong, and North Vietnam—aimed at ending the war and restoring peace.[2] South Vietnam had consistently refused to recognize Viet Cong's Provisional Revolutionary Government (PRG), so references to it were confined to a document signed by the United States and North Vietnam.

The South Vietnamese were presented with a separate document that did not refer to the Viet Cong's provisional government. The Paris Peace Accords provided for a ceasefire throughout Vietnam, but it was never respected until the fall of Saigon in 1975. Fatefully, the United States agreed to withdraw all its troops and advisors and dismantle all its bases, within 60 days. In return, North Vietnam agreed to release all US and other prisoners of war. Both sides also agreed to withdraw all foreign troops from Cambodia and Laos. At that point, the fate of the pro-US regimes was sealed.

The trajectory of war in Afghanistan during the decade of Soviet occupation in the 1980s, and America's 20-year war from 2001, shows remarkable parallels with Vietnam. In April 1978, the People's Democratic Party of Afghanistan, a party closely linked to Moscow, seized power in a coup with the help of a group of Soviet-trained Afghan military officers, and assassinated President Daud Khan and several of his family members. Those events caused deep splits in the country, as well as in the new ruling party, the PDPA, which

---

[2] "Paris Peace Accords Signed," History.com, January 27, 1973.

already had two factions, Khalq (Masses) and Parcham (Banner). The geopolitical significance of the 1978 coup was that the country fell under Soviet domination. But the Kabul regime was extremely unstable due to factional rivalries within the ruling party, its narrow support base, and the widespread anger the communist seizure of power generated in a deeply conservative rural society. In another coup in September 1979, the ruling party's leader, Nur Muhammad Taraki, was removed and died under mysterious circumstances. From then on, Afghanistan began to slide deeper into chaos. The new leader, Hafizullah Amin, was even more unpredictable and authoritarian. The Kabul regime was paralyzed by internal fighting, and rebellions were spreading in the countryside. The Soviet leaders feared a collapse of the Kabul regime, and loss of Afghanistan from their orbit.

Behind the December 1979 invasion of Afghanistan, the Kremlin's motive was to secure that country and consolidate its influence south of the border. Troops loyal to the Afghan leader, Hafizullah Amin, fought fierce battles with Soviet troops who were airlifted to Kabul. Amin was killed, his forces were defeated, the Kremlin's chosen man, Babrak Karmal, the exiled leader of the Parcham faction, was flown to Kabul, and installed as head of the regime. The removal of Amin, who had studied and lived in the United States in the 1960s, and his replacement by Karmal, was supposed to stabilize Afghanistan. Soviet leaders calculated that the new regime that was under total control of Soviet advisors in every government department would obey Moscow's orders. And Soviet occupation forces with loyal Afghan government troops would be able to quell the Mujahideen resistance.

The Soviets miscalculated badly in several respects. Armed with heavy weapons meant for modern urban warfare, Soviet troops did not realize how difficult it would be to fight a guerrilla war in Afghanistan's vast hostile countryside. They underestimated Afghan history, culture, and the tenacity of its people in fighting invaders. Nor did the Kremlin's military planners appreciate that the rebel groups would make use of sanctuaries in neighboring Pakistan, and to a lesser extent Iran. Most of all, the Soviets underrated the capacity and resolve of the United States to fight a proxy war, and in doing so assemble a coalition of European and Arab allies, as well as China. As the Americans had found in Indochina, the Mujahideen fighters who the Soviets were up against had few possessions, lived very frugally, and made great personal sacrifices. As long as they had an AK-47 rifle, and a copy of the Quran to inspire them to fight jihad, they were capable of inflicting extensive damage on the Soviet occupation forces.

As the war dragged on, the Soviets suffered mounting casualties, and loss of morale, while the economy was in sharp decline, and a deepening political crisis in the Kremlin with the death of three leaders, Leonid Brezhnev, Yuri Andropov, and Konstantin Chernenko in under 3 years. Chernenko was succeeded by Mikhail Gorbachev in March 1985 at the relatively young age of 54. Within a year, Gorbachev saw the obvious—the Soviet Union could not go on fighting in Afghanistan indefinitely. The Soviet forces were out by February 1989. The Najibullah regime left behind in Kabul collapsed 3 years later.

After the collapse of communism, Afghanistan went through a particularly turbulent period. Repeated attempts to form a stable government, capable of establishing order in the country with American help, failed due to relentless fighting between rival Mujahideen factions. From the turbulence lasting more than 2 years arose the Taliban, a new generation of young Afghans, who had mostly grown up in refugee camps in Pakistan, and were determined to impose their own brand of fundamentalist Islamic order. Their methods were harsh, and they had the backing of Pakistan's military, which had switched its support from Gulbuddin Hekmatyar's Hizb-i-Islami faction to the Taliban.

By 1996, the Taliban were in control of almost all of Afghan territory. So began the Taliban era in Afghanistan, and their alliance with al Qaeda. Osama bin Laden, who with his men had fought the Soviets in Afghanistan in the 1980s, found a safe sanctuary under Taliban rule. The wealth of bin Laden, and his vehement anti-Americanism, helped assure his dominant position with the Taliban when their regime was subject to severe international sanctions. It was from that position that bin Laden orchestrated his violent campaign against the United States, and the royal family of Saudi Arabia.

America returned to Afghanistan after the September 11, 2001, attacks, and another phase of the conflict began with President George W. Bush ordering reprisal against al Qaeda and the Taliban. With the American-led forces' air supremacy, and use of Northern Alliance foot soldiers, removing the Taliban from Kabul was easy. But in the broader scheme, there were many failures. Al Qaeda and Taliban leaders, and many fighters, escaped to safe havens along the wild Afghan-Pakistan frontier. Others returned with their small weapons to their villages and melted into the communities to which they belonged. The Bush administration insisted from the outset that the Taliban should be wiped out as a force in Afghanistan. Their exclusion from the Bonn peace process was a strategic blunder. Another failure was to introduce the new state structure based on the US presidential system with Karzai as head of state, in a country where centralized government was alien.

Failing to impose central authority, Karzai chose the old method of reaching accommodations with regional warlords to keep himself in power. Promised amnesty for returning Taliban militiamen was not forthcoming, because their reintroduction into society threatened the power of existing tribal chiefs and warlords. As the Americans poured billions of dollars, corruption returned with a vengeance. The Afghan National Army and police never reached the numbers officially recorded. Discipline was always a problem, with soldiers frequently going on unauthorized leave, desertions, and illegal sale of weapons and other military assets. All this drained the state capacity, diminished America's willingness to continue its commitment to Afghanistan, and proved to be a bonanza for the Taliban.

Soon after the invasion of Afghanistan, the Bush administration turned its attention to expanding the war. As part of the war on terror, abductions and torture of people were in full swing. International attention switched to the Guantanamo Bay detention camp. Chapter 5 examines how the George W. Bush administration was further diverted to Iraq to invade and overthrow the Saddam Hussein regime, dissolve the state structure, and create a new state system. Challenges to the US-led coalition in Iraq turned out to be much more serious. The behavior of occupation forces in the Abu Ghraib detention center and the torture regime they ran left the international image of the United States in tatters.

Chapter 6 examines how the United States found itself facing a new and broader challenge in the Arab world. In 2010, the first wave of the Arab Spring came in the form of mass protests against the regime in Tunisia, quickly spreading to Egypt, Libya, Yemen, Syria, and other Gulf states. President Obama's administration was taken by surprise and did not appear to be sure how to deal with the Arab Spring. Obama decided to be selective in where to support popular resistance, and where to back the regime because it was America's ally. Those inconsistent priorities meant that America and allies backed with military means the resistance to Muammar Gaddafi's regime in Libya, where he was overthrown. In Syria, Washington first wanted to overthrow Bashar al-Assad's regime, but later realized that he better be left in power to help in the war against the Islamic State. In Egypt, the military coup which overthrew the democratically elected President, Mohamed Morsi of the Islamic movement Muslim Brotherhood, was staged in Washington's knowledge, returning Egypt to military dictatorship.

All these diversions took a heavy toll on America's military, economic, and moral assets. The American Congress and people increasingly began to question the open commitments in the Middle East without any end in sight. In Afghanistan, meanwhile, the Taliban recovered. Chapter 7 examines how they organized themselves in exile in Pakistan, how they raised funds through donations from Gulf states, fought the American-led international forces and the Afghan National Army, and imposed taxes as they gained more and more territory in Afghanistan. The final chapter shows that coping with the aftermath turned out to be much harder and even more expensive than the invasion and removal of the Taliban from power in Afghanistan.

With each passing year, the cost in terms of economic, military, and moral capital spent was rising. Little surprise that Donald Trump, who had been elected president in 2016, and was facing reelection in 2020, was keen on his pledge to end America's long war. The result was the Doha agreement signed with the Taliban in February 2020, promising America's total withdrawal. Trump was defeated in November 2020, but his successor, President Biden, decided to stay the course. The decision left the Afghan government, which America had installed two decades before, unable to defend itself. As the United States and allies airlifted foreign nationals and thousands of Afghans out of Kabul, the Afghan army equipped with advanced weapons disintegrated. President Ashraf Ghani fled the country, and Taliban soldiers simply walked in and took control in the capital.

Appendix A

America's Long War, 2001–2021

Afghanistan[1]

September 11, 2001	United State attacked
September 18, 2001	President Bush signs Authorization of Military Force
October 7, 2001	Enduring Freedom launched
April 17, 2002	Transitional Afghan Government
2003–2008	Taliban regroup, Bush sends troop reinforcements
2009	Number of US troops peaks under Obama
May 2, 2011	Osama bin Laden killed in Pakistan
June 2011	Obama announces troop withdrawal to begin
September 2014	Announcement of Afghan combat operations to end
October 3, 2015	US bombs Doctors Without Borders clinic in Kunduz
July 6, 2016	Obama slows withdrawal
2017	Trump increases troops
January 28, 2019	Taliban agree on eventual US withdrawal "framework"
February 29, 2020	US and Taliban agreement on withdrawal in Doha
January 15, 2021	Trump announces draw down of troops
April 2021	Biden continues withdrawal
July 2021	Biden moves up deadline
August 6, 2021	Taliban offensive
August 15, 2021	Taliban enter Kabul
August 30, 2021	American troops leave Afghanistan

---

[1] "How September 11, 2001 led to US's longest war," Al Jazeera, September 6, 2021.

Iraq[2]

October 10, 2002	Iraq Authorization of Force approved
March 20, 2003	US-led coalition launches air attacks on Iraq
April 9, 2003	A regime crumbles
May 1, 2003	President Bush declares "Mission Accomplished"
May 23, 2003	Iraqi Army disbanded
June 22, 2003	Organized resistance begins. Saddam's sons killed
December 14, 2003	Saddam Hussein captured
January 24, 2004	WMD search aborted. US admits claims were mistaken
March 31, 2004	Al Qaeda mounts suicide bombing on Shia holy sites
April 28, 2004	Prisoner abuse at Abu Ghraib becomes public
September 8, 2004	Battle for Fallujah between US troops and insurgents
2005	Constitutional referendum, elections and Shi'a majority
June 8, 2006	Al Qaeda leader Abu Musab al-Zarqawi killed
November 5, 2006	Saddam Hussein sentenced to death by hanging
December 30, 2006	Saddam Hussein executed
January 10, 2007	President Bush announces a surge of American troops
August 19, 2007	Suicide bombing kills hundreds of Yazidis near Mosul
December 16, 2007	British forces relinquish control of Basra
December 30, 2007	Nearly four thousand Americans killed since invasion
March 3, 2008	President Ahmadinejad of Iran is welcomed to Baghdad
September 1, 2008	US military hands over security to the Iraqis in Anbar
November 4, 2008	Obama wins the US presidential election
February 1, 2009	Obama announces plans to remove combat brigades
June 30, 2009	US troops withdraw from cities
March 7, 2010	Iraqi parliamentary elections
August 31, 2010	US combat operations end after seven years
December 18, 2011	US announces combat troops leaving Iraq.

However, US troops returned to Iraq at the request of the Iraqi government three years later, when Islamic State fighters overran large parts of Iraq. After the military defeat of the ISIS in 2017, US troops stayed to stabilize the situation.[3]

December 9, 2021	End of the US combat mission, shifts to advisory role [4]

---

[2] "The Iraq War (2003-2011)," Council on Foreign Relations.
[3] "US combat forces to leave Iraq by the end of year," BBC News, July 27, 2021.
[4] "US combat mission in Iraq ends, shifting to advisory role," Al Jazeera, December 9, 2021.

Arab Spring[5]

Tunisia

December 17, 2010	Bouazizi self-immolates after police harassment
January 4, 2011	Bouazizi dies
January 9, 2011	Eleven people die in clashes with security forces
January 14, 2011	President Ben Ali flees to Saudi Arabia after protests
January 17, 2011	Prime Minister Ghannouchi forms unity government
February 27, 2011	Prime Minister Ghannouchi resigns
March 9, 2011	Tunisian court rules Ben Ali's party will be dissolved
October 23, 2011	Polls open nine months after first street protests
January 14, 2012	Celebrations one year after Ben Ali's overthrow

Libya

January 14, 2011	First reports of unrest.
January 16, 2011	Protests erupt in Benghazi after arrest of activists
February 20, 2011	Death toll passes two hundred and thirty
February 25, 2011	Uprising reaches Tripoli. Protests across Middle East
March 9, 2011	Gaddafi warns against air-exclusion zone
March 18, 2011	United Nations backs air-exclusion zone
March 19, 2011	Operation Odyssey Dawn launched
March 23, 2011	NATO takes military command of operation
March 28, 2011	Rebels advance on Sirte, Gaddafi's home city
April 15, 2011	Obama commits to military action
May 1, 2011	British embassy set on fire. Other missions attacked
August 26, 2011	Transitional Council news conference in Tripoli
September 25, 2011	Mass grave of one-thousand-two-hundred and seventy bodies discovered in Tripoli
October 20, 2011	Pinned by NATO air raids, Gaddafi is found and killed
November 20, 2011	Leading Gaddafi regime figures killed, arrested, or flee

Egypt

January 17, 2011	A man sets himself on fire next to Parliament in Cairo
January 25, 2011	Organized protests in Cairo demand Mubarak's removal
January 28, 2011	After four days of protests, Mubarak sacks government
January 31, 2011	Army declares itself allied to protesters

---

[5] "How the Arab Spring unfolded," Al Jazeera, 14 January 2021.

February 1, 2011	Mubarak declares he will not run, but oversee transition
February 2, 2011	Mubarak supporters in a brutal bid to crush protests
February 11, 2011	Mubarak resigns and hands over power to the military
August 1, 2011	Army tanks violently take over Tahrir Square
September 27, 2011	Military regime announces parliamentary elections
November 13, 2011	Violence escalates as protests spread beyond Cairo
November 21, 2011	Violence leaves thirty-three dead, more than two thousand injured
November 29, 2011	Egyptians vote in first free ballot in eighty years
November 30, 2011	Muslim Brotherhood candidates win big in first round
December 5, 2011	Runoff parliamentary elections. No party wins majority
December 7, 2011	New government sworn in by Kamal Ganzouri, appointed as prime minister by military rulers
May 23–24, 2012	First round of the presidential election. Ahmed Shafik and Mohammed Morsi in the lead
June 2, 2012	Hosni Mubarak sentenced to life imprisonment
June 24, 2012	Mohammed Morsi declared winner in the presidential runoff

Bahrain

February 4, 2011	Protesters gather outside the Egyptian embassy to express solidarity with anti-government protesters there
February 14, 2011	"Day of Rage": thousands of people gather demanding constitutional and political reforms
February 17, 2011	"Bloody Thursday": Police clear Pearl Roundabout of estimated fifteen hundred people in tents.
February 26, 2011	The King dismisses several ministers in an apparent attempt to appease the opposition
March 1, 2011	Anti-government rally of tens of thousands of demonstrators called by seven opposition groups
March 14, 2011	Saudi Arabia deploys troops and armored vehicles into Bahrain to quash the unrest
March 15, 2011	Bahrain declares martial law
March 18, 2011	The Pearl Monument—the focal point of the protest movement—is demolished
March 27, 2011	Opposition party Al Wefaq accepts a Kuwaiti offer to mediate
March 29, 2011	Bahraini Foreign Minister denies any Kuwaiti involvement

Saudi Arabia

March 6, 2011	Authorities ban public protests after demonstration by minority Shi'a groups
September 25, 2011	King Abdullah announces cautious reforms, including the right for women to vote and stand for election from 2015

Yemen

January 24, 2011	Police arrest nineteen opposition activists including Tawakkol Karman, female campaigned and Nobel Prize winner, demanding the removal of President Ali Abdullah Saleh
March 8, 2011	More than two thousand prisoners stage a revolt at a prison in the capital, Sanaa, and join protests demanding Saleh's resignation
March 10, 2011	Saleh's promise to create a parliamentary system rejected by the opposition
March 18, 2011	Forty people killed after government forces open fire
April 27, 2011	Security forces shoot at protesters, killing twelve people
June 3, 2011	President Saleh survives an assassination attempt, but is seriously wounded
September 23, 2011	Saleh returns unexpectedly after three months of recovering in Saudi Arabia. Calls for a truce after five days of protests in Sanaa in which a hundred people killed
November 23, 2011	Agreement for an immediate transfer of power pledges immunity for Saleh and family
December 1, 2011	The opposition and Saleh's party agree on the makeup of an interim government
February 27, 2012	Saleh resigns and hands over power to Vice President Abd-Rabbu Mansour Hadi

Syria

March 15, 2011	Major unrest begins when protesters march in Damascus and Aleppo demanding democratic reforms and release of political prisoners
April 9, 2011	Anti-government demonstrations across Syria
April 25, 2011	Tanks are deployed for the first time
April 28, 2011	Hundreds of Ba'ath Party members resign in protest as an increasingly bloody crackdown kills five hundred

June 4, 2011	Security forces kill at least a hundred protesters in two days of violence
June 10, 2011	President Bashar al-Assad says he will not stand down
February 3, 2012	Syrian government launches an attack on Homs
June 16, 2013	Iran sends four thousand troops to help Syrian forces
September 30, 2015	Formal permission is granted by Russia's upper house for air raids in Syria. Al-Assad asks Putin for military aid
March 14, 2016	Putin announces withdrawal of the majority of Russian troops from Syria, saying the intervention has largely achieved its objective

Jordan

January 14, 2011	Protests begin with demands for Prime Minister Samir Rifai's resignation and economic reforms
March 24, 2011	About five hundred protesters set up camps in the main square in the capital Amman
October 7, 2011	Protests start again when former Prime Minister Ahmad Obeidat leads a march of about two thousand people in central Amman. There are also marches in other cities
October 5, 2012	Thousands protest after King Abdullah II dissolved Parliament and called for general election
November 13, 2012	Nationwide demonstrations erupt in response to an increase in fuel prices and other basic goods

Sudan[6]

December 19, 2018	Hundreds protest in the northern city of Atbara against soaring bread prices. Demonstrations triggered by a broader economic crisis spreads to Khartoum and other cities
April 11, 2019	The army overthrows President Omar al-Bashir, ending his thirty years in power.
June 3, 2019	Security forces raid a sit-in protest outside the defense ministry in Khartoum. In the days that follow, opposition-linked medics say more than a hundred people were killed in the assault
June 16, 2019	Omar al-Bashir appears in public for the first time and charged with corruption offenses. He had already been charged with incitement and involvement in killing protesters.
December 14, 2019	A court convicts al-Bashir on corruption charges and sentences him to two years in detention in a reform facility.

---

[6] "Timeline of Sudan's political strife," Arabia News.

Appendix B

Agreement for Bringing Peace to Afghanistan between the Islamic Emirate of Afghanistan which is not recognized by the United States as a state and is known as the Taliban and the United States of America[1]

February 29, 2020 which corresponds to Rajab 5, 1441 on the Hijri Lunar calendar and Hoot 10, 1398 on the Hijri Solar calendar

A comprehensive peace agreement is made of four parts:

1. Guarantees and enforcement mechanisms that will prevent the use of the soil of Afghanistan by any group or individual against the security of the United States and its allies.
2. Guarantees, enforcement mechanisms, and announcement of a timeline for the withdrawal of all foreign forces from Afghanistan.
3. After the announcement of guarantees for a complete withdrawal of foreign forces and timeline in the presence of international witnesses, and guarantees and the announcement in the presence of international witnesses that Afghan soil will not be used against the security of the United States and its allies, the Islamic Emirate of Afghanistan which is not recognized by the United States as a state and is known as the Taliban will start intra-Afghan negotiations with Afghan sides on March 10, 2020, which corresponds to Rajab 15, 1441 on the Hijri Lunar calendar and Hoot 20, 1398 on the Hijri Solar calendar.

---

[1] "Agreement for Bringing Peace to Afghanistan between the Islamic Emirate of Afghanistan which is not recognized by the United States as a state and is known as the Taliban and the United States of America," US State Department, February 29, 2020. This is a true reproduction of a US State Department document, and therefore unedited.

4. A permanent and comprehensive ceasefire will be an item on the agenda of the intra-Afghan dialogue and negotiations. The participants of intra-Afghan negotiations will discuss the date and modalities of a permanent and comprehensive ceasefire, including joint implementation mechanisms, which will be announced along with the completion and agreement over the future political roadmap of Afghanistan.

The four parts above are interrelated and each will be implemented in accordance with its own agreed timeline and agreed terms. Agreement on the first two parts paves the way for the last two parts.

Following is the text of the agreement for the implementation of parts one and two of the above. Both sides agree that these two parts are interconnected. The obligations of the Islamic Emirate of Afghanistan which is not recognized by the United States as a state and is known as the Taliban in this agreement apply in areas under their control until the formation of the new post-settlement Afghan Islamic government as determined by the intra-Afghan dialogue and negotiations.

Part One

The United States is committed to withdraw from Afghanistan all military forces of the United States, its allies, and Coalition partners, including all non-diplomatic civilian personnel, private security contractors, trainers, advisors, and supporting services personnel within 14 months following announcement of this agreement, and will take the following measures in this regard:

A. The United States, its allies, and the Coalition will take the following measures in the first 135 days:

   1. They will reduce the number of U.S. forces in Afghanistan to 8600 and proportionally bring reduction in the number of its allies and Coalition forces.
   2. The United States, its allies, and the Coalition will withdraw all their forces from five military bases.

B. With the commitment and action on the obligations of the Islamic Emirate of Afghanistan which is not recognized by the United States as a state and is known as the Taliban in Part Two of this agreement, the United States, its allies, and the Coalition will execute the following:

1. The United States, its allies, and the Coalition will complete withdrawal of all remaining forces from Afghanistan within the remaining nine and a half (9.5) months.
2. The United States, its allies, and the Coalition will withdraw all their forces from remaining bases.

C. The United States is committed to start immediately to work with all relevant sides on a plan to expeditiously release combat and political prisoners as a confidence building measure with the coordination and approval of all relevant sides. Up to 5000 prisoners of the Islamic Emirate of Afghanistan which is not recognized by the United States as a state and is known as the Taliban and up to 1000 prisoners of the other side will be released by March 10, 2020, the first day of intra-Afghan negotiations, which corresponds to Rajab 15, 1441 on the Hijri Lunar calendar and Hoot 20, 1398 on the Hijri Solar calendar. The relevant sides have the goal of releasing all the remaining prisoners over the course of the subsequent 3 months. The United States commits to completing this goal. The Islamic Emirate of Afghanistan which is not recognized by the United States as a state and is known as the Taliban commits that its released prisoners will be committed to the responsibilities mentioned in this agreement so that they will not pose a threat to the security of the United States and its allies.

D. With the start of intra-Afghan negotiations, the United States will initiate an administrative review of current U.S. sanctions and the rewards list against members of the Islamic Emirate of Afghanistan which is not recognized by the United States as a state and is known as the Taliban with the goal of removing these sanctions by August 27, 2020, which corresponds to Muharram 8, 1442 on the Hijri Lunar calendar and Saunbola 6, 1399 on the Hijri Solar calendar.

E. With the start of intra-Afghan negotiations, the United States will start diplomatic engagement with other members of the United Nations Security Council and Afghanistan to remove members of the Islamic Emirate of Afghanistan which is not recognized by the United States as a state and is known as the Taliban from the sanctions list with the aim of achieving this objective by May 29, 2020, which corresponds to Shawwal 6, 1441 on the Hijri Lunar calendar and Jawza 9, 1399 on the Hijri Solar calendar.

F. The United States and its allies will refrain from the threat or the use of force against the territorial integrity or political independence of Afghanistan or intervening in its domestic affairs.

Part Two

In conjunction with the announcement of this agreement, the Islamic Emirate of Afghanistan which is not recognized by the United States as a state and is known as the Taliban will take the following steps to prevent any group or individual, including al Qaeda, from using the soil of Afghanistan to threaten the security of the United States and its allies:

1. The Islamic Emirate of Afghanistan which is not recognized by the United States as a state and is known as the Taliban will not allow any of its members, other individuals or groups, including al Qaeda, to use the soil of Afghanistan to threaten the security of the United States and its allies.
2. The Islamic Emirate of Afghanistan which is not recognized by the United States as a state and is known as the Taliban will send a clear message that those who pose a threat to the security of the United States and its allies have no place in Afghanistan and will instruct members of the Islamic Emirate of Afghanistan which is not recognized by the United States as a state and is known as the Taliban not to cooperate with groups or individuals threatening the security of the United States and its allies.
3. The Islamic Emirate of Afghanistan which is not recognized by the United States as a state and is known as the Taliban will prevent any group or individual in Afghanistan from threatening the security of the United States and its allies and will prevent them from recruiting, training, and fundraising and will not host them in accordance with the commitments in this agreement.
4. The Islamic Emirate of Afghanistan which is not recognized by the United States as a state and is known as the Taliban is committed to deal with those seeking asylum or residence in Afghanistan according to international migration law and the commitments of this agreement, so that such persons do not pose a threat to the security of the United States and its allies.
5. The Islamic Emirate of Afghanistan which is not recognized by the United States as a state and is known as the Taliban will not provide visas, passports, travel permits, or other legal documents to those who pose a threat to the security of the United States and its allies to enter Afghanistan.

Part Three

1. The United States will request the recognition and endorsement of the United Nations Security Council for this agreement.
2. The United States and the Islamic Emirate of Afghanistan which is not recognized by the United States as a state and is known as the Taliban seek positive relations with each other and expect that the relations between the United States and the new post-settlement Afghan Islamic government as determined by the intra-Afghan dialogue and negotiations will be positive.
3. The United States will seek economic cooperation for reconstruction with the new post-settlement Afghan Islamic government as determined by the intra-Afghan dialogue and negotiations and will not intervene in its internal affairs.

Signed in Doha, Qatar on February 29, 2020, which corresponds to Rajab 5, 1441 on the Hijri Lunar calendar and Hoot 10, 1398 on the Hijri Solar calendar, in duplicate, in Pashto, Dari, and English languages, each text being equally authentic.

Appendix C

Remarks by President Biden on the End of the War in Afghanistan, August 31, 2021[1]

THE PRESIDENT: Last night in Kabul, the United States ended 20 years of war in Afghanistan—the longest war in American history.

We completed one of the biggest airlifts in history, with more than 120,000 people evacuated to safety. That number is more than double what most experts thought were possible. No nation—no nation has ever done anything like it in all of history. Only the United States had the capacity and the will and the ability to do it, and we did it today.

The extraordinary success of this mission was due to the incredible skill, bravery, and selfless courage of the United States military and our diplomats and intelligence professionals.

For weeks, they risked their lives to get American citizens, Afghans who helped us, citizens of our Allies and partners, and others onboard planes and out of the country. And they did it facing a crush of enormous crowds seeking to leave the country. And they did it knowing ISIS-K terrorists—sworn enemies of the Taliban—were lurking in the midst of those crowds.

And still, the men and women of the United States military, our diplomatic corps, and intelligence professionals did their job and did it well, risking their lives not for professional gains but to serve others; not in a mission of war but

---

[1] White House Briefing Room. President Biden's remarks are a true reproduction of the text released by the White House Briefing Room. The text has inaccuracies and corrections as shown.

in a mission of mercy. Twenty servicemembers were wounded in the service of this mission. Thirteen heroes gave their lives.

I was just at Dover Air Force Base for the dignified transfer. We owe them and their families a debt of gratitude we can never repay but we should never, ever, ever forget.

In April, I made the decision to end this war. As part of that decision, we set the date of August 31st for American troops to withdraw. The assumption was that more than 300,000 Afghan National Security Forces that we had trained over the past two decades and equipped would be a strong adversary in their civil wars with the Taliban.

That assumption—that the Afghan government would be able to hold on for a period of time beyond military drawdown—turned out not to be accurate.

But I still instructed our national security team to prepare for every eventuality—even that one. And that's what we did.

So, we were ready when the Afghan Security Forces—after two decades of fighting for their country and losing thousands of their own—did not hold on as long as anyone expected.

We were ready when they and the people of Afghanistan watched their own government collapse and their president flee amid the corruption and malfeasance, handing over the country to their enemy, the Taliban, and significantly increasing the risk to U.S. personnel and our Allies.

As a result, to safely extract American citizens before August 31st—as well as embassy personnel, Allies and partners, and those Afghans who had worked with us and fought alongside of us for 20 years—I had authorized 6000 troops—American troops—to Kabul to help secure the airport.

As General McKenzie said, this is the way the mission was designed. It was designed to operate under severe stress and attack. And that's what it did.

Since March, we reached out 19 times to Americans in Afghanistan, with multiple warnings and offers to help them leave Afghanistan—all the way back as far as March. After we started the evacuation 17 days ago, we did initial outreach and analysis and identified around 5000 Americans who had decided earlier to stay in Afghanistan but now wanted to leave.

Our Operation ~~Allied Rescue~~ [Allies Refuge] ended up getting more than 5500 Americans out. We got out thousands of citizens and diplomats from those countries that went into Afghanistan with us to get bin Laden. We got out locally employed staff of the United States Embassy and their families, totaling roughly 2500 people. We got thousands of Afghan translators and interpreters and others, who supported the United States, out as well.

Now we believe that about 100 to 200 Americans remain in Afghanistan with some intention to leave. Most of those who remain are dual citizens, long-time residents who had earlier decided to stay because of their family roots in Afghanistan.

The bottom line: ~~Ninety~~ [Ninety-eight] percent of Americans in Afghanistan who wanted to leave were able to leave.

And for those remaining Americans, there is no deadline. We remain committed to get them out if they want to come out. Secretary of State Blinken is leading the continued diplomatic efforts to ensure a safe passage for any American, Afghan partner, or foreign national who wants to leave Afghanistan.

In fact, just yesterday, the United Nations Security Council passed a resolution that sent a clear message about what the international community expects the Taliban to deliver on moving forward, notably freedom of travel, freedom to leave. And together, we are joined by over 100 countries that are determined to make sure the Taliban upholds those commitments.

It will include ongoing efforts in Afghanistan to reopen the airport, as well as overland routes, allowing for continued departure to those who want to leave and delivery of humanitarian assistance to the people of Afghanistan.

The Taliban has made public commitments, broadcast on television and radio across Afghanistan, on safe passage for anyone wanting to leave, including those who worked alongside Americans. We don't take them by their word alone but by their actions, and we have leverage to make sure those commitments are met.

Let me be clear: Leaving August the 31st is not due to an arbitrary deadline; it was designed to save American lives.

My predecessor, the former President, signed an agreement with the Taliban to remove U.S. troops by May the 1st, just months after I was inaugurated. It included no requirement that the Taliban work out a cooperative governing arrangement with the Afghan government, but it did authorize the release of 5000 prisoners last year, including some of the Taliban's top war commanders, among those who just took control of Afghanistan.

And by the time I came to office, the Taliban was in its strongest military position since 2001, controlling or contesting nearly half of the country.

The previous administration's agreement said that if we stuck to the May 1st deadline that they had signed on to leave by, the Taliban wouldn't attack any American forces, but if we stayed, all bets were off.

So we were left with a simple decision: Either follow through on the commitment made by the last administration and leave Afghanistan, or say we weren't leaving and commit another tens of thousands more troops going back to war.

That was the choice—the real choice—between leaving or escalating.

I was not going to extend this forever war, and I was not extending a forever exit. The decision to end the military airlift operations at Kabul airport was based on the unanimous recommendation of my civilian and military advisors—the Secretary of State, the Secretary of Defense, the Chairman of the Joint Chiefs of Staff and all the service chiefs, and the commanders in the field.

Their recommendation was that the safest way to secure the passage of the remaining Americans and others out of the country was not to continue with 6000 troops on the ground in harm's way in Kabul, but rather to get them out through non-military means.

In the 17 days that we operated in Kabul after the Taliban seized power, we engaged in an around-the-clock effort to provide every American the opportunity to leave. Our State Department was working 24/7 contacting and talking, and in some cases, walking Americans into the airport.

Again, more than 5500 Americans were airlifted out. And for those who remain, we will make arrangements to get them out if they so choose.

As for the Afghans, we and our partners have airlifted 100,000 of them. No country in history has done more to airlift out the residents of another country than we have done. We will continue to work to help more people leave the country who are at risk. And we're far from done.

For now, I urge all Americans to join me in grateful prayer for our troops and diplomats and intelligence officers who carried out this mission of mercy in Kabul and at tremendous risk with such unparalleled results: an airlift that evacuated tens of thousands to a network of volunteers and veterans who helped identify those needing evacuation, guide them to the airport, and provided them for their support along the way.

We're going to continue to need their help. We need your help. And I'm looking forward to meeting with you.

And to everyone who is now offering or who will offer to welcome Afghan allies to their homes around the world, including in America: We thank you.

I take responsibility for the decision. Now, some say we should have started mass evacuations sooner and "Couldn't this have be done—have been done in a more orderly manner?" I respectfully disagree.

Imagine if we had begun evacuations in June or July, bringing in thousands of American troops and evacuating more than 120,000 people in the middle of a civil war. There still would have been a rush to the airport, a breakdown in confidence and control of the government, and it still would have been a very difficult and dangerous mission.

The bottom line is: There is no evacuation from the end of a war that you can run without the kinds of complexities, challenges, and threats we faced. None.

There are those who would say we should have stayed indefinitely for years on end. They ask, "Why don't we just keep doing what we were doing? Why did we have to change anything?"

The fact is: Everything had changed. My predecessor had made a deal with the Taliban. When I came into office, we faced a deadline—May 1. The Taliban onslaught was coming.

We faced one of two choices: Follow the agreement of the previous administration and extend it to have—or extend to more time for people to get out; or send in thousands of more troops and escalate the war.

To those asking for a third decade of war in Afghanistan, I ask: What is the vital national interest? In my view, we only have one: to make sure Afghanistan can never be used again to launch an attack on our homeland.

Remember why we went to Afghanistan in the first place? Because we were attacked by Osama bin Laden and al Qaeda on September 11th, 2001, and they were based in Afghanistan.

We delivered justice to bin Laden on May 2nd, 2011—over a decade ago. Al Qaeda was decimated.

I respectfully suggest you ask yourself this question: If we had been attacked on September 11, 2001, from Yemen instead of Afghanistan, would we have ever gone to war in Afghanistan—even though the Taliban controlled Afghanistan in 2001? I believe the honest answer is "no." That's because we had no vital national interest in Afghanistan other than to prevent an attack on America's homeland and their fr-—our friends. And that's true today.

We succeeded in what we set out to do in Afghanistan over a decade ago. Then we stayed for another decade. It was time to end this war.

This is a new world. The terror threat has metastasized across the world, well beyond Afghanistan. We face threats from al-Shabaab in Somalia; al Qaeda affiliates in Syria and the Arabian Peninsula; and ISIS attempting to create a caliphate in Syria and Iraq, and establishing affiliates across Africa and Asia.

The fundamental obligation of a President, in my opinion, is to defend and protect America—not against threats of 2001, but against the threats of 2021 and tomorrow.

That is the guiding principle behind my decisions about Afghanistan. I simply do not believe that the safety and security of America is enhanced by continuing to deploy thousands of American troops and spending billions of dollars a year in Afghanistan.

But I also know that the threat from terrorism continues in its pernicious and evil nature. But it's changed, expanded to other countries. Our strategy has to change too.

We will maintain the fight against terrorism in Afghanistan and other countries. We just don't need to fight a ground war to do it. We have what's called over-the-horizon capabilities, which means we can strike terrorists and targets without American boots on the ground—or very few, if needed.

We've shown that capacity just in the last week. We struck ISIS-K remotely, days after they murdered 13 of our servicemembers and dozens of innocent Afghans.

And to ISIS-K: We are not done with you yet.

As Commander-in-Chief, I firmly believe the best path to guard our safety and our security lies in a tough, unforgiving, targeted, precise strategy that goes after terror where it is today, not where it was two decades ago. That's what's in our national interest.

And here's a critical thing to understand: The world is changing. We're engaged in a serious competition with China. We're dealing with the challenges on multiple fronts with Russia. We're confronted with cyberattacks and nuclear proliferation.

We have to shore up America's competitive[ness] to meet these new challenges in the competition for the twenty-first century. And we can do both: fight terrorism and take on new threats that are here now and will continue to be here in the future.

And there's nothing China or Russia would rather have, would want more in this competition than the United States to be bogged down another decade in Afghanistan.

As we turn the page on the foreign policy that has guided our nat-—our nation the last two decades, we've got to learn from our mistakes.

To me, there are two that are paramount. First, we must set missions with clear, achievable goals—not ones we'll never reach. And second, we must stay clearly focused on the fundamental national security interest of the United States of America.

This decision about Afghanistan is not just about Afghanistan. It's about ending an era of major military operations to remake other countries.

We saw a mission of counterterrorism in Afghanistan—getting the terrorists and stopping attacks—morph into a counterinsurgency, nation building—trying to create a democratic, cohesive, and unified Afghanistan—something that has never been done over the many centuries of Afghanistan's history.

Moving on from that mindset and those kind of large-scale troop deployments will make us stronger and more effective and safer at home.

And for anyone who gets the wrong idea, let me say it clearly. To those who wish America harm, to those that engage in terrorism against us and our allies, know this: The United States will never rest. We will not forgive. We will not forget. We will hunt you down to the ends of the Earth, and we will—you will pay the ultimate price.

And let me be clear: We will continue to support the Afghan people through diplomacy, international influence, and humanitarian aid. We'll continue to push for regional diplomacy and engagement to prevent violence and instability. We'll continue to speak out for basic rights of the Afghan people, especially women and girls, as we speak out for women and girls all around the globe. And I've been clear that human rights will be the center of our foreign policy.

But the way to do that is not through endless military deployments, but through diplomacy, economic tools, and rallying the rest of the world for support.

My fellow Americans, the war in Afghanistan is now over. I'm the fourth President who has faced the issue of whether and when to end this war. When I was running for President, I made a commitment to the American people that I would end this war. And today, I've honored that commitment. It was time to be honest with the American people again. We no longer had a clear purpose in an open-ended mission in Afghanistan.

After 20 years of war in Afghanistan, I refused to send another generation of America's sons and daughters to fight a war that should have ended long ago.

After more than $2 trillion spent in Afghanistan—a cost that researchers at Brown University estimated would be over $300 million a day for 20 years in Afghanistan—for two decades—yes, the American people should hear this: $300 million a day for two decades.

If you take the number of $1 trillion, as many say, that's still $150 million a day for two decades. And what have we lost as a consequence in terms of opportunities? I refused to continue in a war that was no longer in the service of the vital national interest of our people.

And most of all, after 800,000 Americans serving in Afghanistan—I've traveled that whole country—brave and honorable service; after 20,744 American servicemen and women injured, and the loss of 2461 American personnel, including 13 lives lost just this week, I refused to open another decade of warfare in Afghanistan.

We've been a nation too long at war. If you're 20 years old today, you have never known an America at peace.

So, when I hear that we could've, should've continued the so-called low-grade effort in Afghanistan, at low risk to our service members, at low cost, I don't think enough people understand how much we have asked of the 1% of this country who put that uniform on, who are willing to put their lives on the line in defense of our nation.

Maybe it's because my deceased son, Beau, served in Iraq for a full year, before that. Well, maybe it's because of what I've seen over the years as senator, vice president, and president traveling these countries.

A lot of our veterans and their families have gone through hell—deployment after deployment, months and years away from their families; missed birthdays, anniversaries; empty chairs at holidays; financial struggles; divorces; loss of limbs; traumatic brain injury; posttraumatic stress.

We see it in the struggles many have when they come home. We see it in the strain on their families and caregivers. We see it in the strain of their families when they're not there. We see it in the grief borne by their survivors. The cost of war they will carry with them their whole lives.

Most tragically, we see it in the shocking and stunning statistic that should give pause to anyone who thinks war can ever be low-grade, low-risk, or low-cost: 18 veterans, on average, who die by suicide every single day in America—not in a far-off place, but right here in America.

There's nothing low-grade or low-risk or low-cost about any war. It's time to end the war in Afghanistan.

As we close 20 years of war and strife and pain and sacrifice, it's time to look to the future, not the past—to a future that's safer, to a future that's more secure, to a future that honors those who served and all those who gave what President Lincoln called their "last full measure of devotion."

I give you my word: With all of my heart, I believe this is the right decision, a wise decision, and the best decision for America.

Thank you. Thank you. And may God bless you all. And may God protect our troops.

Bibliography (Summary)

US Government Documents

"Agreement for Bringing Peace to Afghanistan between the Islamic Emirate of Afghanistan which is not recognized by the United States as a state and is known as the Taliban and the United States of America," US State Department, February 29, 2020.

Burgess, Lt General Ronald, "Annual Threat Assessment: Statement Before the Armed Services Committee," February 16, 2012

Bush, George W, "President's Address to the Nation," January 10, 2007, The White House Archives.

Bush, President George H.W., "Address Before a Joint Session of the Congress on the State of the Union," January 29, 1991a, The American Presidency Project, University of California Santa Barbara.

———., "Remarks to the American Legislative Exchange Council," March 1, 1991b, The American Presidency Project.

"China and the Afghan Resistance," Weekly summary of the US Defense Intelligence Agency, March 6, 1981.

"Circular Telegram from the Department of State to Certain Posts," November 15, 1963, Office of the Historian.

Collins, Shannon, "Desert Storm: A Look Back," January 11, 2019, US Department of Defense.

Daggett, Stephen, "Costs of Major US Wars," June 29, 2010, Congressional Research Service.

Defense Secretary Leo Panetta's statement, "Hearing to Receive Testimony of the US Strategy in Afghanistan and Iraq," Senate Armed Services Committee, September 22, 2011.

"Foreign Relations, 1961-1963, South Asia," US Department of State Archive.

"Iraq Liberation Act of 1998," October 31, 1998.

Joint Resolution S.J.23 Authorization for Use of Military Force, September 14, 2001.

Katzman, Kenneth and Blanchard, Christopher M., "Iraq: Oil-for-Food Program, Illicit Trade and Investigations," June 14, 2005, Congressional Research Service Report.

"Memorandum from Stephen O. Fuqua of the Bureau of International Security Affairs, Department of Defense to the Deputy Assistant Secretary of Defense for International Security Affairs," February 8, 1963, US Office of the Historian.

"Military Advisors in Vietnam: 1963," John F. Kennedy Presidential Library.

"Operation Iraq Freedom," US Naval History and Heritage Command.

"Overview – Rule of Law," United States Courts (Washington, DC: Administrative Office of the United States Courts).

"President Signs Authorization for Use of Military Force Bill," September 18, 2001, George W. Bush White House Archives.

"Quarterly Report to US Congress" (SIGAR: Special Inspector General for Afghanistan Reconstruction), January 30, 2021.

"Rapprochement with China, 1972," Office of the Historian (Washington, DC: US State Department).

"Remarks by the President on National Security," May 21, 2009 10:28 AM, Obama White House Archives.

Report of the Senate Select Committee on Intelligence, "Committee Study of the Central Intelligence Agency's Detention and Interrogation Program," December 9, 2014.

"Sadat on Arms to Afghan Freedom Fighters" (Washington, DC: Joint Chiefs of Staff Message Center, US Defense Department, September 23, 1981).

"Secretary Hillary Rodham Clinton Testimony to the Senate Foreign Relations Committee," June 23, 2011.

"Statement by the President on the End of Combat Mission in Afghanistan," White House Press office, Washington, DC, December 28, 2014.

"Text of Bush Speech," May 1, 2003, CBS News.

"Text: Pentagon Briefing with Secretary Rumsfeld," Washington Post, November 19, 2001.

The following documents were used from the "Ronald Reagan Presidential Library and Museum," Simi Valley, California.

―― Remarks welcoming the British Prime Minister Margaret Thatcher, February 26, 1981

―― Remarks at the State Banquet for President Ziaul Haq of Pakistan, December 7, 1982

―― Radio address on defense spending, February 19, 1983.

―― Address on foreign policy, October 20, 1984.

——— Welcoming King Fahd of Saudi Arabia in the White House, February 11, 1985.
"S.J. Resolution 23 – Authorization for Use of Military Force," September 18, 2001.
"Taguba Report: AR 15-6 Investigation of the 800th Military Police Brigade – Certified Copy," May 27, 2004, The Torture Database.
"The Global War on Terrorism: The First 100 Days," US State Department Archive.
"Tora Bora Revisited: How We Failed To Get bin Laden And Why It Matters Today," The US Senate Foreign Relations Committee Report, November 30, 2009.
"TORTURE (18 U.S.C. 2340A)," US Department of Justice Archives.
"U-2 Overflights and the Capture of Francis Gary Powers, 1960," Office of the Historian, The US State Department.
"U-2 Spy Plane Incident," The Eisenhower Presidential Library.
"Vietnam War US Military Fatal Casualty Figures," US National Archives.

Afghanistan Papers

Whitlock, Craig, *The Afghanistan Papers: A Secret History of the War* (New York: Simon & Schuster, 2021).
——— Who Are the Bad Guys?
——— Afghan Nation-Building Project.

Iraq Papers

Ehrenberg, John, McSherry, J. Patrick, Sanchez, Jose Ramon, Sayej, Caroleen Marji (editors), *The Iraq Papers* (New York: Oxford University Press, 2010).
———, Blix, Hans, "Briefing to the United Nations Security Council," March 7, 2003.
———, Bush, George W., "Ultimatum to Iraq," March 17, 2003.
———, "Declaration of France, Germany, and Russia on War with Iraq," March 5, 2003.
———, Kagan, Robert, "American Power – A Guide for the Perplexed, Commentary, April 1996 (Excerpt).
———, Kissinger, Henry, "A False Dream," Los Angeles Times, February 24, 1991 (Excerpt).
———, "Part I: The Iraqi Insurgency, 2004-2007, United States Marine Corps.
———, "Rumsfeld Blames Iraq Problems on Packets of 'Dead-Enders,'" Associated Press, June 18, 2003, 188-190.
———, 2005 Constitution of Iraq, 306-313.

National Security Archive (Georgetown University, Washington, DC)

"New Light in a Dark Corner: Evidence on the Diem Coup in South Vietnam, November 1963" (Washington, DC: National Security Archive, George Washington University).

Pardo-Maurer, Roger, "Greetings from scenic Kandahar," Roger Pardo-Maurer letter from Kandahar, August 11-15, 2002.

The Following Documents Were from the NSA Document Collection Titled The Soviet Withdrawal from Afghanistan:

The Soviet Withdrawal from Afghanistan, "Memorandum of Conversation: Reagan-Gorbachev, Second Plenary Meeting, Geneva, November 19,1985."

—— "Powell letter to Shultz, April 15, 1988."

—— "Memorandum of Conversation between Secretary Baker and Eduard Shevardnadze, March 20, 1990."

"Transcript of Kennedy-Lodge meeting tape, August 15, 1963," in "New Light in a Dark Corner," Document 03 (Washington, DC: National Security Archive, George Washington University).

US Embassy cable, "Ambassador raises bin Laden with Foreign Secretary, Shamshad Ahmad," Islamabad, October 6, 1998.

—— "Osama bin Laden: Charge reiterates U.S. concerns to key Taliban official, who sticks to well-known Taliban position," Islamabad, December 19, 2000, in Update: The Taliban File Part IV, August 18, 2005.

"US Sets "Decapitation of Government" As Early Goal of Combat," in The Iraq War – Part I: The US Prepares for Conflict, 2001, posted on September 22, 2010.

Wilson Center Digital Archive

Bunzel, Cole, "Explainer: The Islamic State in 2021," December 10, 2021, Wilson Center.

"Discussion Between Mao Zedong and Ho Chi Minh, Changsha (Hunan), May 16, 1965," (Washington, DC: Wilson Center History and Policy Program Digital Archive, CWIHP).

"Note by the East German Embassy in Hanoi on a Conversation with Ambassadors of the other Socialist States in the Soviet Embassy on 2 April 1965, April 25,

1965," Vietnam War document collection (Washington, DC: Wilson Center History and Policy Program Digital Archive, CWIHP).

"Note on the Conversation between the Romanian Party and Government Delegation led by Leon Gheorghe Maurer and Soviet Leader Nikita Khrushchev," September 27, 1964, the Sino-Soviet Split, 1960-1984 collection, History and Public Policy Program (Washington, DC: Wilson Center History and Policy Program Digital Archive).

"Obama on Syria: Assad must go." Wilson Center, March 24, 2013.

"Politburo on Afghanistan," November 13, 1986, in document collection Soviet Invasion of Afghanistan (History and Public Policy Program Digital Archive, Wilson Center, Washington, DC).

"Record of Conversation from Premier Zhou's Reception of the North Korean Ambassador, Pak Se-chang, August 6, 1964, 4 pm," Vietnam War document collection (Washington, DC: Wilson Center History and Policy Program Digital Archive, CWIHP).

"Timeline: The Rise, Spread and Fall of the Islamic State," October 28, 2019, Wilson Center.

Other Archives

"Agreement on the Cessation of Hostilities in Viet-Nam," July 20, 1954, UN Peacemaker.org.

"al Qaeda in Iraq," Britannica.

"Ali Abdullah Saleh," Britannica.

"Anglo-Afghan Wars," Britannica.com.

Barry, Ben, "Understanding the Taliban's Military Victory," International Institute of Strategic Studies, August 19, 2021.

Coleman, David and Silverstone, Marc, "Lyndon B. Johnson and the Vietnam War," Presidential Recordings (Charlottesville, VA: Miller Center, University of Virginia).

"Collective defense – Article 5," North Atlantic Treaty Organization.

Correll, John T., "The Weinberger Doctrine," Air & Space Forces Magazine, March 1, 2014.

Crawford, Neta C., "Afghanistan's Rising Death Toll Due to Airstrikes, 2017-2020," Costs of War Project, Watson Institute, Brown University, December 7, 2020.

"Egypt and Israel Treaty of Peace," March 26, 1979, UN Peacemaker.org.

"Egypt's President Sadat visit in Israel, November 1977," IDF Archives.

"Egypt uprising of 2011," Britannica.

"First Resolution of the 56th UN General Assembly (2001)," September 12, 2001, Avalon Project, Yale Law School.

"Iraq Timeline: Since the 2003 War," United States Institute of Peace.

"Jasmine Revolution: Tunisian History," Britannica.
"Libya revolt of 2011," Britannica.
Michaels, Julia, "Understanding Abu Ghraib: Accountability, the United States, and the Continuity of Torture," Thesis, Scholarly and Creative Work from DePauw University, 2020.
"Military expenditure by country as percentage of gross domestic product," SIPRI 2018.
"Mohamed Bouazizi: Tunisian street vendor and protester," Britannica.
"Oil-for-Food," UN Office for Iraq Program.
"Operation DESERT STORM," US Army Center of Military History.
Peters, Gretchen, "Haqqani Network Financing: The Evolution of an Industry," Combating Terrorism Center, West Point.
"Politics, Popular Culture and the 2011 Egyptian Revolution," (Coventry, UK: University of Warwick).
"Security Council Condemns, in 'Strongest Terms,' Terrorist Attacks on United States," Resolution 1368, September 12, 2001, United Nations.
"Statement by the Secretary General of NATO Lord Robertson; September 11, 2001: Attack on America," Avalon Project, Yale Law School.
"The State of the Union Address Delivered Before a Joint Session of the Congress" by President Jimmy Carter, January 23, 1980, American Presidency Project.
Farrell, Theo, "How the Taliban won," Australian Institute of International Affairs, October 10, 2021.
"Unrest in 2011: January 25 Revolution," Britannica.
UN Security Council Resolution 1970, February 26, 2011.
"Washington Consensus," Britannica.com.
"World Bank GDP 2020," World Bank.

Miscellaneous Sources

"A timeline of key events in Egypt since the 2011 uprising," Associated Press, March 25, 2018.
"ACLU comment of release of Trump administration lethal force use," ACLU, May 1, 2021.
"Admiral Mike Mullen interview," Charlie Rose Show, June 14, 2011.
Airwars.org.
Blum, William and Gibbs, David N., translation of Zbigniew Brzezinski's interview in Le Nouvel Observateur (Paris), January 15-21, 1998, International Politics, 37, no 2, 2000, 241–242.
Brunstetter, Daniel, "Over-the-Horizon Counterterrorism: New Name, Same Old Challenges." November 24, 2021.
"Casualties and Statistics of the Vietnam War," (Mountain View, CA: Study.com).

"Constitutional history of Iraq," ConstitutionNet.
Davis, Daniel L, "Trump Came This Close to Getting Afghanistan Right," October 25, 2018, The American Conservative.
"Death of a Dictator: Bloody Vengeance in Sirte," Human Rights Watch, October 16, 2012.
Drone Warfare, "Bureau of Investigative Journalism."
"Endless Torment: The 1991 Uprising in Iraq And Its Aftermath," June 1992, Human Rights Watch.
Ferguson, Niall, "After Vietnam: Richard Nixon, Henry Kissinger, and the Search for a Strategy to End the Vietnam War," October 26, 2017 (Yorba Linda, CA: Richard Nixon Foundation).
Friedman, Benjamin H., and Logan, Justin, "Disentangling from Syria's Civil War," Defense Priorities, Washington, DC, May 2019.
"Getting Away With Torture: Bush Administration and Mistreatment of Detainees," July 12, 2011, Human Rights Watch.
"Global Conflict Tracker: Civil War in Syria," Council on Foreign Relations, Updated January 18, 2022.
Gopal, Anand and Strick van Linschoten, Alex, "Ideology in the Afghan Taliban," Afghan-Analyst.org.
Greenspan, Jesse, "The Gulf of Tonkin Incident, 50 Years Ago, August 1, 2014, History.com.
"Guantanamo by the Numbers," May 2018, ACLU.
Giustozzi, Antonio, "The Taliban and the 2014 Presidential Elections in Afghanistan," Conflict, Security and Development.
"History of Drone Warfare," Bureau of Investigative Journalism.
"Iraq invades Kuwait," History.com.
Isenberg, David, "Imperial Overreach: Washington's Dubious Strategy to Overthrow Saddam Hussein," November 17, 1999, Policy Analysis No 360, Cato Institute, Washington, DC.
"The Geneva Accords of 1988 (Afghanistan)," signed on April 14, 1988, insidetheColdWar.org.
Kross, Peter, "The Assassination of Ngo Dinh Diem," HistoryNet.
Kurdistan Region Presidency.
"Laos and the CIA's "Secret War" in the Most Bombed Country Per Capita," August 17, 2021, War History Online.
Maizland, Lindsay, "US-Taliban Peace Deal: What to Know," Council on Foreign Relations, Washington, DC, updated March 2, 2020.
McMahon, Robert, "The Impact of the Oil-for-Food Scandal," May 11, 2006, Council on Foreign Relations.
Mustermann, Erik, "Deadly Legacy of US Bombing Campaign in Vietnam War," December 10, 2018, War History Online.
———, "The First Gulf War: Ten Fast Facts," August 21, 2016, War History Online.
"National Liberation Front," Spartacus Educational.

Norrlof, Carla, Hegemony, Oxford Bibliographies, September 2015.
"1 November 1964: Bien Hoa Air Force Base Attacked," in VIETNAM The Art of War.
"Omar Khadr Case," July 30, 2015, last edited July 8, 2019, Canadian Encyclopedia.
Otterman, Sharon, "Iraq: Oil-for-Food Scandal," Council on Foreign Relations, October 28, 2005.
"Overkill: Reforming the Legal Basis for the US War on Terror," Report No. 5, International Crisis Group, September 17, 2021.
"Paris Peace Accords Signed," History.com, January 27, 1973.
"Pathet Lao," Britannica.
"Project for the New American Century," Militarist-Monitor.
"Putin's Gamble: Russia's 2014 Invasion of Crimea – A Short History," History.co.uk.
"Refugees from Afghanistan: The world's largest single refugee group," Amnesty International, November 1999.
"Report On Torture And Cruel, Inhuman and Degrading Treatment Of Prisoners At Guantanamo Bay, Cuba," July 2006 (New York: Center for Constitutional Rights).
Rosenberg, Jennifer "When Did the US Send First Troops to Vietnam?, ThoughtCo.
Schmidt, Brian C., "Hegemony: A conceptual and theoretical analysis" (Berlin: Dialogue of Civilizations Research Institute, 2018).
"Secret War in Laos," Legacies of War.
Shamsi, Hima, "Trump's Secret Rules for Drone Strikes and Presidents' Licence to Kill," Just Security, May 3, 2021.
Suchkov, Maxim A., "Why is Russia seeking to expand its military bases in Syria?," Middle East Institute, Washington, DC, June 1, 2020.
"Supreme Court Says Guantanamo Bay Military Commissions Are Unconstitutional," June 29, 2006, ACLU.
"The Fall of Baghdad," April 2003, Encyclopedia.com.
"The Guantanamo Trials," Human Rights Watch.
"The Iraq War: 2003 – 2011," The Council on Foreign Relations.
"The Viet Cong," alpha history.
"Timeline of Chemical Weapons Activity, 2012–2021," Arms Control Association, last reviewed in May 2021.
"US: Landmark Supreme Court Ruling on Detainees: Guantanamo Inmates Have Right to Challenge Detention," Human Rights Watch, June 12, 2008.
"Viet Cong," Britannica.
"Vietnam War: Allied Troop Levels, 1960-73" (Long Beach, CA: American War Library).
"Vietnam War Casualties (1955-1975)," MilitaryFactory.com.
"Vietnam War Timeline," History.Com.
Zenko, Micah, "Obama's Final Drone Strike Data," Council on Foreign Relations, January 20, 2017.

Articles and Books

Abel, Richard L., *Law's Wars: The Fate of the Rule of Law in the US "War on Terror,"* (Cambridge, UK: Cambridge University Press, 2018).
Assaad, Ragul, "How will Tunisia's Jasmine Revolution Affect the Arab World?," Brookings op-ed, January 24, 2011.
Bennett-Koufie, Peter, "Hegemonic Overreach in the British Empire: Economic Distress, Hegemonic Overreach, and the Fall of Singapore," Inquiries Journal, 2017, volume 9, number 04.
Buley, Benjamin, *The New American Way of War: Military Culture and the Political Utility of Force* (New York: Routledge, 2007).
Cole, Juan, "The Real Problem with the Iraq War: It was illegal," Informed Comment.
———, "Obama: The Tides of War are Receding," Informed Comment, June 23, 2011.
Constable, Pamela, *Playing with Fire: Pakistan at War with Itself* (New York: Random House, 2011).
Cooley, John, *Afghanistan, America and International Terrorism* (London: Pluto Press, 2002).
Ellsberg, Daniel, *Secrets: A Memoir of Vietnam and the Pentagon Papers* (New York: Viking Penguin, 2003).
Fair, C. Christine, *Fighting to the End: The Pakistan Army's Way of War* (New York: Oxford University Press, 2014).
Falk, Richard, Andersson, Stefan (Ed), *Revisiting the Vietnam War and International Law – Views and Interpretations of Richard Falk* (Cambridge: Cambridge University Press).
Farmer, Ben, "Afghan election: Hamid Karzai's rival crosses ethnic divide," Telegraph, August 13, 2009.
Femia, Francesco and Werrell, Caitlin, "Syria: Climate Change, Drought and Social Unrest," The Center for Climate and Security, Washington, DC.
Fukuyama, Francis, *The End of History and the Last Man* (London: Hamish Hamilton, 1992).
Gates, Robert, *From the Shadows: The Ultimate Insider's Story of Five Presidents and How They Won the Cold War* (New York: Simon & Schuster, 1997).
Gelvin, James L, *The Arab Uprisings: What Everyone Needs to Know* 2nd ed (New York, NY: Oxford University Press, 2015).
Grabar, Henry, "What the US Bombing of Cambodia Tells Us About Obama's Drone Campaign," Atlantic, February 14, 2013.
Haass, Richard N, "The Age of Nonpolarity: What Will Follow US Dominance," Foreign Affairs, May/June 2008.
"Haqqani Network," Mapping Militant Organizations, Stanford University, updated November 8, 2017.

Hashim, Ahmed S, "Iraq's Civil War," in *Current History* Vol. 106, No. 696, January 2007, University of California Press, 3-10.

Hoffman, Bruce, "The War on Terror 20 Years on: Crossroads or Cul-De-Sac?," March 18, 2021 (London: Blair Institute for Global Change).

Jalali, Ali Ahmad and Grau, Lester W, *The Other Side of the Mountain: Mujahideen Tactics in Soviet-Afghan War* (Quantico, VA: Military Press, 2000).

Johnson, Chalmers, "The Largest Covert Operation in CIA History," History News Network, George Washington University.

Johnson, Thomas H, "The Prospects for Post-Conflict Afghanistan: A Call of the Sirens to the Country's Troubled Past," Strategic Insights, Volume V, Issue 2, February 2006.

Kalb, Marvin, "It's Called the Vietnam Syndrome, and It's Back," January 22, 2013 (Washington, DC: Brookings Institution).

Kennedy, Paul, *The Rise and Fall of the Great Powers: Economic Change and Military Conflict from 1500 to 2000,* First ed (New York: Random House, 1987).

Kitfield, James, "Obama: The Reluctant Warrior on Libya," Atlantic, March 18, 2011.

Lake, Eli, "The 9/14 Presidency," Reason, April 6, 2010.

Laub, Zachary, "Backgrounder: The Islamic State," last updated August 10, 2016, Council on Foreign Relations.

Leake, Elisabeth, *The Defiant Border: The Afghan-Pakistan Borderlands in the Era of Decolonization, 1936–1965* (Cambridge, UK: Cambridge University Press, 2016).

Lexington, "The Kuwait war plus 20," Economist, February 12, 2011.

Lizza, Ryan, "Leading From Behind," New Yorker, April 26, 2011.

MacAskill, Ewen and Burkeman, Oliver, "Power vacuum that has taken US by surprise," Guardian, April 11, 2003.

Macleod, Hugh, "Inside Deraa," Al Jazeera, April 19, 2011.

Malkasian, Carter, *The American War in Afghanistan: a history* (New York: Oxford University Press, 2021).

Maley, William, *The Afghanistan Wars* (London, UK: Macmillan/Red Globe, 2021).

Mariet D'Souza, Shanthie, "Afghan Peace Talks and the Changing Character of Taliban Insurgency," ISAS Brief No 291, Institute of South Asian Studies, Singapore, July 26, 2013.

Mearsheimer, John, *The Tragedy of Great Power Politics* (New York: WW Norton, 2001).

Murphy, Eamon, *The Making of Terrorism in Pakistan: Historical and Social Roots of Terrorism* (New York: Routledge, 2013).

Oezel, Yasemin, "The Impact of the "Unipolar Moment" on US Foreign Policies in the Mid-East," E-International Relations, September 13, 2015.

Owen, Taylor and Kiernan, Ben, "Bombs Over Cambodia: New Light on US Air War," Asia-Pacific Journal: Japan Focus, Volume 5, Issue 5, May 2, 2007.

Paterson, Pat (Lieutenant Commander), "The Truth About Tonkin," Naval History Magazine, Volume 22, Number 1, February 2008 (Annapolis, Md, US Naval Institute).

Pedaliu, Effie, "Forty five years after the fall of Saigon, the Vietnam War still holds lessons for US foreign policy" (London: Phelan US Centre, the London School of Economics).

Podhoretz, Norman, "Making the World Safe for Communism," Commentary Magazine, April 1976.

Polk, William, "Understanding Syria: From Pre-Civil War to Post Assad," Atlantic, December 10, 2013.

Rashid, Ahmed, *Taliban: Islam, Oil and the New Great Game in Central Asia, Revised Edition* (London: IB Tauris, 2008).

Riedel, Bruce, *Deadly Embrace: Pakistan, America, and the Future of the Global Jihad* (Washington, DC: Brookings Institution Press, 2011).

Riedel, Bruce and Singh, Pavneet, US-China Relations: Seeking Strategic Convergence with Pakistan, Brooking Institute Policy Paper Number 18.

Rubin, Barnett, *Afghanistan: What Everyone Needs to Know* (New York, NY: Oxford University Press, 2020).

Rubin, Barnett, Antonio Giustozzi, principal author of chapter "More War, Insurgency, and Counterinsurgency," in *Afghanistan: What Everyone Needs to Know* (New York, NY: Oxford University Press, 2020)

Ruthven, Malise, book review article, "How to Understand ISIS," reviewing Marc Lynch, "The New Arab Wars" and Fawaz Gerges, "ISIS: A History," in New York Review of Books, June 23, 2016.

Rose, Leo E, and Husain, Noor A, (Ed), *United States–Pakistan Relations* (Institute of East Asian Studies, University of California, Berkeley, 1985).

Roy, Olivier, "Rivalries and Power Plays in Afghanistan: The Taliban, the Shari'a and the Pipeline," *Middle East Report* no. 202 (Winter 1996).

Russian General Staff, *The Soviet Afghan War: How A Superpower Fought and Lost*, translated and edited by Lester Grau and Michael Gress (Lawrence: University Press of Kansas, 2002).

Sauer, Pjotr "Putin annexes four regions of Ukraine in major escalation of Russia's war," Guardian, September 30, 2022.

van Schendel, Willen, *A History of Bangladesh* (Cambridge, UK: Cambridge University Press, 2009).

Sirrs, Owen L, *Pakistan's Inter-Services Intelligence Directorate: Covert Action and Internal Operations* (New York: Routledge, 2018).

Stafford Smith, Clive, *Bad Men: Guantanamo Bay and the Secret Prisons* (London: Phoenix, 2007).

Tadman, Kyle, "An American Provocation: US Foreign Policy during the Soviet-Afghan War," Western Illinois Historical Review Volume V, Spring 2013.

Taylor, Alan, "Operation Desert Storm: 25 Years Since the First Gulf War," Atlantic, January 14, 2016.

"The Arab Spring – a timeline," PEN/Opp magazine, published by Swedish PEN.

"The Diem Coup," (Charlottesville, VA: Miller Center, University of Virginia).

"Timeline: How the Arab Spring Unfolded," Al Jazeera, January 14, 2021.

"Timeline of the revolution in Egypt," DW.
"Timeline: The Major Events of the Arab Spring," NPR, January 2, 2012.
Thomsen, Peter, *Wars of Afghanistan: Messianic Terrorism, Tribal Conflicts, and the Failures of Great Powers* (New York: PublicAffairs, 2011).
Tripathi, Deepak, *Breeding Ground: Afghanistan and the Origins of Islamist Terrorism* (Washington, DC: Potomac, 2011).
"Violent Protests rock Libyan city of Benghazi," France 24, February 16, 2011.
Waldman, Matt, "The Sun in the Sky: The relationship between Pakistan's ISI and Afghan insurgents," Crisis States Research Centre, London School of Economics, June 2010.
Westad, Odd Arne, *The Global Cold War*, (Cambridge, UK: Cambridge University Press, 2005).
Wolfsfeld, Gadi, Segev, Elad, and Sheafer, Tamir, "Social Media and the Arab Spring: Politics Comes First," International Journal of Press/Politics Vol 18 Issue 2 (Sage, 2013), 117.
World Almanac of Islamism 2014, American Foreign Policy Council (New York, NY: Rowman & Littlefield, 2014), 1043.
Yousaf, Mohammad (Brigadier, retired) and Adkin, Mark, *Afghanistan: The Bear Trap* (Barnsley, UK: Leo Cooper, 2001).

News

"A chronology of US aid suspension to Pakistan," News of Pakistan, July 22, 2019.
Adetunji, Jo, "British firms urged to "pack suitcases" in rush for Libya business," Guardian, October 21, 2011.
"Agreement on Afghanistan signed in Geneva," Washington Post, April 15, 1988.
"A Timeline of US Aid to Pakistan," Newsweek, October 20, 2009.
"A timeline of US troop levels in Afghanistan since 2001," Military Times.
"Barack Obama announces total withdrawal of US troops from Iraq," October 21, 2011, Associated Press cited in the Guardian.
Borger, Julian, and Hopkins, Nick, "West training Syrian rebels in Jordan," Guardian, March 8, 2013.
"Bush announces opening of attacks," CNN, October 7, 2001.
"Bush delivers ultimatum", CNN, September 21, 2001.
"Bush denies torture of terror suspects," NPR, October 5, 2007.
"Bush says he wants to close Guantanamo," CBS News, May 8, 2006.
"CIA tactics: What is 'enhanced interrogation'?," BBC News, December 10, 2014.
Cohen, Zackery, "Amnesty Report: ISIS armed with US weapons," CNN, December 9, 2015.
"Confidential documents show failure of Bush, Obama administrations during Afghanistan war," Associated Press, December 9, 2019.

Denselow, James, "The US departure from Iraq is an illusion," Guardian, October 25, 2011.

"Elements of civil war in Iraq," February 2, 2007, BBC News.

"Ex-Abu Ghraib Interrogator: Israelis Trained US to Use "Palestinian Chair" Torture Device," Democracy Now, April 7, 2016.

"Facts about Khadr and the Charges," Globe and Mail, October 10, 2010.

Glass, Andrew, "Nixon authorized invasion of Cambodia, April 28, 1970," POLITICO, April 28, 2015.

Gregory, Andy, "Taliban peace deal: what is the Doha agreement signed by the Trump administration?," Independent, August 19, 2021.

Haddad, Mohammed, "Guantanamo Bay explained in maps and charts," Al Jazeera, September 7, 2021.

Hafezi, Parisa and Solomon, Erica, "US considers no-fly zone after Syria crosses nerve gas "red line,"" Reuters, June 15, 2013.

Hakimi, Aziz, "Af-Pak: What Strategic Depth?," openDemocracy, February 4, 2010.

Hersh, Seymour M., "Torture At Abu Ghraib," New Yorker, April 30, 2004.

"How ISIS Is Filling A Government Vacuum in Syria with An Islamic State," November 4, 2014, Huffington Post.

"Hundred days of war in Ukraine – A timeline," CBS News, June 3, 2022.

Ishfaq, Sarmad, "South Asia's Most Notorious Militant Groups," Diplomat, December 31, 2019.

"ISIL weapons traced to US and Saudi Arabia," Al Jazeera, December 14, 2017.

"Israeli interrogators 'in Iraq'," BBC, July 3, 2004.

"'It's Time To End This Forever War.' Biden Says Forces to Leave Afghanistan By 9/11," NPR, April 15, 2021.

"Just a few bad apples?," Economist, January 22, 2005.

Kaplow, Larry, "History of US Responses to Chemical Weapons Attacks in Syria," NPR, April 13, 2018.

Keneally, Meghan, "What Trump has said about Afghanistan," August 21, 2017, ABC News.

"Key dates in US war in Afghanistan since September 11, 2001," CBC.

Kiely, Eugene and Farley, Robert, "Timeline of US Withdrawal from Afghanistan," FactCheck.Org, August 17, 2021.

Klaidman, Daniel, "Drones: The Silent Killers," Newsweek, May 28, 2012.

"Last US troops withdraw from Iraq," BBC News, December 19, 2011.

"Libya: France recognizes rebels as government," BBC News, March 10, 2011.

"Libya Profile – Timeline," BBC News, March 15, 2021.

"Libya: Pro-Gaddafi forces attack rebel-held Ras Lanuf," BBC News, March 7, 2011.

Liptak, Kevin and Vazquez, Maegan, "Biden announces end of combat mission in Iraq as he shifts US foreign policy focus," CNN, July 26, 2021.

Lister, Tim, "Abbottabad — The military town where bin Laden hid in plain sight," CNN, May 2, 2011.

MacAskill, Ewen and Borger, Julian, "Iraq war was illegal and breached UN Charter," Guardian, September 16, 2004.

McGreal, Chris, "Libyan rebels in retreat as Gaddafi attacks by air, land and sea," Guardian, March 10, 2011.

"Mullah Omar: Taliban Leader 'died in Pakistan in 2013'," BBC, July 29, 2015.

"Mullah Omar is Dead: Father of Afghanistan's Taliban Died in Pakistan," NBC, July 29, 2015.

Ninan, Rina, and Taylor, Marisa, "Secretary Clinton says Syrian President Assad 'Must Go.'" ABC News, April 1, 2012.

"Obama Announces Iraq Exit Plan," VOA News, November 2, 2009.

"Obama to Seek Congressional Approval for Action Against Syria," NPR, August 31, 2013.

"Obama: US underestimated rise of ISIS in Iraq and Syria," 60 Minutes, CBS News, September 28, 2014.

"Pakistani agents 'funding and training' Afghan Taliban," BBC, June 13, 2010.

"President Obama Turns to Congress on Syria," NPR, August 31, 2013.

Priest, Dana and Gellman, Barton, "US Decries Abuse but Defends Interrogations," Washington Post, December 26, 2002.

"Principles, Standards, and Procedures For US Direct Action Against Terrorist Targets," New York Times data archive.

"Q&A: What is the Coalition of the Willing," from the Council on Foreign Relations, cited in New York Times, March 28, 2003.

"Quetta Shura Taliban (QST)," Afghan War News.

"Remembering Mohamed Bouazizi: The man who sparked the Arab Spring," Al Jazeera, December 17, 2020.

Ritchie, L Carol, "US Says Syria's Chemical Weapons Stockpile Is Destroyed," NPR, August 18, 2014.

Rosenberg, Carol, "The Cost of Running Guantanamo Bay: $13 million Per Prisoner," New York Times, September 18, 2019, reproduced by The Pulitzer Center.

Ross, Alice, "Drones may predate Obama, but his resolute use of them is unmatched," Guardian, November 18, 2015.

Rubin, Alissa J, "Did the War in Afghanistan Have to Happen," New York Times, August 23, 2021.

Savage, Charlie, "Trump's Secret Rules for Drone Strikes Outside War Zones Are Disclosed," New York Times, May 1, 2021.

Sheehan, Edward RF, "Why Sadat packed off the Russians," New York Times, April 6, 1972.

Shelbourne, Mallory, "Study shows US weapons given to Syrian rebels ended up in ISIS hands," Hill, December 14, 2017.

Sly, Liz and Bahrampour, Tara, "Libya gains control of more rebel territory," Washington Post, March 13, 2011.

Sly, Liz and Warrick, Joby, "Gaddafi's forces push back rebels in key town; world leaders call for his ouster," Washington Post, March 29, 2011.

Smith, Saphora, "US officials misled public on Afghan war, according to the Washington Post," NBC, December 9, 2019.
Sommerlad, Joe, "What is the Haqqani network linked to the Taliban and al-Qaeda?," Independent, September 7, 2021.
Starr, Barbara, Yellin, Jessica and Carter, Chelsea J, "White House: Syria crosses 'red line' with use of chemical weapons on its people," CNN, June 14, 2013.
"Taliban defy Bush ultimatum," Guardian, September 21, 2001.
"Taliban momentum broken in Afghanistan, says Clinton," BBC News, June 23, 2011.
Tawfeeq, Mohammed, "Hundreds of thousands protest US troop presence in Iraq," January 24, 2020, CNN.
"The Bombing of Laos: By the Numbers," ABC News, September 6, 2016.
"The Death of Gaddafi," Al Jazeera, October 20, 2011.
"The Guantanamo Docket," New York Times.
"Text of George Bush's State of the Union speech," Guardian, September 21, 2001.
"Timeline: Oil-for-Food Scandal," BBC News, September 7, 2005.
"Timeline: Yemen's Uprising," Al Jazeera, March 21, 2011.
Timm, Jane C, "Factcheck: Trump is right, ISIS did lose almost all its territory in Iraq and Syria," NBC News.
"Transcript of President Bush's Remarks" from the East Room of the White House, September 6, 2006, NPR.
Treyz, Catherine, "European distraction led to Libya mess," CNN, March 11, 2016.
"Trump signs order to keep Guantanamo Bay prison open," BBC, January 31, 2018.
"The United States has offered Pakistan a military and economic package," UPI, June 15, 1981.
"US and UK Bomb Targets in Afghanistan: Bush: 'Battle Joined'," New York Times, October 8, 2001.
"US combat forces to leave Iraq by the end of year," BBC News, July 27, 2021.
"US ends Iraq combat mission," Graphic News.
"US-led combat mission in Iraq ends, shifting to advisory role," Al Jazeera, December 9, 2021.
"US recognises Libyan opposition group," Al Jazeera, July 15, 2011.
Declan Walsh, "Strategic Balochistan become a target in war against Taliban," Guardian, December 21, 2009.
Yusufzai, Rahimullah, "Analysis: Khalilzad emerges as the king-maker in Afghanistan," Gulf News, June 13, 2002.

Index

Abbottabad, 13, 35, 60, 111
Abdullah, Abdullah, 14, 109, 110
Abu Ghraib, 46–49, 127, 130
Abu Hanifa mosque, 78
Afghan communism, 57
Afghan conflict, vii, viii, 102, 124
Afghan invasion, vii, x, 9, 51–53, 58, 59, 85, 122–125, 127, 128
Afghanistan, 1, 18, 35, 51, 65, 84, 101, 122, 129, 135, 141
Afghanistan-Pakistan theater, 79
Afghanistan Papers, 14, 58–63, 111–114, 116, 117
Afghanistan War, 59, 101, 109, 110
Afghan National Army, 102, 127
Afghan-Pakistan border, 59, 101
Afghans, viii, x, 3, 10, 14, 55, 58, 63, 64, 108–110, 118, 119, 122, 123, 126, 128, 141, 142, 144, 146
Afghan trap, 52
African Union, 93
Air-exclusion zone, 66, 70, 71, 91, 93, 98, 131
AK-47, 58, 125

Al-Assad, Bashar, 89, 95, 96, 98–100, 127, 134
Al-Assad, Hafez, 89, 96
Al-Baghdadi, Abu Bakr, 35, 79
Aleppo, 100, 133
Algeria, 43, 85, 86, 89
Ali, Liyaquat, 5
Al-Islam, Saif, 90, 91
Al-Mada newspaper, 71
Al-Muhandis, Abu Mahdi, 82
Al Qaeda, xiii, xiv, 1–3, 12, 14, 35, 37, 38, 40, 45, 51, 57–65, 74, 77–79, 81, 85, 101, 104, 106, 111, 112, 114, 126, 130, 138, 145
Al Qaeda in Mesopotamia, 78
Al-Sadr, Muqtada, 77, 78, 81, 82
Al-Sisi, Abdel Fattah, 88, 89
Al-Sistani, Grand Ayatollah Ali, 78
Al-Zarqawi, Abu Mus'ab, 78, 130
America, 2, 16, 35, 51, 65, 84, 104, 121, 129, 135, 144
American Civil Liberties Union (ACLU), 40, 43, 48
Amin, Hafizullah, 123, 125
Anbar, 77, 130

Andropov, Yuri, 53, 126
Anglo-Afghan War (1839–1842), 122
Anglo-Afghan War (1878–1880), 122
Anglo-Afghan War (1919), 123
Annan, Kofi, 43, 71, 74
Anti-Vietnam War Movement, 19
Arabian Peninsula, 68, 89, 111, 145
Arab-Israeli War, vii, ix, xi, 1973
Arab nationalists, 70
Arab Socialist Ba'ath Party, 96
Arab Spring, 83–100, 127, 131–134
Arms Control Association, 100
Auckland, Lord, 122
Authorization for Use of Military Force (AUMF), 36, 37, 39
Awami League, 5

B

Ba'athist state, 65, 85
Ba'ath Party, 66, 76, 96, 133
Badakhshan, 108
Baghdad, 46, 68, 70, 74–76, 78, 81, 82, 114, 130
Baghdad Pact, 6, 7
Bagram air base, 61
Bahrain, 86, 132
Balkh, 108
Baloch, 5
Balochistan, 104, 105
Bangladesh War, 9
Banias, 97
Baradar, Mullah, 105
Barcelona, 75
Basra, 75, 114, 130
Ben Ali, Zine al-Abidine, 83–85, 87, 131
Benghazi, 89–91, 93, 131
Beyda, 89
Bhutto, Benazir, 6
Bhutto, Zulfiqar Ali, 5, 6, 9
Biden, Joe, 35, 40, 45, 46, 51, 82, 117–119, 128, 129, 141–148

Bien Hoa air base, 25
Bin Laden, Osama, xiii, 1–3, 12, 13, 35, 42, 57–60, 106, 111, 112, 114, 126, 129, 142, 145
Blair, Tony, 2, 73, 74
Blix, Hans, 74
Bosnia, 40, 64
Bouazizi, Mohamed, 83, 131
Bremer, Paul, 76
Brezhnev, Leonid, 53, 126
Britain, xiv, 11, 17, 67, 75, 92, 110, 122, 123
Brunstetter, Daniel, 46
Brzezinski, Zbigniew, xi, xii, 9, 52, 53
Buddhist Crisis, 25
Buley, Benjamin, 32, 33
Bundy, William, 26
Burgess, Ronald, 113
Bush, George H.W., 11, 67–70, 72, 73, 80
Bush, George W., viii, xiii–xv, 1–4, 12–14, 35–40, 42–48, 51, 58–63, 65, 72–76, 79–81, 88, 91, 101, 102, 126, 127, 129, 130

C

Cairo, 53, 86–88, 90, 131, 132
Cambodia, vii, xi–xiii, xv, 19, 20, 26–33, 55, 124
Cameron, David, 92, 94
Camp David Accords, 88
Carter, Jimmy, xi, xii, 9, 10, 14, 19, 51–53, 55, 65, 98, 124
Casey, William, 54, 55
Cavagnari, Louis Sir, 123
CENTCOM, 62
Center for Constitutional Rights, 40, 42
Central Asia, 3, 57, 89
Central Intelligence Agency (CIA), xi, 7, 13, 14, 25, 27, 36–39, 51, 52, 54, 55, 66, 71, 76, 111

Chalabi, Ahmed, 76
Chamberlain, Neville Sir, 122
Charlie Rose Talk Show, 112
Cheney, Dick, 37, 76
Chernenko, Konstantin, 53, 126
Chief Executive Officer, 109
China, ix, xi, xii, 2, 5, 7–9, 17, 18, 22, 24, 29, 30, 52–54, 71, 75, 96, 125, 146
CIA pipeline, 54
Clapper, James, 113
Clinton, Bill, 28, 57, 69, 70, 72, 80, 98
Clinton, Hillary, 92, 97, 113, 115
Clinton presidency, 79
Coalition Provisional Authority (CPA), 76, 79
Cold War, vii, viii, 2, 5, 10, 11, 16, 18, 29, 36, 51, 55, 88
Conein, Lucien, 25
Containment, 25, 69–73
Convention against Torture, 38
Crocker, Ryan, 61
Czechoslovakia, 56

Damascus, 96, 97, 99, 133
Davis, Krissie, 114
Day of Rage, 86, 90, 94, 132
Delta Oil, 57
Democratic Constitutional Rally (RCD), 84
Deobandi, 3, 103
Deraa, 96, 97
Detainee Treatment Act of 2005, 43
Diem, Ngo Dinh, 20, 24, 25
Disraeli, Benjamin, 122
Dobbins, James, 60
Doctors Without Borders, 114, 129
Doha agreement, 102, 117, 128
Don, Tran Van, 25
Dostum, Abdul Rashid, 3
Dowson, John, 114

Drone attacks, 39, 44, 111
Drone strikes, 44–46
Duhok, 81
Duma, 97, 99
Dunford, Joseph, 116

Eastern Bloc, 17
Eastern Europe, ix, 56
East Germany, 56
East-West confrontation, vii, xiii
Eggers, Jeffrey, 59
Egypt, 11, 53, 67, 85–90, 96, 127, 131–132
Eisenhower administration, 7, 8
Eisenhower, Dwight, 8, 20
ElBaradei, Mohamed, 86
Election Commission, 109
Ellsberg, Daniel, 22
End game, 111–115
Enlai, Zhou, 22
Erbil, 80, 81
Europe, ix, 2, 16, 17, 74, 96
European Parliament, 75
European Union, xiv, 2, 17, 18, 63, 91, 92

Fahim, Mohammed, 14
Falk, Richard, 20–22
Fallujah, 77, 130
Far East, ix, 19
Farrell, Theo, 102, 103
Federal Reserve, 71
First Gulf War (January–February1991), 47, 65, 74
Fletcher, Yvonne, 92
Florig, Dennis, 15, 16, 19, 121, 123
Ford, Gerald, 31, 72
Fort Mayer, 116
France, xi, 8, 11, 12, 23, 74, 89, 91–93, 95, 97

Franks, Tommy, 60, 62
Free Officers, 87, 90
French Indochina, 124
Frontier Corps, 59
Fukuyama, Francis, 18

G

Gaddafi, Muammar, 85, 89–93, 127, 131
General Accountability Office, 71, 72
Germany, viii, ix, 12, 16, 56, 62, 74
Ghani-Abdullah coalition, 110
Ghani, Ashraf, 64, 109, 110, 118, 119, 128
Ghannouchi, Mohamed, 84, 131
Ghazni, 63
Gheit, Ahmed Aboul, 87
Ghouta, 99
Giap, Vo Nguyen, 22, 23
Golan Heights, 96
Gonzales, Alberto, 38, 48
Gorbachev, Mikhail, 53, 55, 56, 126
Greater Middle East, xiv, 84, 89
Guantanamo Bay, 36–44, 127
Gulf Cooperation Council (GCC), 95
Gulf of Tonkin, 19–21, 23
Gulf War, 68–70, 73

H

Haass, Richard, 18, 62
Habeas corpus, 43
Haig, Alexander, 28
Hairatan Bridge, 56
Halabja, 81
Hammond, Philip, 93
Haqqani, Jalaluddin, 106, 107
Haqqani network, 104–108
Haqqani, Sirajuddin, 106, 107
Haq, Ziaul, 6, 9, 52
Haynes, William, 38
Hegemonic Overreach, 15, 16, 19

Helmand, 112, 114, 115
Hikmatyar, Gulbuddin, 10, 108
Hizb-i-Islami, 108, 126
Ho Chi Minh trail, 26, 27
Hood, Jay, 40
House of Representatives, 1, 114
Hungary, 56
Hussein, Saddam, xv, 46, 62, 65–79, 81, 84, 89, 127, 130
Hyde, Henry, 72

I

Idir, Mustafa Ait, 42
Imperial Overreach, 15, 69
Imperial Overstretch, 15, 16, 19
India-Pakistan War, 8, 1965
India-Pakistan War, 8, 1971
Indochina, vii, xi–xiii, xv, 19, 20, 23, 26, 28, 30, 33, 68, 121, 124, 125
International Contact Group on Libya, 92
International Covenant on Civil and Political Rights, 42
International Monetary Fund (IMF), 88
International Security Assistance Force (ISAF), 102
Inter-Services Intelligence (ISI), 6, 7, 10, 54, 105, 107
Iran, 7, 9, 10, 57, 66, 67, 71, 80, 82, 84, 85, 96, 97, 105, 109, 125, 130, 134
Iranian revolution, 16
Iranian Revolutionary Guards, 108
Iran-Iraq War, 66
Iraq, vii, xv, 2, 18, 33, 43–45, 47, 62, 65–82, 84, 85, 89, 91, 93, 97, 100, 111, 112, 114, 127, 130, 145, 148
Iraqi Kurdistan, 66, 80
Iraqi occupation, 47, 68
Iraqi Parliament, 80, 82
Iraq Liberation Act, 69

Islamic revolution, 9, 66
Islamic State, 78, 79, 82, 97, 98, 100, 127, 130
Islamic State of Iraq and Syria (ISIS), 35, 79, 82, 85, 86, 97, 100, 111, 117, 130, 141, 145, 146
Israel, 47, 67, 70, 88, 89, 96, 98

Jaish Muhammad, 78
Jalalabad, 12, 114
January 25th Revolution, 86
Japan, viii, ix, 19
Jasmine Revolution, 83, 84, 86
Jinnah, Muhammad Ali, 5
Johnson administration, 20, 21, 27
Johnson, Lyndon, 19–23, 25–27, 30, 31
Joint Meeting Parties (JMP), 94
Jordan, 71, 98, 134

Kacem, Rafik Belhaj, 83
Kagan, Robert, 72
Kalb, Marvin, 32, 33
Kandahar, 12, 14, 43, 58, 59, 102
Karachi, 57, 108
Karmal, Babrak, 53, 123, 125
Karpinski, Janis, 47
Karzai, Hamid, 14, 61, 63, 64, 101–104, 109, 126
Kashmir, 5, 10
Kayani, Ashfaq Parvez, 6
Kennedy, John F., 8, 20, 25
Kennedy, Paul, xiii, 15, 121
Kent State University, 29
Kerry, John, 109
Khadr, Omar, 41, 42, 44
Khalilzad, Zalmay, 14, 117, 118
Khalq (Masses), 125
Khan, Amanullah, 123

Khan, Ayub, 5, 8
Khan, Daud, ix, x, 14, 106, 124
Khan, Dost Mohammad, 122
Khan, Habibullah, 123
Khan, Ismail, 3
Khan Sheikhoun, 99
Khan, Sher Ali, 122
Khan, Yahya, 5
Khan, Yaqub Ali, 122, 123
Khmer Rouge, xii
Khost, 106
Khrushchev, Nikita, 8, 29
Khyber Pakhtunkhwa, 107
Kissinger, Henry, ix, 9, 27–29, 35, 36, 72, 73
Kosovo, 64
Kremlin, 53, 55, 56, 123, 125, 126
Kunduz, 12, 107, 114, 129
Kurdistan region, 80, 81
Kushner, Jared, 115
Kuwait, 47, 65–70, 72, 73, 86, 132

Laird, Melvin, 29
Lao Patriotic Front, 26
Lao People's Liberation Army, 26
Laos, vii, xi–xiii, xv, 19, 26–28, 31, 55, 124
Latakia, 97
League for the Independence of Vietnam, 19
Lebanon, 91
Lessons Learned, 59, 62, 63
Libya, xv, 2, 44, 45, 84–86, 89–94, 127, 131
Libyan civil war, 91
Libyan embassy, 92
Limited war, 46
Lockerbie, 92
Lodge, Henry Cabot, 25
Lucenti, Martin, 40
Lytton, Lord, 122

M

Macnaghten, William Hay Sir, 122
Madrassahs, 3, 10
Madrid, 75
Mahdi Army, 77, 78, 81
Mandela, Nelson, 75
Mansour, Adly, 89
Mansour Hadi, Abd Rabbu, 95, 133
Marine Corps, 59, 77
Massoud, Ahmad Shah, 3, 109
McKenna, Andrew, 114
McNamara, Robert, 21–23
Mearsheimer, John, 17
Mebazaa, Fouad, 84
Memorandum of Notification (MON), 37
Middle East, vii, ix, x, xiv, xv, 2, 18, 33, 57, 67, 68, 79, 84, 85, 89, 91, 93, 96, 127, 131
Military Commissions Act of 2006, 43
Minh, Duong Van, 25
Minh, Ho Chi, 24, 26, 27
Miran Shah Shura, 107, 108
Mirza, Iskander, 5
Misrata, 93
Mohajir, 5
Morocco, 85, 86
Morsi, Mohamed, 88, 89, 127, 132
Mosul, 75, 79, 82, 114, 130
Mubarak, Hosni, 85–88, 131, 132
Mujahideen, vii, xi, xiii, 2, 3, 9–12, 51–57, 65, 106, 125, 126
Mullen, Mike, 112
Musharraf, Pervez, 4, 6, 104
Muslim Brotherhood, 86, 88, 127, 132
Mutassim, 93
Mutual Defense Assistance Agreement, 6, 7

N

Najaf, 77
Najeeb, Atef, 96
Najibullah, vii, xii, 2, 55–57, 126
Nasiriyah, 76
Nasser, Gamal Abdel, 87, 90
National Assembly, 5, 61, 110
National Association for Change, 86
National Democratic Party, 87
National Front for the Liberation of the South (NFL), 24
Nationalism, xiii
Nationalist, vii, xi, 5, 28, 66, 70, 77, 118, 124
National Press Club, 32, 116
National Security Council, 29, 37, 59
National Transitional Council (NTC), 92
National Unity Government, 109
NATO, ix, 4, 18, 60, 64, 74, 93, 106, 112, 116, 131
Nazimuddin, Khwaja, 5
Nechla, Mohammed, 40, 41
Neoconservatives, 2, 14, 18, 72, 73, 84
New Yorker, 47, 92
New York Times, 12, 21, 40, 43–46, 48, 74, 88, 101
Nixon, Richard, vii, ix, 9, 27–29, 31, 36
Niyazov, Saparmurat, 57
Nol, Lon, xii, 28, 29
Northern Alliance, 12–14, 46, 57, 101, 126
North Vietnam, xi–xiii, 20–26, 28–30, 32, 124
North Waziristan, 106, 107

O

Obama administration, 39, 45, 59, 60, 87, 91, 97, 99, 111, 112
Obama, Barak, viii, 13, 27, 35, 39, 43–45, 59, 60, 63, 65, 80–82, 87, 88, 91, 93, 98–100, 109, 111–115, 118, 127, 129–131
Obama presidency, 39, 80

Oman, 67, 86
Omar, Mullah, 13, 60, 102, 104, 105
Operation Desert Shield, 67
Operation Desert Storm, 65–67
Operation Iraqi Freedom, 73–76
Operation Plan 34A, 21, 22
Organization for the Prohibition of Chemical Weapons (OPCW), 99, 100
Organization of Petroleum Exporting Countries (OPEC), vii, ix, 31

P

Pahlavi, Reza, 9
Pakistan, xiii, 1, 3–13, 23, 35, 39, 42–45, 52–60, 89, 101, 104–108, 111, 112, 116, 125–127, 129
Pakistani Military Academy, 13
Paktia, 104
Paktika, 104
Palestinian National Authority, 86
Pan Am Flight 103, 92
Panetta, Leon, 111, 112
Paracha, Saifullah, 44
Parcham (Banner), 125
Pardo-Maurer, Roger, 58, 59
Paris Peace Accords, xii, 124, 1973
Pashtun, 3, 10, 13, 14, 58, 108, 109, 118
Pathet Lao, xii, 26, 27
Pentagon, 58, 72, 76, 102, 111, 116
Pentagon Papers, 21, 22
People's Democratic Party of Afghanistan (PDPA), 124
People's Democratic Republic of Yemen, 89, 94
Persian Gulf, 9, 66
Peshawar, 7, 54, 107, 108
Peshawar Shura, 107–108
Pink Revolution, 94
Podhoretz, Norman, 31, 33

Pompeo, Mike, 117
Powell, Colin, 38, 56
Powers, Gary, 7, 8
President Biden, 35, 46, 51, 82, 117–119, 128, 129, 141–148
President Clinton, 69, 80
Project for the New American Century (PNAC), 2, 18, 72, 88
Provisional Revolutionary Government (PRG), xii, 25, 124
PT-boat attacks, 20, 21
Putin, Vladimir, xiv, 74, 76, 134

Q

Qanooni, Younus, 14
Qatar, 67, 117, 139
Quetta, 54, 104–108
Quetta Shura, 104, 105, 107, 109
Quran, 3, 125

R

Rabbani, Burhanuddin, 3, 14, 112
Rahbari Shura, 104
Rahman, Abdur, 123
Rahman, Mujibur, 6
Raphael, Arnold, 11
Raqqa, 79, 82
Reagan presidency, 54, 124
Reagan, Ronald, xi, 10, 11, 19, 32, 33, 52–54, 56, 72, 80
Rendition, 37
Reprisal, 1–14, 21, 22, 51, 59, 65, 126
Rice, Condoleezza, 37
Robertson, Lord, 4
Rogers, William, 29
Roland, Matthew, 114
Romney, Mitt, 114
Rubin, Barnett, 60, 101, 103
Rumsfeld, Donald, 38, 40, 58, 60, 62, 77, 102
Russian General Staff, 54, 55

S

Sadat, Anwar, 53, 87–89
Safed Koh, 59
Saigon, 25, 31, 119, 124
Saleh, Abdullah, 85, 94, 95, 133
Samarra, 78
Sana'a, 94, 95
Sanchez, Ricardo, 47, 66
Sar-e-Pul, 108
Sarkozy, Nicolas, 92
Saudi royal family, 53, 58
Savage, Charlie, 45, 46
Schwarzkopf, Norman, 67
Scud missiles, 67, 68
Se-chang, Pak, 22
Sectarian violence, 77, 79–81
Senate, 1, 32, 37, 38, 59, 112–114, 116
September 11, 2001 (9/11 attacks, events of 9/11), viii, x, xiii, xiv, 1–14, 33, 36, 39, 46, 51, 59, 64, 65, 69, 111, 126, 129, 145
Sevan, Benon, 71, 72
Shafik, Ahmed, 88, 132
Shah, Zahir, ix, x, 13, 14, 106, 110
Shcherbakov, Ilya, 23
Shi'a, 66, 69, 70, 77–80, 82, 85, 96, 130, 133
Shultz, George, 56, 72
Sibley, Forrest, 114
Sidi Bouzid, 83
Sihanouk, Norodom, 28
Sindhis, 5
Sino-Soviet split, 29
Sirte, 93, 131
Soleimani, Qasem, 82
Somalia, 39, 44, 45, 111, 145
South Asia, vii, ix, 8, 107, 108
Southeast Asia Collective Defense Treaty, 23
Southeast Asia Treaty Organization (SEATO), 6
South Vietnam, vii, xi, xii, 19, 20, 23–26, 28–32, 124
Soviet-Afghan War (1979–1989), 121
Soviet casualties, 55
Soviet Union, vii, ix–xii, 2, 5–9, 11, 12, 16–18, 28, 29, 52, 55, 56, 66, 68, 88, 89, 96, 110, 122–124, 126
Spain, 74, 75
Special Inspector General for Afghanistan Reconstruction (SIGAR), 59, 61
Speer, Christopher, 42
State Department, 3, 4, 7, 8, 38, 60, 63, 66, 76, 117, 135, 144
Stockholm International Peace Research Institute (SIPRI), 79, 80
Stoletov, Nikolai, 122
Sudan, 86, 134
Sulaymaniyah, 81
Suleiman, Omar, 87
Sunni, 3, 77–81, 85, 106
Syria, xv, 2, 18, 35, 44, 45, 67, 79, 80, 82, 84, 86, 89, 95–100, 127, 133–134, 145
Syrian Democratic Forces (SDF), 97
Syrian Revolution 2011, 96

T

Taft, William, 38
Taguba, Antonio, 47, 48
Tahrir Square, 86, 87, 90, 132
Tajik, 3, 12, 109
Taliban, 1, 35, 51, 65, 85, 101, 126
Taliban regroup, 63, 103–105, 111, 129
Tantawi, Mohamed Hussein, 88
Taraki, Nur Muhammad, 125
Tikrit, 75, 81, 82
Tora Bora, 12, 59, 60
Torture, 36–40, 42, 46–49, 93, 96, 127
Tripoli, 90, 91, 93, 131
Trump, Donald, 35, 39, 40, 43, 45, 46, 82, 99, 100, 115–119, 128, 129
Trump, Donald Jr., 115
Trump, Ivanka, 115

Trump presidency, 43
Tunis, 83
Tunisia, 83–87, 89, 90, 92, 127, 131
Tunisian parliament, 84
Tunisian Revolution, 85
Turkey, 7, 8, 80, 97, 123

Ukraine, v, ix, xiii, xiv
Umm Hawsh, 100
UN Charter, 73, 74
UN Commission on Human Rights, 42
UN General Assembly, 4
UNICEF, 71
United Kingdom, 8, 62, 66, 71, 91–93, 97, 98
United States, 1, 16, 36, 51, 65, 84, 101, 123
Unocal, 57
UN Oil-for-Food program, 71
UN Security Council, 4, 9, 66, 68, 71, 75, 91
UN weapons inspector in Iraq, 75
Uoc, Nguyen Dinh, 22
Uprisings, 69, 70, 77–79, 83–86, 90–93, 95–97
US administration, 2, 77, 84, 88, 112
US-Afghan War (2001-2021), 121
US-centric, v, 33, 121
US military police, 47
US military prison, 47
USS Abraham Lincoln, 75
USS *Maddox*, 20
US Special Forces, 20, 27, 60
USS Porter, 99
USSR, ix, x, xii, xxii, 7–10, 17, 18, 52, 56, 68, 123
USS Ross, 99
USS *Turner Joy*, 21
US-Taliban agreement, 117
U-2, 7, 8, 21
Uzbek, 3, 12, 13, 59

Viet Cong, xi, 24–26, 28, 31, 124
Vietnam, 19, 35, 52, 67, 113, 121
Vietnam Syndrome, v, ix, xiii, xiv, xix, xxi, xxii, 19–22, 32, 33, 68, 121, 123
Vietnam War, xi, xiii, xv, xxi, 19, 20, 22, 29–32, 35, 52, 67–69, 73, 113, 124
Viet Minh, 19, 26
Volcker Commission, 71, 72
Volcker, Paul, 71, 72

War on Soviet communism, 51–57
Washington Post, 38, 39, 58, 59, 102
Wassom, Herbert, 11
Watergate, vii, 31
Weinberger, Caspar, 32, 33
Weinberger Doctrine, 32
West Asia, vii, ix, 89
Western Alliance, xiv
West Point Military Academy, 46
Wolesi Jirga, 61, 110
World War II (WWII), 2, 16, 18, 19, 28, 39, 69

Xinjiang Province, 7

Yemen, 39, 43–45, 85, 94–95, 127
Yemen Arab Republic (North Yemen), 89, 94

Zadran, 106
Zaeef, Abdul Salaam, 1
Zakir, Abdullah, 105
Zedong, Mao, 24, 29
Zintan, 89, 90

Ingram Content Group UK Ltd.
Milton Keynes UK
UKHW022146130323
418513UK00006B/351